CONTRACT NEGOTIATIONS

Skills, Tools, and Best Practices

Gregory A. Garrett

CCH INCORPORATED
Chicago

A WoltersKluwer Company

Editorial Director: Aaron M. Broaddus
Cover and Interior Design: Craig Arritola

ISBN 0-8080-1246-0

4025 W. Peterson Ave.
Chicago, Illinois 60646-6085
1 800 248 3248
http:// www.cch.com

A Wolters Kluwer Company

Contents

Appendices

Preface

This one-of-a-kind book provides a comprehensive treatment of contract negotiations, with a compelling discussion of what skills, tools, and best practices are needed to become a master contract negotiator. There are many books written on the basics of negotiations, a few books specific to contract negotiations, but, this is the only book which thoroughly discusses the entire contract negotiation process - from beginning to end - with more than 200 best practices from U.S. federal government, commercial, and multinational/global business sectors.

If you are involved with negotiating business deals - large or small - this book is for you! The target audience for this book includes: contract managers, contract negotiators, contract administrators, sales managers, account mangers, price/cost analysts, subcontract managers, purchasing managers, supply-chain managers, project managers, and real estate agents - in both the public and private business sectors.

Gregory A. Garrett has skillfully blended his 25 years of highly successful business experience planning, negotiating, documenting, and managing more than $30 Billion of complex deals, in both the public and private business sectors worldwide. In addition to the wealth of proven contract negotiation best practices, there are 50+ contract negotiation tactics and countertactics, 25+ contract negotiation templates/forms, and numerous real-world case studies. I consider this book worth its weight in gold! Few business skills are as important to both buyers and sellers and have such significant impact either positive or negative, as one's ability to negotiate a great deal!

I am Professor Emeritus in Contracting Management from the Air Force Institute of Technology (AFIT), the graduate school of the Air Force. During my tenure with AFIT from 1975 to 1994 I taught thousands of students. When I taught negotiation I used three different texts in the classroom and had ten more on my reading shelves. I would have coveted a text like Contract Negotiations: Skills, Tools, and Best Practices.

Not only is this book a great companion to Mr. Garrett's three other books: *World Class Contracting, Capture Management Life-Cycle: Winning More Business, and Managing Complex Outsourced Projects,* but for the first time he brings all the process, tools, and best practices of contract negotiation into a single text. What a dream come true for a contract management educator or anyone involved in contract negotiations.

This text is really needed in our professional literature. Sales personnel and educators write most of the books I have read, about the topic of negotiation. This is the first text authored by someone who has actually experienced the contract negotiation process from virtually every angle: buyer, seller, U.S. Government, commercial, multinational, and global. What a refreshing change of pace!

William C. Pursch, Ph.D., CPCM
President, Pursch Associates
Past National President, National Contract Management Association (NCMA)

Dedications

To my wife Carolyn for her patience, love, and support. She is the best negotiator!

To my three children: Christopher, Scott, and Jennifer for their love, support, and constant testing of my personal negotiation skills.

In memory of my late grandfather, Mr. Albert H. Wolf, a highly successful business man, a man of great passion, a patient fisherman, and an astute negotiator.

Acknowledgements

To my parents for their love, support, and confidence in my success! To all of my customers, team members, and suppliers who I have had the pleasure of working with and learning what to do and what not to do! Special thanks to the following individuals for their friendship, support and advice:

> Mr. William C. Pursch, Ph.D., CPCM
> Mr. W. Gregor Macfarlan, CPCM
> Mr. Ken Martin, Esq.
> Mr. Charles E. Rumbaugh, Esq.
> Mr. Dennis Knapp
> Mr. Tom Reid, Esq.
> Mr. Philip E. Salmeri, CPCM
> Dr. Rene G. Rendon, CPCM, C.P.M.

Special thanks to Mrs. Barbara Hanson for her outstanding administrative support. Many thanks to Mr. Aaron Broaddus and the entire CCH Incorporated team for their excellent editing, cover design, and marketing of the book!

About the Author

Gregory A. Garrett, is a respected international educator, best-selling author, and practicing industry leader. He has successfully led more than $30 Billion of high-technology contracts and projects during the past 25 years. He has taught, consulted, and led contract and project teams in more than 40 countries. He has served as a lecturer for The George Washington University Law School and the School of Business and Public Management. He is the President and CEO, of Garrett Consulting Services.

At Lucent Technologies, Mr. Garrett served as Vice President, Program Management, North America, Wireless. He also served as Chairman, Lucent Technologies Project Management Leadership Council, representing more than 2,000 Lucent project managers globally, and Director, Global Program Management Platform at the company headquarters.

At ESI International, Mr. Garrett served as Executive Director of Global Business, where he led the sales, marketing, negotiation, and implementation of bid/proposal management, project management, commercial contracting, and government contract management training and consulting programs for numerous Fortune 100 multinational corporations, government agencies and small businesses worldwide, including: ABB, AT&T, Bell-South, Boeing, IBM, Inter-America Development Bank, Israel Aircraft Industries, Lucent Technologies, Motorola, NCR, NTT, Panama Canal Commission, SBC, United States Trade Development Agency, United Nations, and the United States Department of Defense.

Formerly, Mr. Garrett served as a highly decorated military officer for the United States Air Force, awarded more than 17 medals, badges, and citations. He completed his active duty career as the youngest Acquisition Action Officer, in the Colonel's Group Headquarters USAF, the Pentagon. He was the youngest Division Chief and Professor of Contracting Management at the Air Force Institute of Technology where he taught advanced courses in contract administration and program management to more than 5,000 people from the Department of Defense and NASA.

Previously, he was the youngest Procurement Contracting Officer for the USAF Aeronautical Systems Center, where he led more than 50 multi-million dollar negotiations and managed the contract administration of over $15 billion in contracts for major weapon systems. He served as a Program Manager at the Space Systems Center, where he managed a $300 million space communications project.

Mr. Garrett is a Certified Purchasing Manager (CPM) of the Institute for Supply Management (ISM). He is a Certified Project Management Professional (PMP) of the Project Management Institute (PMI) and has received the prestigious PMI Eric Jenett Project Management Excellence Award. He is a Certified Professional Contracts Manager (CPCM), a Fellow, and member of the Board of Advisors of the National Contract Management Association (NCMA). He has received the NCMA National Achievement Award, NCMA National Educational Award, and the Blanche Witte Memorial Award for outstanding service to the contract management profession.

A prolific author, Mr. Garrett co-authored the book *Managing Contracts for Peak Performance* (NCMA, 1991), authored the best-selling book *World-Class Contracting* (3d Ed., CCH Incorporated, 2003), authored the book *Managing Complex Outsourced Projects* (CCH, Incorporated, 2004), and co-authored the book *The Capture Management Life-Cycle* (CCH, Incorporated, 2003). He has also authored more than 50 published articles on bid/proposal management, supply chain management, contracting, and project management.

Mr. Garrett resides in Oakton, Virginia with his wife Carolyn and three children - Christopher, Scott, and Jennifer.

Introduction

While more and more business transactions are conducted via electronic means including: e-marketplaces, e-catalogs, and e-auctions the majority of the dollars are still spent in a relatively few large complex negotiated deals. The vital few, the trivial many. While all business deals are important, some are clearly more important than others. For both buyers and sellers, ensuring you get the most favorable outcome from each of the big deals is critical to the success of your organization.

This book provides a comprehensive treatment of the challenging world of contract negotiations. The book discusses today's dynamic performance-based business environment in both the public and private business sectors. Further, the book provides an engaging discussion of the competencies/skills, which must be mastered to become a world class contract negotiator.

In addition, the book features a proven effective contract negotiation process, supplemented with numerous tools, forms/templates, and case studies. The book discusses all aspects of contract negotiation planning, conducting contract negotiations, documenting contract negotiations, and forming contracts. Finally, the book contains detailed discussions of proven effective contract negotiation best practices in various marketplaces:

- U.S. federal government contracts
- U.S. commercial contracts
- Multinational and global contracts

This book will answer many key questions, which you may have regarding contract negotiations, including:

- What skills do you need to become a master contract negotiator?
- How do you build a better relationship while conducting complex contract negotiations?
- What are the most effective strategies, tactics, and counter-tactics to achieve success in contract negotiations?
- How should you deal with obstacles you face when planning or conducting contract negotiations?

- What contract negotiation best practices should you apply and when?
- What are the similarities and differences between U.S. federal government and U.S. commercial contract negotiations?
- How do you create a successful performance-based contract?

The New Performance-Based Buying & Selling Environment - The World We Live In!

INTRODUCTION

The world we live in, is a world of constant change with increasingly demanding customers in both the public and private business sectors. The world we live in, is a world of tremendous technology, which allows for rapid voice, data, and video communications at the speed of light nearly everywhere globally. The world we live in, is a world of buyers and sellers with business rules, regulations, policies, standards, contracts, laws, and enforcement agencies. The world we live in, is a matter of facts and perceptions in which some people, organizations, and companies get more than they deserve, while most get less than they deserve. The world we live in, is influenced by each and every individual and their respective ability to leverage their knowledge, experience, and skills to benefit themselves, their organization/company, and our society. One's ability to leverage or negotiate, in both their personal and professional life, is often key to their success.

In this brave new challenging, fast-paced, electronically enhanced world we live in, business is becoming less personal and more automated, which like most things provides both challenges and opportunities. Today, far fewer people are directly involved in business to business transactions, whether in buying or selling, as a result of the increased use of automated/electronic tools, hardware, software and integrated enterprise applications providing Internet-based solutions. In both the public and private business sectors, increasingly simple, routine, and indirect business transactions are highly automated via e-marketplaces, allowing for the use of electronic search catalogs, e-auctions, procurement cards, and electronic-funds transfer. However, the majority of the expenditures of most organizations in both the public and private business sectors, are still completed via a relatively few large, complex, competitively negotiated deals.

CAPS OUTSOURCING RESEARCH RESULTS

The most recent cross-industry benchmarking studies conducted by the Center for Advanced Purchasing Studies (CAPS), which included hundreds of companies from 25 major industries including: aerospace/defense, construction, engineering, manufacturing, financial services, telecommunications, and utilities, provides the following information regarding the use of outsourcing and electronic procurement.[1]

Table 1-1

CAPS Research Cross-Industry Benchmarking Summary (August 2002 - November 2003 Reports)	
Findings/Descriptions	**Avg.**
Outsourcing spend as a percent of sales $	40.39%
Active suppliers that account for 80% of the purchase $	9.47%
Active suppliers that are e-enabled	12.50%
Purchase spend - EDI	11.60%
Purchase spend - B2B e-commerce	5.88%
Purchase spend - Strategic alliances	21.68%
Purchase spend - e-auctions	2.21%
Purchase spend - Procurement cards	1.20%
Purchase spend - Minority owned business	2.98%
Purchase spend - Women owned business	2.25%
Purchase spend - Other small business	12.84%

CAPS OUTSOURCING RESEARCH RESULTS — ASSESSMENT

The CAPS Outsourcing Research results reflected in Table 1-1 indicates that outsourcing is increasing across all industries and now accounts for an average of more than 40 percent of company expenditures compared to company sales revenue. Further, the CAPS outsourcing research verifies that companies are increasingly reducing their supplier base. Less than 10 percent of their suppliers typically account for 80 percent of purchases. In addition, the research demonstrates that 82 percent of the purchases are awarded to large businesses and only 18 percent of the purchases are awarded to small businesses. While 18 percent of the purchases are awarded to small businesses only a little over 5 percent of total purchases were awarded to diversity suppliers (minority owned businesses and women owned businesses).

Clearly, the CAPS Cross-Industry Benchmarking Summary conveys the strong message that companies primarily in the commercial or private business sector, are selecting fewer suppliers, primarily large businesses, in order to be able to increase their leverage or negotiation power to obtain lower prices, reduce cycle-times, and gain more favorable terms and conditions on their business deals. It is also somewhat surprising to learn that as of late 2003 only 12.5 percent of active suppliers are e-enabled and only 11.6 percent are using electronic data interchange (EDI), to facilitate buyer and seller communication and electronic funds transfer.

E-MARKETPLACES: PRODUCTS, SERVICES, & PROCESSES

Products, services, or solutions purchased electronically should be selected carefully, properly evaluating the opportunities and risks. One of the key items concerning this selection is the degree of digitalization of the products, processes, and transaction partners (see Figure 1-1).[2]

Figure 1-1. The E-Procurement Cube

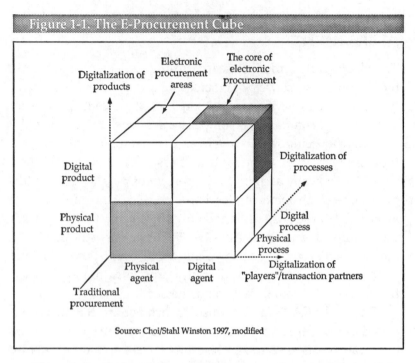

Source: Choi/Stahl Winston 1997, modified

Electronic marketplaces are able to cover most phases of the sourcing process. The sourcing process is supported by web-based information and communication technologies, which means a completely digitalized process. Typically, the products and services bought and sold on these e-marketplaces are either digital or physical products/services. Digitalized products like software are easier to handle on e-marketplaces, because they can be distributed electronically. More and more traditional industries, like steel, paper, mining, and automotive are becoming digitalized.

TYPES OF E-MARKETPLACES

e-Marketplaces do not arise like regular markets. A service provider must create the market and be responsible for rules, access, and technology. Service providers are neutral parties who provide the infrastructure and tools that allow buyers, sellers, and subcontractors to communicate, thus facilitating the outsourcing process. e-Marketplaces are usually divided into vertical marketplaces (focused on one industry's products and services) and horizontal marketplaces (focused on multi-industries products and services). Further, e-Marketplaces are usually categorized as a buyer-oriented marketplace, a neutral marketplace, or a seller-oriented marketplace, as illustrated in Figure 1-2.[3] While e-Marketplaces are indeed a growing part of the world we live in, they are usually limited to the buying and selling of relatively simple commercial-off-the-shelf (COTS) products and services, which typically represent 20 percent to 50 percent of an average organization's spending.

Figure 1-2. E-Marketplaces

Model	Architecture	Horizontal Example	Vertical Example
"Traditional" E-Purchasing		Buying Homepage	Internet EDI
Buyer Orientated Marketplace		Global Trading Web (worldwide network for buyers)	Covisint (joint venture of GM, Ford, DaimierChrysler)
Neutral Marketplace		Allago (marketplace for indirect material of Dresdner Bank)	FreeMarkets (auctions in different branches)
Seller-Oriented Marketplace		Grainger (selling of MRO-goods)	Omnexus (Selling platform of BASF, Bayer, DOW, etc)
E-Selling		Dell (here: B2B-business for computers)	Gehe pharmaceuticals

(E-Marketplaces spans the Buyer Orientated, Neutral, and Seller-Oriented rows)

Internal clients only: *internal buyer-driven e-marketplace*

Access of external clients: *open buyer-driven e-marketplace*

Source: Boston Consulting Group 2000, modified

E-MARKETPLACES ENABLERS

e-Marketplace enablers have been developed to help companies create e-marketplaces on the Internet. Most market enablers supply software and consulting. Two major infrastructure providers - Ariba and FreeMarkets - provide best-in-class examples of e-marketplace enablers.

ARIBA: ENABLING E-MARKETPLACES

During the past few years, Ariba has transformed itself from a pure buy-side solution provider into a technology platform for building and powering Internet trading exchanges. Ariba accomplished their transformation via major acquisitions, including acquiring Tradex - an exchange solution and Trading Dynamics - an auction solution. Ariba is continually expanding its product offerings from automation of the transactional buying activities of indirect materials/services into automation of strategic and direct materials buying by acquiring Supplier Market.

Ariba has also established partnerships with sell-side solution companies, including InterWorld and CardoNet, and supply chain management companies, such as IBM and I2Technologies. With these partnerships, Ariba platforms now fully cover buy-side, sell-side, exchange and auction, and supply chain optimization solutions.[4]

FREEMARKETS: AUCTION ENABLER

FreeMarkets operates a buyer-focused auction exchange focused on the multi-trillion dollar procurement marketplace for industrial parts, raw materials, and commodities. FreeMarkets service essentially creates a custom market for the direct materials or other goods that its clients purchase in a particular auction. FreeMarkets combines its Bid Ware technology with knowledge of supply markets to help clients obtain lower prices and make better purchasing decisions for simple off-the-shelf products.

THE NEW PERFORMANCE-BASED SUPPLY ENVIRONMENT

In both the public and private sectors, 50% to 80% of the total value of purchases are transacted via competitive negotiated performance-based contracts. In both the public and private sectors, we are witnessing increased use of outsourcing, privatization, and competitive sourcing combined with the increased use of performance-based contracts. Today, more than ever Buyers are requiring customized integrated solutions, often composed of hardware, software, and professional services - which are

Chapter 1

provided by an integrated supply team. All of these forces are transforming the marketplace, while placing greater risks on both parties. Sellers are being asked to agree to increasingly demanding performance-based contracts, often with significant penalties for failure to perform. Buyers are also taking greater risks, because they are increasingly outsourcing their capabilities to other parties, thus losing some direct control over their success or failure. Business is becoming less mono a mono and more integrated and team oriented. Figure 1-3, describes The World We Live In and how the forces of technology and regulations are impacting and forming a new performance-based supply environment.

As shown in Figure 1-3, The World We Live In, the public business sector composed of Federal, State, and local government agencies is adopting more and more commercial buying practices in its quest to reduce acquisition cycle-time, reduce costs, and increase customer satisfaction. Similarly, the private business sector is moving to create better defined and integrated buying and selling processes to increase speed to market, reduce operating costs, improve profitability, and increase customer loyalty.

Figure 1-3. The World We Live In

	Supply Drivers	New Performance-Based Supply
Technology	■ Growth of Internet architecture ■ Continued growth of voice/data/video wireless communications ■ Use of e-Marketplaces ■ Growth of enterprice applications for e-procurement automated sales tools, and customer relationship management (CRM)	**Pros** + New products and services + Wider range of products and services + More modular products and services + Reduced prices + Improved performance + Faster products introductions
Regulation	■ U.S. Govt. increased use of commercial buying practices ■ U.S. Govt. increased us of past performance as a major factor in best value source selection process ■ Increased competition ■ Increased enforcement of procurement ethics	**Cons** - More complexity - Higher cost of integration - Less reliability - Accelarated pace of change - Rapid obsolescence - Less personal contact

Clearly, the public and private business sectors are converging via technology and regulations, resulting in the increased use of large, complex performance-based contracts, which are competitively negotiated. There is no denying the increased trend of organizations awarding large, complex performance-based contracts, which typically comprise the bulk of most organizations expenditures for buyers and revenue for sellers. Thus, winning these large complex performance-based contracts is indeed critical to sellers. But, winning is not enough, sellers must ensure they are able to negotiate a fair and reasonable deal that will allow them to make an appropriate profit. For buyers, selecting the right seller, prime contractor with subcontractors, is of critical importance. But, selecting the right supplier is not enough, buyers must ensure the seller honors its commitments and meets or exceeds the mutually agreed to performance-based metrics for quality, technical, cost, schedule, and customer satisfaction.

Simply stated, performance-based contracts (PBCs) are documented business arrangements, in which the buyer and seller agree to: a performance work statement, a set of performance-based metrics, and a quality assurance surveillance plan as a means to evaluate seller provided products, services, and/or solutions. Increasingly PBCs are being used instead of more detailed "how to" product and services specifications.

The practice of performance-based contracting is not new. However, it was conceptually revitalized in U.S. federal government contracting in April 1991, when the Office of Federal Procurement Policy (OFPP) issued a policy letter emphasizing the use of performance requirements and quality standards in defining contract requirements, source selection, and quality assurance.[5] The OFPP policy letter stemmed from a growing body of evidence that the U.S. federal government does not effectively procure its goods and services.

In the commercial or private business sector, performance-based contracts have been successfully used for years in the procurement of products. Today, the private business sector is also increasingly using performance-based contracts to acquire professional services and integrated solutions, which require a mix of products (hardware and software) and services often delivered in a highly customized manner. The real key to making

PBCs work is the requirement for the seller to truly understand the customer's needs, then be able to work with the customer to translate their needs into a performance work statement (PWS), a quality assurance surveillance plan (QASP), performance-based metrics, and contractual incentives. Chapter 6 will provide a much more detailed discussion of both the opportunities and challenges associated with the growing use for PBCs, plus how and when to use PBCs most effectively in your contract negotiations.

CMI AND ISM STUDIES SHOW NEED FOR NEGOTIATION SKILLS

In two research-based studies commissioned by the Contract Management Institute (CMI), a not-for-profit, educational/research group supported by the National Contract Management Association (NCMA), and surveys commissioned by the Institute for Supply Management (ISM), formerly the National Association of Purchasing Management (NAPM), between 2000 - 2003, the following trends were discovered.

The ISM and CMI year 2000 surveys showed for every 100 surveyed contract management/purchasing professionals, concerning their roles:[6]
- 90 indicate "more time sensitive"
- 85 indicate "more responsibility"
- 85 indicate "more team-oriented"
- 85 indicate "more strategic"
- 80 indicate "more use of performance-based metrics"

The CMI year 2001 study, which distributed surveys to 3,180 business professionals in both the public and private sectors, received 872 completed surveys - a 27 percent response rate, statistically a valid survey. The CMI year 2001 study and survey titled: Performance Metrics for the Contract Management Discipline, received survey responses from a diverse, experienced, and well educated pool of business professionals throughout the United States and some internationally.

The CMI year 2001 survey, Performance Metrics for the Contract Management Discipline, included the following key demographics from their respondents:[7]

- Public sector (35%); private sector government (37%); private sector-non-government (21%); educational, not-for-profit, and other (7%)
- 15 years or more of experience (75%)
- 20 years or more of experience (50+%)
- Education: high school (1%); some college (10%); under graduate (33%); masters degree (45%); postgraduate degree (9%)

In the CMI year 2001 survey, one of the most significant questions asked, which respondents had to write-in their answers, was "[w]hich metrics do you believe your organization will use in the next 3 to 5 years to evaluate personnel performance?" The respondents' Top 10 choices:

- Business judgment
- Decision-making
- Problem-solving
- Negotiation skills
- Customer service
- Integrity/ethics
- Education
- Interpersonal relations
- Responsiveness
- Communications[8]

Clearly, the research-based studies commissioned by CMI and ISM indicate the growing use of performance-based metrics in the buying and selling environment in both the public and private business sectors.

Likewise, the CMI year 2001 study demonstrates the general acknowledgement of the real importance of negotiation skills within the contract management/purchasing discipline.

CONTRACT NEGOTIATION SKILLS GAP

Today, there is a growing shortage of highly skilled, demonstrated successful master contract negotiators. Unfortunately, in both the public and private business sectors, many master contract negotiators have retired, are retiring, or are retirement eligible. With the growth of technology tools in our new supply environment we have fewer people directly involved in the buying and selling processes. Today, as a result of our being more technology dependent, we have far fewer available highly skilled contract negotiators. Combine the aforementioned statement, with the increased use of large complex outsourced performance-based contracts, requiring more highly skilled contracts negotiators, the result is a growing contract negotiation skills gap.

Having spent most of the last 25 years planning, negotiating, documenting, and managing some of the world's most complex contracts and projects and having the great fortune to travel and teach more than 20,000 business professionals from over 40 countries about bid/proposal, contract, and project management my experience and research both indicate the compelling need for improved contract negotiation skills - to ensure each party gets what they want, when they want it, at a fair and reasonable price. The alternative is not acceptable - bad deals, late delivery, financial losses, reduced consumer confidence, and negative economic impacts!

SUMMARY

In this chapter, we have examined the world we live in. We have discussed the new performance-based supply environment, its opportunities and challenges. Further, we have reviewed several studies and surveys conducted and/or commissioned by the Center of Advanced Purchasing Studies (CAPS), the Institute for Supply Management (ISM), and the Contract Management Institute (CMI). All of the research discussed, demonstrates that the majority of simple, routine, commercial off-the-shelf business transactions are being conducted electronically increasingly via e-marketplaces. However, the research also shows that the majority of most organizations expenditures are being spent via large competitively negotiated performance-based contracts.

Clearly, based upon the CMI year 2001 study and experience, negotiation skills are extremely important for people involved in the new performance-based buying and selling environment. Unfortunately, it is also clear from the studies, demographics, and experience that worldwide we have far fewer master contract negotiators to handle the increasingly large complex performance-based deals, resulting in a real negotiation skills gap.

The intent of this book is to serve as a tool to increase awareness, understanding, and sharpen the skills required to become a master contract negotiator. Chapter 2 provides a unique Contract Negotiator's Competencies Model, with a comprehensive discussion of the specialized skills and critical knowledge and skill areas required to become a master contract negotiator!

QUESTIONS TO CONSIDER

- How much money does your organization spend via e-marketplaces, procurement cards, e-auctions, and e-catalogs?

- How much money does your organization spend via large complex negotiated contracts?

- Is your organization using performance-based contracts with your customers and/or suppliers?

- How important are contract negotiation skills to ensure business success?

- How well do you negotiate?

- Does your organization have the number and level of skilled master contract negotiators needed?

ENDNOTES

1   Center of Advanced Purchasing Studies, Cross-Industry Benchmarking Report, 2003.
2   Choi and Stahl, e-Marketplaces and the e-Procurement Cube, Winston, 1997.
3   Boston Consulting Group, e-Marketplaces Report, Boston MA, 2000.
4   Kalakota, Ravi and Robinson, Marcia, e-Business 2.0, Addison-Wesley, Boston MA, 2001.
5   Office of Management and Budget, Office of Federal Procurement Policy, Policy Letter, Performance-Based Contracting, April 1991.
6   Contract Management Institute and Institute of Supply Management 2000 study, The Role of Contract Management/purchasing Professionals, Vienna VA, 2001.
7   Contract Management Institute 2001 Study: Performance Metrics for the Contract Management Discipline, Vienna VA, 2002.
8   Ibid

Contract Negotiation Competencies: The Skills to Win

INTRODUCTION

Everyone has an opinion as to what skills are needed to become a master negotiator. Some people believe you are either born a negotiator or not. Other people believe negotiation, especially contract negotiation, is a skill which can only be mastered by highly trained lawyers. Mark H. McCormack, inventor of sports management and best-selling author of "What They Don't Teach You at Harvard Business School," has stated the perfect negotiator should have:

- Faultless people sense
- A strong competitive streak
- A view of the big picture
- An eye for the crucial detail
- Unimpeachable integrity.[1]

I submit to you, like any skill, contract negotiation can be learned and mastered. Further, professional and personal growth in any aspect of life, typically involves a combination of education, experience, and risk-taking. For those whose business and professional livelihood depends upon success in contract negotiation, skill is more than a nicety - it is a vital necessity. With the growing use of outsourcing in the both the public and private sectors, the ability to negotiate a good deal is becoming a vital element for success at many levels of business management.[2]

Wherever you work, and whatever you do, it is nearly impossible to avoid the need to negotiate in some fashion. Contract negotiation is an area full of traps lying in wait for the untrained or ill prepared. Unfortunately, many novice or apprentice negotiators are often taken advantage of by business-savvy master contract negotiators. In fact, some apprentice contract negotiators will complete a deal thinking they did well, when in reality they lost badly. Some say, ignorance is bliss, but, in contract negotiation it is just bad business.

The intent of this book is not to advocate one way of negotiating deals. Rather, this book suggests contract negotiation is a dynamic process, which requires certain mastery of skills - understanding how, when, what, and why to use specific strategies, tactics, and countertactics in a tailored way for each unique business situation. Likewise, this chapter offers a unique model (Figure 2-1) to help visualize the competencies or skills, which are required to evolve from an apprentice negotiator, intermediate negotiator, to a master negotiator.

Figure 2-1. The Contract Negotiator's Competencies Model

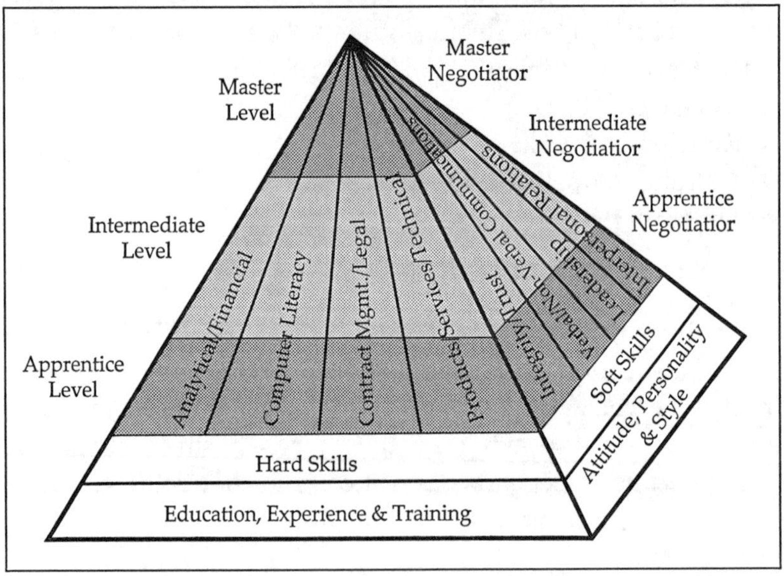

THE CONTRACT NEGOTIATOR'S COMPETENCIES MODEL

Figure 2-1, the Contract Negotiator's Competencies Model, is a visual tool designed to illustrate the following:

- Three levels of contract negotiation mastery
  - Apprentice (1st level) - lowest
  - Intermediate (2nd level) - middle
  - Master (3rd level) - highest
- Two categories of competencies, each with four specialized skills areas
  - Hard Skills
    - Analytical/financial
    - Computer literacy   } Specialized Skill Areas (SSAs)
    - Contract management/legal
    - Product/service/technical

  - Soft Skills (Category)
    - Integrity/trust
    - Verbal/non-verbal communications   } Specialized Skill Areas (SSAs)
    - Leadership
    - Interpersonal relations

It is possible for someone to be considered a master contract negotiator, without truly mastering all of the specialized skill areas. However, based upon extensive research and experience most people who attain mastery of contract negotiation have typically mastered at least three of the four specialized skill areas (SSAs) in each of the two categories of competencies - hard skills and soft skills.

THE SKILLS TO WIN — SELF-ASSESSMENT SURVEY

Fill out the following self-assessment survey to evaluate your hard and soft skills, necessary to be a master contract negotiator. Your answers will help you to determine whether you have the required skills and what areas you may need for improvement. Circle the number that best reflects where you fall on the scale (1 = Low to 5 = High) the higher the number, the more the skill you possess. When you have completed the self-assessment survey add up your numbers on the following worksheet and put the total in the space provided.[3]

The Skills to Win: Self-Assessment Survey

I am a person of high integrity.				
1	2	3	4	5
I always act as a true business professional, especially in contract negotiations.				
1	2	3	4	5
I ensure all of my business partners and team members act honestly, ethically, and legally, especially when involved in contract negotiations and contract formation.				
1	2	3	4	5
I verbally communicate clearly and concisely.				
1	2	3	4	5
I am an effective and persuasive contract negotiator.				
1	2	3	4	5
My written communications are professional, timely, and appropriate.				
1	2	3	4	5
I am an excellent team leader.				
1	2	3	4	5
I consistently build high performance teams, which meet or exceed business requirements.				
1	2	3	4	5
I am willing to compromise when necessary to solve problems.				
1	2	3	4	5
I confront the issues, not the person, in a problem-solving environment.				
1	2	3	4	5
I recognize the power of strategies, tactics, and countertactics and use them frequently in contract negotiations.				
1	2	3	4	5
I am able to achieve my desired financial results in contract negotiations.				
1	2	3	4	5
I understand various cost estimating techniques, numerous pricing models, and how to apply each when negotiating financial arrangements.				
1	2	3	4	5
I understand generally accepted accounting practices and how to apply them when negotiating deals.				
1	2	3	4	5

I am highly computer literate, especially with electronic sales tools, and/or electronic procurement tools.

1	2	3	4	5

I am knowledgeable of e-marketplaces, vertical and horizontal trade exchanges, e-auctions, and how to use them to buy or sell products/services.

1	2	3	4	5

I understand the contract management process and have extensive education, experience, and professional training in contract management.

1	2	3	4	5

I have extensive education, experience, and training in contract law.

1	2	3	4	5

I have extensive education, experience, and training in our organization's products and services.

1	2	3	4	5

I am considered a technical expert in one or more areas.

1	2	3	4	5

Skills to Win Self-Assessment Survey Worksheet

Questions #	Self-Assessment Score (1-5)
1.	
2.	
3.	
4.	
5.	
6.	
7.	
8.	
9.	
10.	
11.	
12.	
13.	
14.	
15.	
16.	
17.	
18.	
19.	
20.	

Grand Total Score: _____

Skills to Win Self-Assessment Survey Scoring

90+:	You have the knowledge and skills of a master contract negotiator.
80 - 90:	You have the potential to become a master contract negotiator, after reviewing the specialized skill areas and determining in which areas you need to improve your skills. You are an intermediate contract negotiator.
65 - 79:	You have basic understanding of successful contract negotiation skills. You need to improve numerous skills to reach a higher level of mastery of contract negotiations. You are an apprentice contract negotiator.
0 - 64:	You have taken the first step to becoming a master contract negotiator. You have a lot of specialized skills areas you need to improve. With time, dedication, and support (education, experience, and training) you can become a master contract negotiator. [4]

THE HARD SKILLS

Traditionally, when most people think about the skills required to become a master contract negotiator they often focus on what I refer to as the hard skills. The hard skills are essentially a competency category composed of four specialized skill areas (SSAs), including:

- Analytical/financial skills
- Computer literacy skills
- Contract management/legal skills
- Products/services/technical skills

Based upon extensive research and experience I have concluded the aforementioned SSAs are key to becoming a master contract negotiator in the world of e-business. For each of the respective SSAs, I will provide a brief summary, and a listing of the top ten critical knowledge and skills areas (KSAs), necessary to become a master contract negotiator.

ANALYTICAL/FINANCIAL SKILLS

When buying or selling products, services, and/or solutions in either the public or private business sectors, it is important to possess a mastery of certain analytical and financial skills. Don't worry be happy - you do not need to be a math major or an expert in probability and statistics. However, you do need to be comfortable working with numbers and percentages and understand how cost, profit, and price are determined and evaluated by each party involved in contract negotiations. In many team-based contract negotiations one member of the team often serves as the analytical/ financial expert, including: a price/cost analysts, finance managers, or chief financial officers (CFOs).

Form 2-1, Checklist of Critical Analytical and Financial Knowledge and Skills Areas, is provided to summarize some of the many specialized areas of knowledge and skills required to become a master contract negotiator. The following checklist is by no means all inclusive, rather it provides a simple, yet effective means of listing ten of the important knowledge and skills areas (KSAs), which based upon research and experience, have proven to be vital to successfully negotiating complex business deals.

Form 2-1 Checklist. 10 Critical Analytical & Financial Knowledge & Skills Areas (KSAs)

☐ Understand the concepts of opportunity costs, sunk costs, fixed costs, variable costs, direct costs, indirect costs, etc.

☐ Able to execute basic mathematical processes (addition, subtraction, multiplication, division, and percentages)

☐ Understand the elements of cost, profit, and price

☐ Understand various pricing methods, including:

　☐ Cost-based pricing (CBP)

　☐ Activity-based pricing (ABP)

　☐ Value-based pricing (VBP)

☐ Able to evaluate cost proposals

☐ Understand cost estimating relationships (CERs)

☐ Able to quantify the total value or best value of an offer in comparison to other offers

☐ Understand the following terms, methods, and techniques:

　☐ Life cycle costing (LCC)

　☐ Economic order quantity (EOQ)

　☐ Expected monetary value (EMV)

　☐ Net present value (NPV)

　☐ Return on inventory (ROI)

Continue on Next Page

☐ Accounts receivable (AR)

☐ Return on assets (ROA)

☐ Earned value (EV)

☐ Days of sales outstanding (DSO)

☐ Lump-sum agreement (LSA)

☐ Able to apply generally accepted accounting principles and practices

☐ Able to achieve desired financial results in contract negotiation

COMPUTER LITERACY SKILLS

In this age of e-business, computer literacy skills are essential. Again, don't worry be happy! You don't need a degree in computer science, however, you must be able to effectively operate in a digital world. In order to become a master contract negotiator it is important to be able to effectively communicate electronically.

Today, computer literacy is usually the biggest challenge for some middle-age and senior adults. Most people under the age of 30 years old, have grown up using computers in their primary education (elementary, middle, and senior high schools) and in their secondary education (undergraduate, graduate, and postgraduate). Plus, many adults use computers every day on their jobs, for some using computers is a key aspect of their occupation. Further, computers are rapidly becoming an essential ingredient in nearly every aspect of our lives at home, at work, in the automobile, while traveling by plane, train, bus, or boat.

So, the real question is how much do you need to know about computer hardware, software, programming, and troubleshooting? The answers to the previous multi-part question are: some, little to none, and some/who to call. Form 2-2, Checklist of Critical Computer Literacy Knowledge and Skills Areas (KSAs), provides a brief summary of ten of the key essential aspects one must master to be able to successfully negotiate complex contracts to buy or sell products, services, and solutions in the world of e-business.

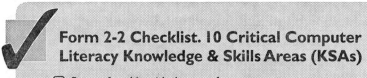

Form 2-2 Checklist. 10 Critical Computer Literacy Knowledge & Skills Areas (KSAs)

- [ ] Be comfortable with the use of computers
- [ ] Understand and be able to operate basic elements/components of computer hardware: keyboard, mouse, monitor, central processor unit (CPU), CD-ROM drive, disk drive, etc. on workstation or lap-top computers
- [ ] Understand and be able to operate basic computer software applications:
  - [ ] Word processing
  - [ ] Spreadsheets
  - [ ] Graphics/charts
  - [ ] Calculator
  - [ ] e-mail
- [ ] Understand and be able to:
  - [ ] Send documents/files
  - [ ] Read documents/files
  - [ ] Edit documents/files
  - [ ] Store/save documents/files
- [ ] Understand and be able to operate more advanced/specialized software applications designed for:
  - [ ] e-procurement
  - [ ] e-sales
  - [ ] e-bids/proposals/capture management
  - [ ] e-pricing
- [ ] Be able to do some customizing of software applications
- [ ] Understand and be able to use the following:
  - [ ] Customized web Portals
  - [ ] Net-marketplaces
  - [ ] Vertical trade exchanges
  - [ ] Horizontal trade exchanges
  - [ ] The World Wide Web
  - [ ] Intranet web sites

Continue on Next Page

☐ Be able to electronically:
 ☐ Create and send documents/files
 ☐ Transfer funds
 ☐ Provide/obtain signatures
 ☐ Obtain proposal and/or contract reviews and approvals
 ☐ Create and send audio/video/photographs
☐ Use wireless computer technology:
 ☐ Be able to use cell phone/mobile phone to send/receive voice/data/video
 ☐ Be able to use wireless networks to send/receive information 24/7/365 globally
☐ Know who and how to contact people to provide timely technical support and/or perform all of the above actions for you

CONTRACT MANAGEMENT/LEGAL SKILLS

As a business professional who negotiates contracts, you will encounter contracts in two ways. As a seller (the provider of goods or services in return for compensation), contracts will be sources of business opportunities. As a buyer (the purchaser of goods or services), contracts will be the means of obtaining the goods and services needed to conduct your business. You will face uncertainty and risk in both types of encounters, so managing contracts effectively is essential. That process is called contract management: the art and science of managing a contractual agreement throughout the contracting process.

Business organizations must strive for the most efficient use of their resources—labor, capital, and money. In an age of ever greater specialization, buyers must make strategic decisions about how best to obtain the goods and services they need. Often, procuring materials, components, parts, finished goods, and services from other companies proves more practical than making or providing them in-house. This practice of obtaining goods and services from outside the organization is commonly called outsourcing. These make-or-buy decisions are an important part of design and production planning and general business operations.

Outsourcing has become a hot topic in business management today, with more and more companies using contracts to help reduce costs, capitalize expenses, improve quality, and increase profitability. The decision to buy goods or services rather than produce them in-house can be a fateful one, however. The buyer will depend on the seller, an entity not entirely under the buyer's control. Therefore, the buyer will face an element of uncertainty and risk. What if the seller cannot deliver on time, within budget, and according to specifications? To what extent does the seller depend on other companies (subcontractors) to deliver the goods and services needed by the buyer?

Market-based societies developed the legal concept of a contract in response to this critical problem of seller-related risk. Thus, contracts became tools for managing uncertainty and risk. Contracts enable buyers and sellers to enforce their agreements through the power of government, thereby reducing (but not eliminating) the risks associated with commercial transactions of goods and services. But because the idea of a contract as both social convention and legal construct has developed over hundreds of years in many different societies and legal systems, contracting concepts are quite complex.

Remember that contracts are first and foremost about developing and maintaining a professional business partnership between the buyer and the seller. Secondarily, contracts are the written documents that confirm and communicate the agreement between the buyer and seller. Thus, to understand contracts fully can take years of specialized study and professional practice. However, as a business professional who manages contracts, you cannot take years to become an expert in contract law; you must learn quickly to operate in the world of contracts as an intelligent layperson.

Think about approaching contract management this way: although not every project involves a contract, almost every contract can be considered a project. Aside from routine retail transactions, virtually all contracts satisfy the four criteria for being a project:

- They are goal-oriented
- They involve the coordinated undertaking of related activities
- They are of finite duration, with a beginning and an end
- They are unique—each different from the next

In managing contracts as projects, it is essential to break down the process into smaller steps that can be handled easily. Thus, the contract management process comprises three common phases, and the phases comprise six major steps for the buyer and six major activities for the seller. This process is summarized in Figure 2-2.

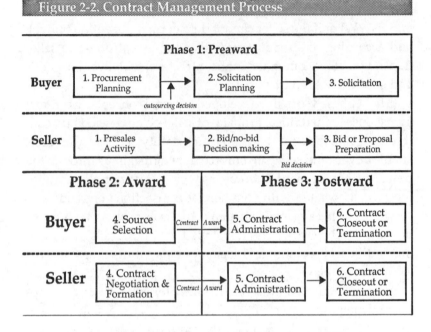

Figure 2-2. Contract Management Process

CONDUCTING THE PREAWARD PHASE

The contract management preaward phase includes procurement planning, market research, requirements determination, the make-or-buy decision, solicitation, bid/no-bid decision making, and bid or proposal preparation. This phase is vital in creating successful business relationships.

The preaward phase has three major activities or steps for the buyer:
- Step 1: Procurement planning
- Step 2: Solicitation planning
- Step 3: Solicitation

Three major activities or steps are also involved for the seller:
- Step 1: Presales activity
- Step 2: Bid/no-bid decision making
- Step 3: Bid or proposal preparation

Figures 2-3 and 2-4 illustrate the contract management process steps for the buyer and seller, respectively.

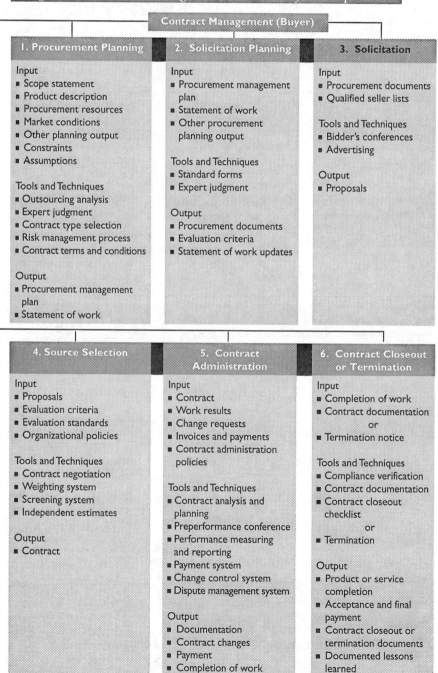

Figure 2-3. Contract Management Process: Buyer's Steps

Contract Management (Buyer)

1. Procurement Planning

Input
- Scope statement
- Product description
- Procurement resources
- Market conditions
- Other planning output
- Constraints
- Assumptions

Tools and Techniques
- Outsourcing analysis
- Expert judgment
- Contract type selection
- Risk management process
- Contract terms and conditions

Output
- Procurement management plan
- Statement of work

2. Solicitation Planning

Input
- Procurement management plan
- Statement of work
- Other procurement planning output

Tools and Techniques
- Standard forms
- Expert judgment

Output
- Procurement documents
- Evaluation criteria
- Statement of work updates

3. Solicitation

Input
- Procurement documents
- Qualified seller lists

Tools and Techniques
- Bidder's conferences
- Advertising

Output
- Proposals

4. Source Selection

Input
- Proposals
- Evaluation criteria
- Evaluation standards
- Organizational policies

Tools and Techniques
- Contract negotiation
- Weighting system
- Screening system
- Independent estimates

Output
- Contract

5. Contract Administration

Input
- Contract
- Work results
- Change requests
- Invoices and payments
- Contract administration policies

Tools and Techniques
- Contract analysis and planning
- Preperformance conference
- Performance measuring and reporting
- Payment system
- Change control system
- Dispute management system

Output
- Documentation
- Contract changes
- Payment
- Completion of work

6. Contract Closeout or Termination

Input
- Completion of work
- Contract documentation
  or
- Termination notice

Tools and Techniques
- Compliance verification
- Contract documentation
- Contract closeout checklist
  or
- Termination

Output
- Product or service completion
- Acceptance and final payment
- Contract closeout or termination documents
- Documented lessons learned

Adapted from: World-Class Contracting, 3d Ed., Gregory A. Garrett, CCH Incorporated, 2003

Figure 2-4. Contract Management Process: Seller's Steps

Contract Management (Buyer)

1. Presales Activity	2. Bid/No-Bid Decision Making	3. Bid or Proposal
Input	Input	Input
■ Customer identification	■ Solicitation	■ Solicitation
■ Customer needs determination	■ Buyer -Specific information	■ Analysis of solicitation
■ Evaluation of competitors	■ Competitive analysis report	■ Competitive analysis report
	■ Seller's strategic objectives and plans	■ Past proposals
Tools and Techniques		
■ Proactive sales management	Tools and Techniques	Tools and Techniques
■ Market research	■ Risk assessment	■ Compliance matrix
■ Competitive analysis	■ Opportunity assessment	■ Standard terms and conditions
	■ Risk management team process	■ Past proposals
Output		■ Lessons-learned database
■ Potential and existing customer lists	Output	■ Executive summary
■ Customer-focused sales plan	■ Bid/no-bid decision	
■ Competitive analysis report	■ Justification document for bid/no-bid decision	Output
		■ Bid or proposal
		■ Supporting documentation
		■ Oral presentation

4. Contract Negotiation and Formation	5. Contract Administration	6. Contract Closeout or Termination
Input	Input	Input
■ Solicitation	■ Contract	■ Completion of work
■ Bid or proposal	■ Work results	■ Contract documentation
■ Buyer's source selection process	■ Change requests	or
■ Seller's past performance	■ Invoices and payments	■ Termination notice
■ Previous contracts	■ Contract administration policies	
■ Competitive analysis report		Tools and Techniques
	Tools and Techniques	■ Compliance verification
Tools and Techniques	■ Contract analysis and planning	■ Contract documentation
■ Contract negotiation process	■ Preperformance conference	■ Contract closeout checklist
■ Highly skilled negotiators	■ Performance measuring and reporting	or
■ Market and industry practices	■ Payment system	■ Termination
■ Legal review	■ Change control system	
	■ Dispute management system	Output
Output		■ Product or service completion
■ Contract	Output	■ Acceptance and final payment
or	■ Documentation	■ Contract closeout or termination documents
■ Walk away	■ Contract changes	■ Documented lessons learned
	■ Payment	
	■ Completion of work	

Adapted from: World-Class Contracting, 3d Ed., Gregory A. Garrett, CCH Incorporated, 2003.

Buyer Step 1: Procurement Planning

Procurement planning is determining what to procure and when. The first contract management problem for the buyer is to decide which goods and services to provide or perform in-house and which to outsource. This *make-or-buy decision* requires consideration of many factors, some of which are strategically important. The decision to buy creates a project that will be implemented in cooperation with an outside organization that is not entirely within the buyer's control. As a result, an element of uncertainty and risk will be introduced for the buyer.

The relationship between buyer and seller is as legal, if not economic, equals. The contract binds them to one another but does not place one under the other's managerial control. Sometimes the seller's economic position may be so powerful, however, that the terms and conditions (Ts and Cs) of the contract are ineffective in protecting the interests of the buyer.

For the seller, the contract will present an opportunity to succeed, but it also will pose great risks. The seller may find that the buyer has specified its needs inadequately or defectively; the seller's marketing department has oversold its products, services, or capabilities; faulty communication has transpired between the two parties during contract formation; or more likely, some combination of all three has occurred. In any of these cases, performance may be much more demanding than originally contemplated and may even be beyond the seller's capabilities. In addition, the buyer may wield great economic power, which effectively outweighs the contract Ts and Cs designed to protect the seller from the buyer's potentially unreasonable demands.

All the communication breakdowns, misunderstandings, conflicts, and disputes that can occur within virtually every organization also can occur between organizations, often with greater virulence and more disastrous effect. Although the contract is intended to provide a remedy to the injured party if the other fails to fulfill its contractual obligations, it is not a guarantee. Legal remedies may be uncertain and, even if attained, may not fully compensate the injured party for the other party's failure.

The outsourcing decision can be a critical one for any organization. After the decision to contract for goods or services is made, the buyer must plan carefully and implement the decision properly.

Buyer Step 2: Solicitation Planning

In the course of planning, the buyer must—
- Determine how to specify its requirements or deliverables
- Identify potential sources
- Analyze the sources of uncertainty and risk that the purchase will entail
- Develop the Ts and Cs of the contract
- Choose the methods for selecting a seller and for proposal evaluation, negotiation, and contract formation
- Arrange for effective administration of the contract

Developing a statement of work (SOW) and the specifications that are usually included in it is one of the most difficult challenges in procurement planning. First, the buyer must understand its own requirements—quite often a difficult task. Second, the buyer must be able to communicate those requirements, typically in the form of either specific deliverables or some form of a level of effort, to others outside the buyer's organization—an even more difficult task. Developing and communicating performance-based requirements is one of the most critical functions in contract management.

Buyer Step 3: Solicitation

Buyers may request bids, quotes, tenders, or proposals orally, in writing, or electronically through procurement documents generally called *solicitations*. Solicitations can take the following forms: request for proposals, request for quotations, request for tenders, invitation to bid, invitation for bids, and invitation for negotiation.

Solicitations should communicate the buyer's needs clearly to all potential sellers. Submitting a high-quality solicitation is vital to the buyer's success. Better solicitations from the buyer generally result in having better bids, quotes, proposals, or tenders submitted by the seller in a more timely manner. Poorly communicated solicitations often result in delays, confusion, fewer bids or proposals, and lower-quality responses. Increasingly, buyers are using electronic data interchange and electronic commerce to solicit offers from sellers of products and services worldwide.

Seller Step 1: Presales Activity

Presales activity is the proactive involvement of the seller with prospective and current buyers. Presales activities include identifying prospective and current customers, determining their needs and plans, working to influence their needs and desires, and evaluating competitors. Presales activities include conducting market research, benchmarking both products and processes against the best companies in industry, and performing competitive analysis reports.

Seller Step 2: Bid/No-Bid Decision Making

Making the bid/no-bid decision should be a two-part process: evaluating the buyer's solicitation, the competitive environment, and your company and assessing the risks against the opportunities for a prospective contract. This step is critical to the contract management process; however, far too many companies devote too little time and attention to properly evaluating the risks before they leap into preparing bids and proposals.

Effectively managing this risk is one of the keys to the success of sellers in today's highly competitive global business environment. Several world-class companies have developed tools and techniques to help their business managers in evaluating the risks versus the opportunities of potential contracts. The tools they use involve risk identification, risk analysis, and risk mitigation.

Seller Step 3: Bid or Proposal Preparation

Bid or proposal preparation is the process of developing offers in response to oral or written solicitations or based on perceived buyer needs. Bid and proposal preparation can range from one person writing a one or two-page proposal to a team of people developing a multivolume proposal of thousands of pages that takes months to prepare.

Chapter 2

CONDUCTING THE AWARD PHASE

Based on the solicitation, the buyer must evaluate offers (bids, proposals, tenders), select a seller, negotiate terms and conditions, and award the contract. Buyers commonly call this step *source selection*. The seller negotiates the Ts and Cs with the buyer and helps form the contract.

Buyer Step 4: Source Selection

Clearly, seller selection is one of the most important decisions a buyer will make. Contract success or failure will depend on the competence and reliability of one or more key sellers and their subcontractors. Procurement planners must identify potential sources of goods and services, analyze the nature of the industry and market in which they operate, develop criteria and procedures to evaluate each source, and select one for contract award. No single set of criteria or procedures is appropriate for all procurements; thus, to some extent, original analyses must be made for each contract.

Source selection may be as simple as determining which competing set of bid prices is the lowest. On the other hand, it may involve weeks or even months of proposal analysis, plant visits, prototype development, and testing. The selection may be accomplished by one person, or it may require an extended effort by a panel of company managers.

Today, companies are spending more time planning and conducting source selection than ever before. The industry trend is toward more comprehensive screening and selection of fewer suppliers for longer duration contracts.

Seller Step 4: Contract Negotiation and Formation

After a source is selected, the parties must reach a common understanding of the nature of their undertaking and negotiate the Ts and Cs of contract performance. The ideal is to develop a set of shared expectations and understandings. However, this goal is difficult to attain for several reasons. First, either party may not fully understand its own requirements and expectations. Second, in most communication, many obstacles prevent achieving a true "meeting of the minds." Errors, miscues, hidden agendas, cultural differences, differences in linguistic use and competence, haste, lack of clarity in thought or expression, conflicting objectives, lack of good faith (or even ill will), business exigencies—all these factors can and do contribute to poor communication.

In any undertaking, uncertainty and risk arise from many sources. In a business undertaking, many of those sources are characteristic of the industry or industries involved. Because one purpose of a contract is to manage uncertainty and risk, the types and sources of uncertainty and risk must be identified and understood. Then buyer and seller must develop and agree to contract terms and conditions that are designed to express their mutual expectations about performance and that reflect the uncertainties and risks of performance. Although tradition and the experiences of others provide a starting point for analysis, each contract must be considered unique.

The development of appropriate terms and conditions is an important aspect of contract negotiation and formation (common terms and conditions include period of performance, warranties, intellectual property rights, payments, acceptance/ completion criteria, and change management). Some organizations spend a lot of time, perhaps months, selecting a source, but they hurry through the process of arriving at a mutual understanding of the contract Ts and Cs. A "let's get on with it" mentality sets in. It is true that contracts formed in this way sometimes prove successful for all concerned. However, when both sides involve large organizations, difficulties can arise from the different agendas of the functional groups existing within each organization's contracting party.

Some world-class companies have developed internal electronic systems to help their contract managers in negotiating, forming, and approving their contracts.

CONDUCTING THE POSTAWARD PHASE

The steps in the postaward phase are the same for both buyer and seller: contract administration and contract closeout or termination.

Buyer and Seller Step 5: Contract Administration

Contract administration is the process of ensuring compliance with contractual terms and conditions during contract performance and up to contract closeout or termination.

After award, both parties must act according to the terms and conditions of their agreement; they must read and understand their contract, do what it requires of them, and avoid doing what they have agreed not to do.

Best practices in contract administration include:

- Reading the contract
- Ensuring that all organizational elements are aware of their responsibilities in relation to the contract
- Providing copies of the contract to all affected organizations (either paper or electronic copies)
- Establishing systems to verify conformance with contract technical and administrative requirements
- Conducting preperformance (or kickoff) meetings with the buyer and the seller
- Assigning responsibility to check actual performance against requirements
- Identifying significant variances
- Analyzing each such variance to determine its cause
- Ensuring that someone takes appropriate corrective action and then follows up
- Managing the contract change process
- Establishing and maintaining contract documentation: diaries and telephone logs, meeting minutes, inspection reports, progress reports, test reports, invoices and payment records, accounting source documents, accounting journals and ledgers, contracting records, change orders and other contract modifications, claims, and routine correspondence

Periodically, buyer and seller must meet to discuss performance and verify that it is on track and that each party's expectations are being met. This activity is critical. Conflict is almost inescapable within and between organizations. The friction that can arise from minor misunderstandings, failures, and disagreements can heat to the boiling point before anyone on either side is fully aware of it. When this happens, the relationship between the parties may be irreparably damaged, and amicable problem resolution may become impossible. Periodic joint assessments by contract managers can identify and resolve problems early and help to ensure mutually satisfactory performance.

Some world-class companies use electronic systems to assist them with contract monitoring, performance measurement, progress reporting, and contract compliance documentation.

BUYER AND SELLER STEP 6: CONTRACT CLOSEOUT OR TERMINATION

After the parties have completed the main elements of performance, they must settle final administrative and legal details before closing out the contract. They may have to make price adjustments and settle claims. The buyer will want to evaluate the seller's performance. Both parties must collect records and prepare them for storage in accordance with administrative and legal retention requirements.

Unfortunately, contracts are sometimes terminated due to the mutual agreement of the parties or due to the failure of one or both of the parties to perform all or part of the contract. After a termination notice is received, the parties must still go through the same closeout actions as for a completed contract.

CONTRACT MANAGEMENT AND LEGAL SKILLS SUMMARY

Like projects, contracts must be managed effectively to be successful. Business professionals are responsible for managing contracts—how you will be affected by a particular contract and how you will manage it depends on whether you are acting as the buyer or the seller of the product or service. Form 2-3 provides a brief summary of ten of the critical contract management and legal knowledge and skill areas.

Form 2-3 Checklist. 10 Critical Contract Management/Legal Knowledge & Skills Areas (KSAs)

☐ Understand the entire contract management process (preaward, award, and postaward phases)

☐ Understand and be able to execute the six-steps required of both buyers and sellers throughout the entire contract management process

☐ Understand and be able to appropriately tailor the following terms and conditions for a specific deal:

  ☐ Acceptance criteria

  ☐ Changes management

  ☐ Delivery

  ☐ Dispute resolution method

  ☐ Force majeure

  ☐ Indemnification

  ☐ Intellectual property rights

  ☐ Invoicing and payments

  ☐ Pricing and discounts

  ☐ Taxes

  ☐ Terminations

  ☐ Warranties

☐ Understand the essential elements to form a legal and binding contract

☐ Be able to draft a legal & binding contract with all appropriate terms and conditions.

☐ Understand who you need to contact, and when to get the appropriate support, to form a successful performance-based contract (technical, financial, and legal support)

☐ Understand the choice of law, and all applicable federal, state, and/or local laws, regulations, and policies which you must adhere to/comply with

☐ Understand the penalties for violations of any or all laws, regulations, or policies

☐ Be able to effectively resolve any contractual dispute

☐ Obtain professional certification in contract management and/or law degree

Products/Services/Technical Skills

In the world of business, contract negotiators, whether representing the buyer or seller, should be knowledgeable of the respective products, services, and technical aspects of each to create the best deal. While product, service, and technical expertise is not required, certainly the more knowledgeable a contract negotiator is about what they are buying or selling the better. Having some product, service, and technical knowledge can be a real key advantage during negotiations. In many team-based complex contract negotiations, there will often be one or more product, service, or technical experts, including: engineers, scientists, product managers, and/or project managers. Remember, the key aspect is to leverage your organization's knowledge/expertise of the marketplace, the products, services, and technical features to negotiate a best-value deal.

Form 2-4, Checklist of 10 Critical Products/Services/Technical Knowledge and Skills Areas (KSAs), is a brief summary of ten of the key items which can be effectively leveraged by buyers and sellers. The items included in Form 2-4 are essential to ensure the buyer receives the quality product, service, and/or solution they desire, for a fair and reasonable price, while allowing the seller to achieve an appropriate profit based upon their performance and assumption of risk.

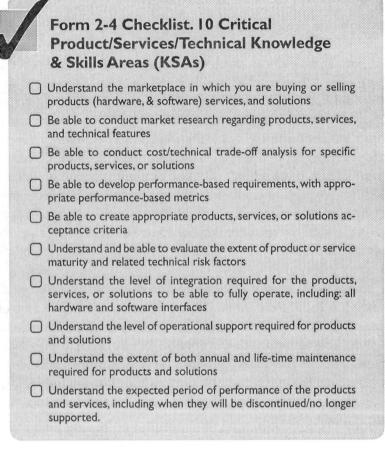

Form 2-4 Checklist. 10 Critical Product/Services/Technical Knowledge & Skills Areas (KSAs)

- ☐ Understand the marketplace in which you are buying or selling products (hardware, & software) services, and solutions

- ☐ Be able to conduct market research regarding products, services, and technical features

- ☐ Be able to conduct cost/technical trade-off analysis for specific products, services, or solutions

- ☐ Be able to develop performance-based requirements, with appropriate performance-based metrics

- ☐ Be able to create appropriate products, services, or solutions acceptance criteria

- ☐ Understand and be able to evaluate the extent of product or service maturity and related technical risk factors

- ☐ Understand the level of integration required for the products, services, or solutions to be able to fully operate, including: all hardware and software interfaces

- ☐ Understand the level of operational support required for products and solutions

- ☐ Understand the extent of both annual and life-time maintenance required for products and solutions

- ☐ Understand the expected period of performance of the products and services, including when they will be discontinued/no longer supported.

THE SOFT SKILLS

Usually, when most individuals consider the skills necessary to become a master contract negotiator they focus on the hard skills, as previously discussed. However, the soft skills, which many people believe are more about an individual's attitude, personality, and style, have a significant bearing on one's ability to consistently be successful when negotiating complex contracts. The soft skills are essentially a competency category composed of four specialized skills areas (SSAs) including:

- Integrity/trust skills
- Verbal/non-verbal communication skills
- Leadership skills
- Interpersonal relation skills

Based upon extensive research and experience I have concluded the aforementioned SSAs are vital to becoming a master contract negotiator. Each of the respective SSAs is composed of ten critical knowledge and skill areas (KSAs).

INTEGRITY/TRUST SKILLS

In the words of Mark H. McCormack, inventor of sports management and best-selling author, "Integrity in a negotiator is like consistency in an athlete. It is not apparent right away and it takes time for other people to appreciate it. But it is a talent or skill nonetheless, because if you are known for your integrity, the other side will be often more willing to accommodate you."[5]

Said simply, an individual of integrity is an individual who has principles and lives by them. Said differently, an individual of integrity is an individual who builds trust by managing expectations and honoring commitments on a consistent basis.

One of the biggest challenges in creating and maintaining a successful long-term business partnership is building trust. Trust is like quality; it is difficult to accurately describe, but you know it when it's there.

Trust is typically earned by doing what you say you are going to do on a repeated basis; in other words, by honoring commitments. A company can also instill trust when it comes to the rescue of another company in a time of urgent business need.

Building trust in business partnerships can take years to accomplish, but sometimes can be lost very quickly.

One of the key elements of building trust is how a company, whether buyer or seller, manages the expectations of its business partner(s). Expectations are assumptions or beliefs about future events. They are usually hopeful and optimistic. Sometimes expectations are pessimistic "plans for the worst."

In our current dynamic high-speed world of e-business, expectations are incredibly high. Too often, people leap to expect the impossible to be achieved without knowing all the facts or details. Of course, sometimes companies can create virtual miracles but, in many cases, fall well short of their customers' unrealistic expectations.

No one in business can avoid setting expectations. Everything companies say or do – or don't say or do — sets some form of expectation in the minds of others. Most companies try to set expectations through their advertising and marketing. However, companies' real market expectations are typically set by their actual performance in comparison to their promises, commonly referred to by results-oriented business leaders as the hype-to-results index. The real key to successfully managing expectations and honoring commitments is understanding the process.[6]

The process of managing expectations is primarily a communication process. The following diagram (figure 2-5) depicts a variety of simple ways to describe the essential elements. Understanding the managing expectations process is good; applying it is even better. Unfortunately, because of the speed of business today, companies frequently react to partial information based upon inaccurate assumptions, rather than truly listening and understanding their customers' needs and desires. Often, sellers do not properly distinguish the real difference between a buyer's needs vs. a buyer's desires.

Figure 2-5. The Managing Expectations Process

Ask	Align	Fulfill
Clarify Expectations	Control Expectations	Meet or Exceed Expectations

Listen ⟩ Understand ⟩ Negotiate ⟩ Agree ⟩ Communicate

■ Surface explicit & Implicit expectations ■ Surface assumptions	■ Compare expectations to reality ■ Resolve gaps ■ Communicate differences ■ Re-set expectations ■ Set realistic expectations ■ Document acceptance criteria	■ Meet with customer ■ Obtain agreement that expectations were met ■ Identify gaps

Adapted from:
"Managing Expectations"
by Dorothy Kirk. PM Network. August 2000

Aligning expectations to reality is a critical step in the managing expectations process. Aligning expectations does not mean reducing objectives or requirements to the lowest level. Aligning expectations is about negotiating a challenging but achievable set of objectives for all parties, based upon the realities of the situation (i.e., technology maturity, schedule, budget, scope of work, mutual priorities, and resource availability).

In order to meet or exceed customer expectations, a company must first agree upon, preferably in writing, what is required. These requirements, often referred to as acceptance criteria, include price, schedule, quality, quantity, etc. It is clearly in the best interest of both parties to ensure that the agreed-to products, services, or solutions will meet or exceed the documented acceptance criteria.

Frequent, open, and honest communication is vital to building successful partnerships between companies. When meeting with customers to provide status reports on the business partnership, whether on a contract or program basis, business professionals must learn to deliver the truth, both good and bad. No business partnership goes perfectly, but communicating the good, the bad, and at times the ugly goes a long way to building trust. What a company does to overcome business obstacles and successfully communicate those actions with customers can be vital to building trust even when the final results are not the best.[7]

Form 2-5 Checklist. 10 Integrity/Trust Critical Knowledge & Skills Areas (KSAs)

☐ Listen to the customer

☐ Understand the customer's needs vs. desires

☐ Return phone calls, voice mail messages, and e-mail in a timely manner

☐ Provide regular communication on contract, program, and partnership status

☐ Develop a project plan for every deal (scope of work, integrated schedule, work breakdown structure, responsibility assignment matrix, and acceptance criteria)

☐ Develop a risk management plan

☐ Disclose problems early and mitigate negative impacts

☐ Back up all verbal agreements and conversations with written documentation

☐ Be prepared to deliver both good and bad news at multiple levels, both internally and with customers

☐ Demonstrate passion in honoring commitments

VERBAL/NON-VERBAL COMMUNICATION SKILLS

Clearly one of the most important, if not the most important skill area one must master to achieve consistent success when negotiating complex contracts is communication skills. As a contract negotiator, all aspects of communications are vital to success. According to numerous studies on adult education, most adults retain more of what they see, than what they hear. Likewise, most adults value more how you communicate, than what you communicate. Further, everyone communicates more via non-verbal means than through the spoken word. Finally, to become a master contract negotiator one must think before communicating, especially during contract negotiations, because everything you say, don't say, write, don't write, do, and don't do, will be evaluated by the other side.

Communication Skills:
12 Best Practices

In many business transactions you will be required to provide verbal (oral) and/or written presentations as a part or basis for contract negotiations. In fact, the quality of your presentation may very well be a deciding factor as to whether or not you are even able to get to conduct the negotiation with the other party. Thus, it is worthwhile to consider the following 12 best practices, adapted from George Fuller, Master Contract Negotiator, and author of the book, The Negotiator's Handbook, to ensure your oral and/or written presentation is indeed successful.

1. **Accuracy.** Is your presentation error-free? Many presentations that are sound in all other respects, fall by the wayside in this regard. This is usually due to limited time constraints when preparing the presentation.

2. **Be complete but concise.** How much is enough is a mental hurdle that often leads to loading presentations with all sorts of irrelevant information. The question, "Is anything missing?" is always thought about during proposal preparation, but the counter question of, "Is this overkill?" is often ignored. Sheer volume can spell the death knell for presentations far faster than a slim presentation that's loaded with convincing arguments.

3. **Make it persuasive.** Someone has to be convinced about something to make any presentation a winner. So support what you propose with sound reasoning, and if possible provide solid examples. In short, prove that you can produce what you are proposing.

4. **Don't get fancy.** Fight the tendency to offer more than is necessary to be successful. This can lead to promises that the reviewer knows cannot be fulfilled.

5. **Skip the fluff.** All too often, there's an attempt to cover-up an inadequacy by padding the presentation with fluff that has no relationship to what's being proposed. For instance, a company that has a renowned scientist in its employ will include that person's credentials in every presentation. This creates skepticism when the subject matter of the proposal has no relationship to the individual's area of expertise. This leaves reviewers wondering if this is being done to beef-up an otherwise weak proposal.

6. **Don't ignore problems.** Many presentations accentuate the positive - which is good - but ignore the negative aspects that must be overcome for the project to be a success.

7. **Solve the "right" problems.** Many presentations try to succeed by covering "all of the bases" in every ball park, when the game is just being played on one field. The presentation sounds like, "Here's what you want, but if it isn't, we'll do it your way." This tactic seldom succeeds since it shows a lack of conviction, as well as doubt about what is actually being proposed.

Continue on Next Page

8. **Be creative.** Although you shouldn't wander too far afield, simply laying out a response that minimally complies with what's being sought won't get you very far. After all, most proposals will offer something similar, but the one that wins will have provided some real creativity in demonstrating how to build a better solution.

9. **Watch your numbers.** Long lists of numbers should be placed together in a separate section to provide both better organization and ease of analysis. And don't forget to spend some time thinking about how you will format your data. For example, if you're just indicating a general trend, a graph can be more effective than a lengthy list of numbers.

10. **Combine substance with style.** As any consumer goods manufacturer can tell you, packaging helps sell the product. Therefore, take pains to make your oral or written presentation look good. A proposal strong in substance may overcome the handicap of a sloppy appearance, but you run the risk of a reviewer who thinks that a shabby looking proposal may indicate lousy results down the road.

11. **Remember readability.** It's easy to overlook the potential readership of an oral or written presentation/proposal. This leads to proposals that are targeted toward one person or group, without considering the fact that the actual decision-maker is someone else. This is especially true in technical proposals which are prepared on the assumption that the proposal will be evaluated only by those who understand the technical terminology. However, proposals are often reviewed by people who don't understand technical terms and the jargon of the trade. Therefore, it is prudent to prepare proposals that avoid jargon, do not confuse readers, and are not vague.

12. **Don't waste your efforts.** Preparing both oral presentations and written proposals can be expensive, and time consuming. Therefore, it is important to concentrate your resources on those proposals with the highest possible payoff.[8]

NONVERBAL COMMUNICATION SKILLS

Years of extensive research in communication suggests that nearly 90 percent of the meaning transmitted between two or more people in face-to-face communications is via nonverbal channels.[9] Said differently, only about 10 percent of your message is transmitted by your spoken words. Realizing, most people focus on the words they say, not on how they say it, these statistics indicate the importance of nonverbal contract negotiations skills.

Some communication experts have stated that in a typical 30 minute face-to-face contract negotiation meeting, two people can send over 800 different nonverbal messages.[10] Therefore, it is not surprising that people often do not understand why the other party is not in agreement with them, because their words may say one thing, while their nonverbals communicate something else. In the book Nonverbal Selling Power, Gerhard Gshwandtner discusses the power of recognizing nonverbal communication signals - in yourself and the other parties.

LEVERAGING THE ART OF NONVERBALS IN CONTRACT NEGOTIATIONS

There are three key aspects of nonverbal contract negotiations:
1. Awareness of yourself
2. Awareness of the other side
3. Using nonverbal communication to manage yourself and others.

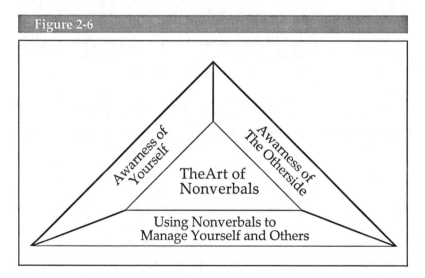

Figure 2-6

Often the question arises, how accurate are nonverbal communications when compared to verbal ones? After analyzing video tapes of conversations, D.A. Humphries, a British researcher, found that groupings of nonverbal gestures proved to be more accurate, truthful representations of the participants' feelings than their words were.

Interpreting nonverbal communication can prove challenging. However, if you study your own nonverbal behavior and that of others daily, you will begin to understand the gesture grouping process.[11] Nonverbal communication skills can prove to be very valuable to mastering contract negotiations, because it allows you to know when people are saying one thing and meaning another. To make sure you are catching and understanding the nonverbal signals your counterpart is sending, Gschwandtner suggests conducting a "body scan." A good formula to follow is to divide the body into five categories:

1. Face and head,
2. Body,
3. Arms,
4. Hands, and
5. Legs.

Figure 2-7. The Language of Nonverbal Communication, describes how groupings of gestures can convey meanings.[12]

The Language of Nonverbal Communication	
Dominance and Power	**Submission and Nervousness**
■ Placing feet on desk	■ Fidgeting
■ Making piercing eye contact	■ Making minimum eye contact
■ Putting hands behind head or neck	■ Touching hands to face, hair, etc.
■ Placing hands on hips	■ Using briefcase to "guard" body
■ Giving a pal-down handshake	■ Giving a palm-up handshake
■ Standing while counterpart is seated	■ Clearing throat
■ Steepling (fingertips touching)	
Disagreement, Anger, and Skepticism	**Boredom and Lack of Interest**
■ Getting red in the face	■ Failing to make eye contact
■ Pointing a finger	■ Playing with objects on desk
■ Squinting	■ Staring blankly
■ Frowning	■ Drumming on table
■ Turning body away	■ Picking at clothes
■ Crossing arms or legs	■ Looking at watch, door, etc.
Uncertainty and Indecision	**Suspicion and Dishonesty**
■ Cleaning glasses	■ Touching nose while speaking
■ Looking puzzled	■ Covering mouth
■ Putting fingers to mouth	■ Avoiding eye contact
■ Biting lip	■ Using incongruous gestures
■ Pacing back and forth	■ Crossing arms and legs
■ Tilting head	■ Moving body away
Evaluation	**Confidence, Cooperation, and Honesty**
■ Nodding	■ Leaning forward in seat
■ Squinting	■ Keeping arms and palms open
■ Maintaining good eye contact	■ Maintaining great eye contact
■ Tilting head slightly	■ Placing feet flat on floo
■ Stroking chin	■ Sitting with legs uncrossed
■ Touching index finger to lips	■ Moving with counterpart's rhythm
■ Placing hands on chest	■ Smiling

Chapter 2

Form 2-6, provides a brief summary of ten of the critical verbal/ nonverbal communications knowledge and skill areas (KSAs) needed to become a master contract negotiator.

✓ **Form 2-6 Checklist. 10 Critical Verbal/ Nonverbal Communications Knowledge & Skills Areas (KSAs)**

☐ Be able to apply the 12 best practices of communications

☐ Be comfortable when communicating to others

☐ Understand the language of nonverbal communication

☐ Know the five categories of the body, for purposes of identifying and grouping gestures to determine meanings

☐ Be able to orally deliver clear, concise, and compelling communications

☐ Be able to prepare effective written proposals

☐ Be able to effectively ask questions during contract negotiations to gain information

☐ Be able to effectively use audio and visual aides to support your oral and written presentations

☐ Practice active listening

☐ Look the part - dress for success

LEADERSHIP SKILLS

Leadership skills are important, especially in team-based contract negotiations. Real leaders know how to "talk the talk," "walk the talk," build leaders at every level, and make a difference. This section was adapted from the book *Managing Complex Outsourced Projects*, by Gregory A. Garrett (CCH Incorporated, 2004).

Step 1: Talk the Talk — To successfully deliver a message, a leader must: (1) know how to deliver the message, (2) pay attention to appearance, and (3) know what to say.

■ *It's in the Delivery* — To improve communications skills, a leaders should:

   ■ *Learn to be a proactive listener.* Think before talking.

- *Deliver messages in person or via telephone.* Do this with passion, commitment, and a positive "can do" attitude; people usually can spot a fake.
- *Use tone, pauses, loudness, pitch, and inflection.* These communicate what is important.
- *Use body language to reinforce verbal communication.* This includes eye contact, hand motions and gestures, and facial expressions.
- *Practice, develop, and refine your communication skills daily.*

- *Look Like a Leader* — Some people foolishly believe that saying the right things makes appearance unimportant. Wrong! Appearance always matters, because it communicates so much. While being physical attractive helps in some instances, how one chooses to dress, stand, sit, and use other non-verbal physical communication methods and techniques has a dramatic impact on how effectively the message is delivered (see Form 2-7).

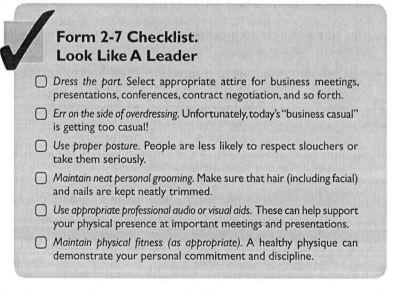

Form 2-7 Checklist.
Look Like A Leader

- ☐ *Dress the part.* Select appropriate attire for business meetings, presentations, conferences, contract negotiation, and so forth.
- ☐ *Err on the side of overdressing.* Unfortunately, today's "business casual" is getting too casual!
- ☐ *Use proper posture.* People are less likely to respect slouchers or take them seriously.
- ☐ *Maintain neat personal grooming.* Make sure that hair (including facial) and nails are kept neatly trimmed.
- ☐ *Use appropriate professional audio or visual aids.* These can help support your physical presence at important meetings and presentations.
- ☐ *Maintain physical fitness (as appropriate).* A healthy physique can demonstrate your personal commitment and discipline.

- *Know What to Say* — To effectively talk the talk, a person also must know what to say. Communicating customer needs versus desires, as well as the status of the marketplace, to team members is vitally important. The company's vision and goals need to be communicated precisely and repeatedly, ensuring that everyone knows their role, responsibilities, and performance metrics for achieving those goals. In addition, the firm's business challenges regarding revenue, expenses, profitability, and loss should be regularly explained. Finally, effective leaders communicate the importance of creating a performance-based contract — and reward results.

Step 2: Walk the Talk — Learning to practice real leadership in team-based contract negotiation is challenging. Leadership is not about micromanagement; it is about becoming a force-multiplier. Novice contract negotiators often make the mistake of doing the work their team members are responsible for doing instead of holding them accountable, providing appropriate coaching/support, or changing personnel when needed. Novice or apprentice contract negotiators frequently fail to quickly recognize team members' strengths and weaknesses, resulting in additional problems and potential negotiation failures. Finally, apprentice contract negotiators are hesitant to remove poor performers or disruptive individuals from their team, instead they allow the ineffective worker to negatively impact team and negotiation results. The following proven best practices can help ensure the motivation of others to accomplish your desired results.

1. Listen to your team members and the other side and understand their needs and desires.
2. Take proactive, appropriate actions to help your team members achieve their needs and desires.
3. Teach team members and the other side about leadership by honoring commitments.
4. Hold people accountable for their actions or inactions and results.
5. Conduct frequent team meetings with all team members either in person or via teleconferencing or the Internet.
6. Display a positive "can do" attitude with a blend of realism and practicality.
7. Conduct frequent customer and supplier meetings with key decision-makers to discuss relationship and performance goals versus results using agreed upon performance metrics.
8. Develop and live by a code of conduct that includes honesty, integrity, mutual respect, and so forth.

9. Develop, document, and distribute the organization's vision statement, goals, and performance metrics and results. Distribute these items via e-mail, posters, web site ads or articles, company newsletters, and CD ROMs. When distributing performance metrics and results, include information about customer satisfaction, product and service quality, employee satisfaction, delivery times, cycle times, revenue, and expenses.

10.Recognize and reward individuals and contract negotiation teams for outstanding performance. Tie pay to performance if possible.

Step 3: Build Leaders at Every Level — One of the best books on leadership is Neal Tichy's *The Leadership Engine.* Tichy discusses the importance of building leaders at every level of a company or organization and provides a simple model that describes typical situational leadership methods used to obtain results. Figure 2-8, The Leadership Pyramid, outlines some of Tichy's primary leadership principles.

Figure 2-8. The Leadership Pyramid

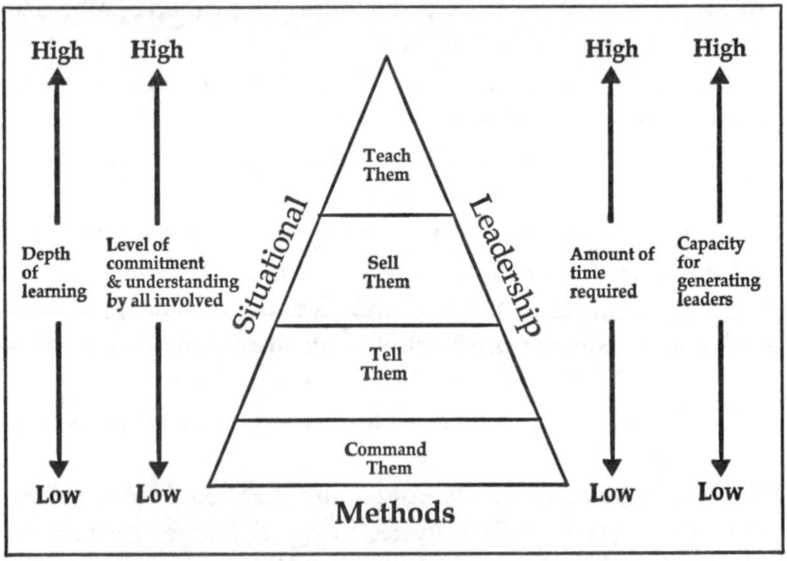

Step 4: Make a Difference — Everyone has encountered individuals they would describe as leaders, people who really do walk the talk (see Form 2-8).

✓ **Form 2-8 Checklist. 10 Critical Leadership Skills Knowledge & Skills Areas (KSAs)**

☐ Unlike self-proclaimed leader "wannabes," real leaders
☐ Have ideas, values, energy, passion, and focus
☐ Lead the team through the tough times
☐ Hold people accountable
☐ Get results
☐ Make decisions
☐ Clearly communicate ideas
☐ Live by a set of values
☐ Build high-performance teams
☐ Accept blame for team failures and give credit and recognition to others for team successes
☐ Take the time to teach others to be leaders

INTERPERSONAL RELATION SKILLS

It has been said, a person learns everything they need to know in preschool or kindergarten. I do not believe that is entirely true; however, I appreciate the importance of learning how to get along with others, especially dealing with difficult people. As related to contract negotiations, interpersonal skills are extremely important, including: building trust, forming partnerships, and resolving conflicts. Interpersonal skills are vital to success both internally, within your organization, and externally with your customers and suppliers.

Building teamwork based upon trust and mutual respect with your team members, suppliers, and customers is critical to successful contract negotiation. The greater the level of respect or confidence your team members and other parties have in your honesty, integrity, and reliability, the easier it will be to create win/win deals. Conversely, without a professional relationship even minor concessions will be very challenging.

Peter B. Stark and Jane Flaherty, consultants, and co-authors of the book *The Only Negotiating Guide You'll Ever Need*, offer the following 15 building blocks for establishing professional relationships based on trust and mutual respect in negotiations.[13]

1. Demonstrate your competence
2. Make sure the nonverbal signals you are sending match the words you are saying
3. Maintain a professional appearance
4. Communicate your good intentions
5. Do what you say you are going to do
6. Go beyond the conventional relationship
7. Listen
8. Over communicate
9. Discuss the undiscussables
10. Provide accurate information, without any hidden agenda
11. Be honest — even when it costs you something
12. Be patient
13. Safeguard for fairness
14. Negotiate for abundance, not scarcity
15. Take calculated risks

Forming partnerships is vital to success in contract negotiations. Partnerships must be internally formed first within the contract negotiation team, then partnerships must be developed with the other parties — customers and suppliers. Unfortunately, it can be very challenging to build partnerships with individuals who do not want to build relationships — some people only care about winning the immediate deal.

Dealing with conflicts and untrustworthy parties is a fact of life. Unfortunately, nearly every organization has a few untrustworthy individuals, some organizations clearly have more than others, and most of us have to find a professional and ethical way to work with them. Conflict is natural, even when dealing with people who are honest and of high integrity. Conflicts often arise out of differences in opinion, viewpoint, organizational goals, personal agendas, etc. The key to conflict management is to treat the conflict as a mutual problem which must be jointly solved by addressing the issue not the person or their position.

✓ **Form 2-9 Checklist. 10 Critical Interpersonal Knowledge & Skills Areas (KSAs)**

☐ Able to work well with others
☐ Be honest
☐ Able to deal with untrustworthy individuals
☐ Able to build strong professional business relationships
☐ Use joint problem solving
☐ Practice active listening
☐ Be respectful to everyone
☐ Practice patience
☐ Honor your commitments
☐ Hold people accountable

SUMMARY

So in retrospect, in this chapter we have provided you a brief review of the skills needed to become a master contract negotiator. Using the Contract Negotiator's Competencies Model we discussed the following:

- Two competency categories (Hard Skills and Soft Skills), each with four Specialized Skill Areas (SSAs)
  - Hard Skills:
    - Analytical/financial
    - Computer literacy
    - Contract management/legal
    - Products/services/technical
  - Soft Skills:
    - Integrity/trust
    - Verbal/nonverbal communication
    - Leadership
    - Interpersonal relations

I have summarized ten critical Knowledge and Skill Areas (KSAs) for each of the eight SSAs. Very few people have truly mastered all of the SSAs and respective KSAs. However, most individuals who demonstrate mastery of complex contract negotiations, have mastered at least 3 of the 4 SSAs in each of the two competency categories - hard skills and soft skills. After reading this chapter, I suggest you go back and complete each of the checklist forms, and see how well you rate your skills. If you score 9 - 10 (excellent - master level), 7 - 8 (good - intermediate level), 4 - 6 (satisfactory - apprentice level), and 0 - 3 (poor - first step).

QUESTIONS TO CONSIDER:

■ What are the most important skills for a master contract negotiator to posses?

■ Is it necessary to have unimpeachable integrity to be a master contract negotiator?

■ What analytical/financial skills are critical to become an effective negotiator?

■ As a person who negotiates contracts how important is it to have excellent oral and written communication skills?

■ Are nonverbal skills really important in face-to-face communications?

■ How important are leadership skills in team-based contract negotiations?

ENDNOTES

1 McCormack, Mark H., Mark H. McCormack on Negotiating, Los Angeles CA, Dove Books, 1995.
2 Ibid
3 Stark, Peter B. and Jane Flaherty, The Only Negotiating Guide You'll Ever Need, New York NY, Broadway Books, 2003.
4 Ibid
5 Ibid Note 1
6 Garrett, Gregory A., World Class Contracting, Chicago IL, CCH Incorporated, 2003.
7 Ibid
8 Fuller, George, The Negotiator's Handbook, Englewood Cliffs, Prentice Hall, 1991.
9 Ibid Note 3
10 Ibid Note 3
11 Nierenberg, Gerard, The Art of Negotiating, New York NY, Penguin Books, 1989.
12 Ibid Note 3
13 Ibid Note 3

The Contract Negotiation Process

INTRODUCTION

So, what is contract negotiation? According to I. William Zartman, author of *The Practical Negotiator*, "it is the process of unifying different positions into a unanimous joint decision, regarding the buying and selling of products and/or services." Zartman states further, "Contract negotiation is a process of making or reaching an agreement without rules about how decisions are made."[1] Extensive experience and research, clearly show that many business professionals fear negotiating contracts.

Why do so many people fear negotiating contracts? The seven most typical responses include:
- It's too hostile and intimidating!
- I like to avoid conflict!
- I do not know enough about contracts!
- I do not know enough about the legal or technical aspects!
- I am not articulate enough!
- I do not want to develop a new challenging skill!

CONTRACT NEGOTIATION — A COMPLEX HUMAN ACTIVITY

As discussed in Chapter 2, contract negotiation is a complex human activity. Successful contract negotiators must:
- Master the art and science, or soft and hard skills, required to become a master negotiator;
- Possess the intellectual ability to comprehend the factors shaping and characterizing the negotiation;

- Be able to adapt strategies, tactics, and countertactics in a dynamic environment;
- Understand their own personalities and personal ethics and values;
- Know their products and services, desired terms and conditions, and pricing strategy; and
- Be able to lead a diverse multi-functional team to achieve a successful outcome.

If accomplishing all of the aforementioned tasks sounds easy, then you are either a highly skilled contract negotiator or somewhat naïve about what it takes to become a master contract negotiator.

Contract Negotiation Approaches

We all negotiate every day—with our friends, our family, our business customers, suppliers, and team members. Some of us negotiate well on occasion with some of the parties in our lives. But most of us do not negotiate consistently well with all of the parties in our personal and professional lives. The fact is there are two basic approaches to contract negotiations: the intuitive approach, and the process approach.

The intuitive contract negotiation approach is usually characterized as unstructured, informal, undocumented, and yielding inconsistent negotiation results. The intuitive contract negotiation approach is also affectionately known as the following:

- The no plan, no clue approach;
- Fly-by-the-seat-of-your pants approach;
- Ad hoc approach;
- Think out-of-the-box approach; or
- Who needs a stinking plan approach.

The contract negotiation process approach is typically characterized as structured, planned, formal, documented, and yielding more consistent negotiation results. Arguably, in the world of contract negotiations, the three most important aspects are planning, negotiating, and documenting the deal.

Contract Negotiation — The Art and Science of the Deal

In contract negotiation, getting to yes means getting past no! As William Ury, the co-author of the best-selling books *Getting to Yes* and *Getting Past No!* states, "Getting around yes, but focusing on common interests not positions, is critical to achieve successful negotiation results."[2] Creating a joint buyer and seller problem solving environment is vital to developing a win/win contract negotiation situation. Remember, the right solution is truly a matter of perspective for both the buyer and the seller. Like the game of chess, contract negotiation requires strategy, tactics, countertactics, stressing one's flexibility and ability to adapt to changing situations while realizing there is more than one way to achieve success. Unlike chess, contract negotiation provides an opportunity for both parties to meet or exceed their respective needs.

Contract Negotiation Objectives (Interests)

Clearly, contract negotiation is about a buyer (an organization purchasing goods or services) selecting a Seller (an organization providing goods or services) and their respective representatives reaching a written agreement to document their relationship: who will do what, where, when, and for how much!

Typically, buyers' contract negotiation objectives include:
- Acquire necessary supplies, services, or solutions of the desired quality, on-time, and at the lowest reasonable price;
- Establish and administer a pricing arrangement that results in payment of a fair and reasonable price; and
- Satisfy needs of the end-user (customer).

Similarly, sellers' contract negotiation objectives usually include:
- Grow profitable revenue (long term vs. short term);
- Increase market share within their respective industry; and
- Deliver quality supplies, services, or solutions to achieve customer loyalty.

While each contract negotiation is unique and there may be some special objectives for certain deals, the previously stated contract negotiations objectives are relatively common for most buyers and sellers.

Contract Negotiation: A Process Approach for Building Successful Business Relationships

Contract negotiation is the process by which two or more competent parties reach an agreement to buy or sell products or services. Contract negotiation may be conducted formally or informally and may involve many people or just two—a representative for the buyer and a representative for the seller. Contract negotiation may take a few minutes or may involve many discussions over days, months, or years.

The desired result of the contract negotiation process is a contract. Contract formation is the process of putting together the essential elements of the contract and any special items unique to a particular business agreement (see Figure 3-1).

Figure 3-1. Contract Negotiation: Essential Elements

Key Inputs	Tools & Techniques	Desired Outputs

▪ Solicitation (RFP, RFQ, etc.)
▪ Bid or proposal
▪ Buyer's source selection process
▪ Seller's past performance
▪ Previous contracts
▪ Competitor profile business ethics/standards of conduct guidelines
▪ Market and industry practices
	▪ Oral presentations
	▪ Highly skilled contract negotiators
	▪ Legal review
	▪ Business case approval
	▪ Contract negotiation formation process
	  ▪ Plan negotiations
	  ▪ Conduct negotiations
	  ▪ Document the negotiation and form the contract
		▪ Contract or walk away

From: *World Class Contracting*, by Gregory A. Garrett, CCH Incorporated, 2003.

KEY INPUTS[3]

The key inputs to negotiations and contract formation consists of the following items:

- ▪ *Solicitation:* The solicitation is either an oral or written request for an offer (Request for Proposal (RFP), Request for Quote (RFQ), Invitation for Bid (IFB), and so on) prepared by the buyer and provided to one or more potential sellers.

- *Bid or proposal:* The bid or proposal is either an oral or written offer by potential sellers to provide products or services to the buyer, usually in response to a solicitation. It also includes all supporting documentation, such as delivery plans, assumptions, and cost/price models.
- *Buyer's source selection process:* Source selection is the process by which a buyer selects a seller or source of supply for products or services. Buyers typically apply evaluation criteria to select the best seller to meet their needs. The source selection process is seldom an uncomplicated one because:
  - Price may be the primary determinant for an off-the-shelf item, but the lowest proposed price may not be the lowest cost if the seller proves unable to deliver the product in a timely manner;
  - Proposals are often separated into technical/delivery and pricing/contractual sections that are evaluated separately; and
  - Multiple sources may be required for critical products.

    Bids or proposals may be simple, requiring only one person to evaluate the sources and select the best alternative, or they may be complex, requiring a panel of experts. In fact, some proposal evaluations may require a consultant's assistance.
- *Source Selectino Evaluation Criteria:* Developing the evaluation criteria for source selection requires three prerequisites. First, the buyer must understand what goods or services it wants to buy. Second, the buyer must understand the industry that will provide the required goods or services. And third, the buyer must understand the market practices of that industry. Market research provides this information.

    The buyer gains an understanding of the required products or services during requirements analysis and development of the specification or statement of work. Understanding the industry means learning about the attributes of the goods or services in question and the firms that make them: What features do those goods or services have? What processes are used to produce or render them? What kinds and quantities of labor and capital are required? What are the cash requirements? Understanding the market means learning about the behavior of buyers and sellers: What are the pricing practices of the market, and what is the range of prices charged? What are the usual terms and conditions of sale?

After gaining an understanding of these issues, the buyer is ready to develop the evaluation criteria by selecting attributes for evaluation.

■ *Source Selection Attributes:* A consumer shopping for an automobile does not evaluate an automobile per se but rather selected attributes of the automobile, such as acceleration, speed, handling, comfort, safety, price, fuel mileage, capacity, appearance, and so forth. The evaluation of the automobile is the sum of the evaluations of its attributes.

An automobile has many attributes, but not all are worthwhile subjects of evaluation. The attributes of interest are those that the consumer thinks are important for satisfaction. The attributes that one consumer thinks are important may be inconsequential to another.

In most procurements, multiple criteria will be required for successful performance for the following reasons: First, buyers usually have more than one objective. For example, many buyers look for both good quality and low price. Second, attributes essential for one objective may be different from those essential for others. For example, in buying an automobile, the attributes essential for comfort have little to do with those essential for quick acceleration.

To complicate matters further, some criteria will likely be incompatible with others. The attributes essential to high quality may be inconsistent with low price; high performance, for example, may be incompatible with low operating cost. Thus, for any one source to have the maximum desired value of every essential attribute—such as highest quality combined with lowest price—may be impossible. If so, the buyer must make trade-offs among attributes when deciding which source is best. These are considerations that make source selection a problem in *multiple attribute decision making*, which requires special decision analysis techniques.[4]

As a rule, source selection attributes fall into three general categories relating to the sources themselves, as entities; the products or services they offer; and the prices they offer. Thus, the buyer must have criteria for each category that reflect the buyer's ideas about what is valuable. The criteria concerning the sources themselves, as entities, are the management criteria; the criteria concerning the products or services offered are the technical criteria; and the criteria concerning the prices of the products or services are the price criteria.

■ *Seller's past performance:* The past performance of a seller is often a critical aspect of contract negotiation. Has the seller delivered previous products and services on time? Has the seller provided high-quality products and services?

Past performance can be regarded as a separate evaluation factor or as a subfactor under technical excellence or management capability. Using the past performance history also reduces the emphasis on merely being able to write a good proposal.

■ *Previous contracts:* Has the seller provided products or services to this buyer in the past? If so, what did the previous contract say? How was it negotiated? Who negotiated it?

■ *Competitor profile:* The competitor profile, developed during the pre-bid phase, provides a written summary of the seller's competitors and their respective strengths and weaknesses compared to the seller's.

■ *Business ethics/standards of conduct guidelines:* In light of numerous recent cases of corporate greed, corruption, and violations of law, ethics is especially important. Every company should have mandatory business ethics policies, procedures, and well-defined standards of conduct. Even the appearance of conflicts of interests should be avoided. All business activities should be conducted in a professional and ethical manner.

■ *Market and industry practices:* Knowing what the competitors are offering (most-favored pricing, warranties, product discounts, volume discounts, and so on) is essential for a successful outcome to negotiation.

Tools and Techniques

The following tools and techniques are used for negotiations and contract formation:

- *Oral presentations:* It is usually better to orally present your bid/proposal to your customer than to merely submit it electronically (e-mail, fax, CD-ROM) or on paper. When preformed by a skilled, knowledgeable, and persuasive individual, oral presentations can help sell your products, services, or solution to the buyer. Oral presentations can be used to address questions and clarify concerns that the buyer may have regarding your proposal.
- *Contract negotiation process:* The contract negotiation process is discussed in detail later in this chapter.
- *Highly skilled negotiators:* Conducting contract negotiation is a complex activity that requires a broad range of skills. Providing negotiators with the best available training in contract negotiation is vital. Top negotiators help their organizations save money and make higher profits.
- *Legal review:* A legal review should be conducted, if not as a regular part of the contract negotiation process, then at least for all key contracts.

CASE STUDY: NORTHROP/GRUMMAN

For more than 25 years, Northrop/Grumman has had an excellent reputation in building or developing highly skilled contract negotiators and negotiation teams. Northrop/Grumman has traditionally ensured their sales managers, contract managers, and contract administrators receive appropriate and timely negotiation training through in-house professional seminars, university-based courses, and attendance at educational conferences and seminars. In addition, Northrop/Grumman has for many years developed and maintained a seasoned and highly skilled major negotiations team to tackle the largest and most important contract negotiations.

The Contract Negotiation Process

The contract negotiation process is composed of three phases: planning negotiations, conducting negotiations, and documenting negotiations. Table 3-1 describes an effective, logical approach to plan, conduct, and document contract negotiations based on the proven best practices of world-class organizations.

Table 3-1. Contract Negotiation Process

Plan the Negotiation	Conduct the Negotiation	Document the Negotiation and Form the Contract
1. Prepare yourself and your team	11. Determine who has authority	21. Prepare the negotiation memorandum
2. Know the other party	12. Prepare the facility	22. Send the memorandum to the other party
3. Know the big picture	13. Use an agenda	23. Offer to write the contract
4. Identify objectives	14. Introduce the team	24. Prepare the contract
5. Prioritize objectives	15. Set the right tone	25. Prepare negotiation results summary
6. Create options	16. Exchange information	26. Obtain required reviews and approvals
7. Select fair standards	17. Focus on objectives	27. Send the contracts to the other party for signature
8. Examine alternatives	18. Use strategy, tactics, and countertactics	28. Provide copies of the contract to affected organizations
9. Select your strategy, tactics, and countertactics	19. Make counteroffers	29. Document lessons learned
10. Develop a solid and approved team negotiation plan	20. Document the agreement or know when to walk away	30. Prepare the contract administration plan

PLAN THE NEGOTIATION

The following ten actions should be performed to properly plan the negotiation:

1. *Prepare yourself and your team:* Ensure that the lead negotiator knows his or her personal and professional strengths, weaknesses, and tendencies as well as those of other team members. (Many self-assessment tools are available, including the Myers-Briggs Type Indicator® assessment. It can provide helpful insight on how an individual may react in a situation because

of personal or professional tendencies.) Preparing a list of the strengths and weaknesses of team members can be an important first step in negotiation planning (see Form 3-1).

Form 3-1. Team Members Strengths, Weaknesses and Interests

Team Member	Team Member
Name	Name
Job Title	Job Title
Phone No.	Phone No.
Fax No.	Fax No.
E-Mail:	E-Mail:
Strengths I	Strengths I
2	2
3	3
Weaknesses I	Weaknesses I
2	2
3	3
Interests I	Interests I
2	2
3	3

Date Prepared:_____   Lead Negotiator:_____

2. *Know the other party:* Intelligence gathering is vital to successful negotiation planning. Create a checklist of things to know about the other party to help the team prepare for negotiation Form 3-2 lists a few suggested questions that you should discuss with your team members to ensure you understand as much as possible about your organization and the other side.

Form 3-2. Things to Know About the Other Party

Buyer and Seller
▪ What is the organization's overall business strategy?
▪ What is its reputation?
▪ What is its current company business environment?
▪ Who is the lead negotiator?
▪ Who are the primary decision makers?
▪ What are their key objectives?
▪ What are their overall contract objectives?
▪ What are their personal objectives?
▪ Who or what influences the decision makers?
▪ What internal organization barriers do they face?

Seller Only
▪ When does the buyer need our products or services?
▪ How much money does the buyer have to spend?
▪ Where does the buyer want our products and services delivered?
▪ What benefits will our products and services provide?
▪ What is our company's past experiences with this buyer?

Date Prepared:_____ Lead Negotiator:_____

3. *Know the big picture:* In the words of Stephen R. Covey, author of *The Seven Habits of Highly Effective People,* "begin with the end in mind." Keep focused on the primary objectives. Be aware that the ability of either party to be flexible on some issues may be limited because of internal policies, budgets, or organizational politics.

   One of the proven best practices to keep the negotiation focused is using interim summaries. The key is not to get caught up in small, unimportant details that take the negotiation off track.

4. *Identify objectives:* Know what both you and the other party want to accomplish. Successful negotiators know that nearly everything affects price, as illustrated in Figure 3-2: changes in schedule, technology, services, terms and conditions, customer obligations, contract type, products, and other contracting elements.

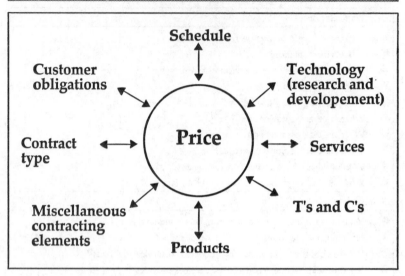

Figure 3-2. Importance of Price

You can easily identify a novice or apprentice negotiator because they always want to discuss price first. An experienced negotiator knows you should agree to all of the terms and conditions (Ts and Cs) first. Price is the last item a master negotiator will discuss and agree to with the other side

Chapter 3

Form 3-3. Objectives Identification

Seller Objectives	Buyer Objectives
Personal I	Personal I
2	2
3	3
4	4
5	5
Professional I	Professional I
2	2
3	3
4	4
5	5
6	6
7	7

Date Prepared:_____   Lead Negotiator:_____

5. *Prioritize objectives:* Although all terms and conditions are important, some are clearly more important than others. Prioritize your objectives to help you remain focused during negotiation. Figure 3-3 shows that various terms and conditions affect cost, risk, and value.

Figure 3-3. Importance of Ts and Cs

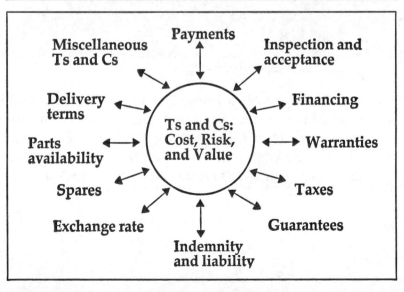

It is important for contract negotiators to truly understand and appreciate that all Ts and Cs contained in the deal have a cost, risk, and value associated with them and their specific wording. The exact wording of the deal is critical in contract negotiations.

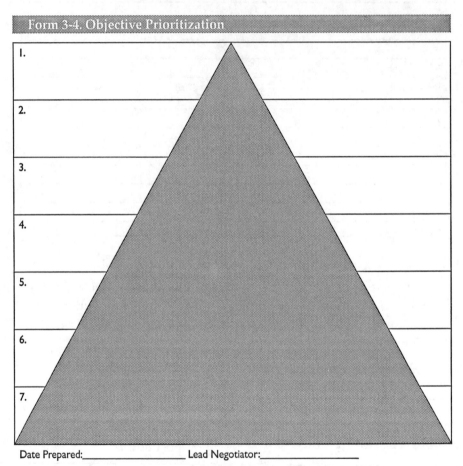

Form 3-4. Objective Prioritization

1.

2.

3.

4.

5.

6.

7.

Date Prepared:_____ Lead Negotiator:_____

6. *Create options:* Creative problem solving is a critical skill of successful negotiators. Seek to expand options; do not assume that only one solution exists to every problem. Conducting team brainstorming sessions to develop a list of options to achieve negotiation objectives is a proven best practice of many world-class organizations (see Form 3-5).

Form 3-5. Create Options for Achieving Negotiation Objectives		
Seller Objectives	**Possible Options**	**Buyer Objectives**

Date Prepared:_____ Lead Negotiator:_____

7. *Select fair standards:* Successful negotiators avoid a contest of wills by turning an argument into a joint search for a fair solution, using fair standards independent of either side's will. Use standards such as the:
   - Uniform Commercial Code;
   - United Nations Convention on Contracts for the International Sale of Goods;
   - American Arbitration Association standards;
   - ISO 9000 quality standards;
   - State, local, and federal laws; and
   - Market or industry standards.
8. *Examine alternatives:* Prepare in advance your alternatives to the important negotiation issues or objectives. Successful negotiators know their best-case, most-likely, and worst-case (walkaway) alternatives for all major objectives (see Form 3-6).

Form 3-6. Objectives and Alternatives:		
Worst Case, Most Likely, and Best Case		
Objective:		
Worst Case	Most Likely	Best Case

←————————————————————————————————→

(Plot your most likely position)

Date Prepared:_____ Lead Negotiator:_____

9. *Select your strategy, tactics, and countertactics:* Negotiation strategies provide the overall framework that will guide how you conduct your negotiation. Negotiation strategies can be divided into two types: win-lose and win-win.

The win-lose negotiation strategy is about winning today, despite the potential long-term effect tomorrow and beyond. Common characteristics of the win-lose strategy include concealing one's own position and interests, discovering the other party's position and interests, weakening the other party's resolve, and causing the other party to modify its position or accept your position on all key issues. Although the win-lose negotiation strategy is not a "politically correct" approach, it is a commonly used negotiation strategy worldwide.

The win-win negotiation strategy is about creative joint problem solving, which develops long-term successful business relationships. The win-win negotiation strategy, however, may sometimes be difficult to accomplish. Among the obstacles to developing the win-win business environment are previous adverse buyer-seller relations, lack of training in joint problem solving and conflict resolution, and complex and highly regulated contracting procedures in some organizations, especially large companies and government agencies.

Winning or losing a contract negotiation is, indeed, a matter of perspective, which is based on your knowledge, experience, and judgment. The only way to know whether you have won or lost a negotiation is to compare the results to your negotiation plan. Did you get what you wanted? Is what you got closer to your best-case, most-likely, or worst-case alternative? Clearly, without a contract negotiation plan, you have no basis against which to evaluate the negotiation outcome.

To achieve your desired contract negotiation results, you need not only a strategy, but also tactics and countertactics, which are a means to a desired end. Chapter 5 provides a more detailed discussion of contract negotiation strategies, tactics, and countertactics.

10. *Develop a solid and approved team negotiation plan:* The conclusion of contract negotiation planning should be the summary and documentation of all planned actions. If necessary, have the negotiation plan reviewed and approved by higher management to ensure that all planned actions are in the best interests of the organization (see Form 3-7).

Form 3-7. Sample Negotiation Planning Summary

Negotiation Information

Location	Date	Time
1	1	1
2	2	2
3	3	3

Key Objectives (Plot your most likely position)

1. Price

Worst Case ————————————————————— Best Case
$10.5M $12.0M $12.5M

2. Payments

Worst Case ————————————————————— Best Case
After Delivery   Progress payments   Advance payments

3. Warranty period

Worst Case ————————————————————— Best Case
36 months   18 months   12 months
                                   Industry average

4.

Worst Case ————————————————————— Best Case

5.

Worst Case ————————————————————— Best Case

6.

Worst Case ————————————————————— Best Case

7.

Worst Case ————————————————————— Best Case

8.

Worst Case ————————————————————— Best Case

9.

Worst Case ————————————————————— Best Case

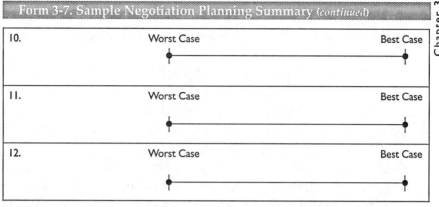

Form 3-7: Sample Negotiation Planning Summary *(continued)*

Possible Tactics and Countertactics		
Objective	Planned Tactics - Buyer	Planned Countertactics - Seller

Contract Price	
Range	
Best Case	
Most Likely	
Worst Case	

Date Prepared:_____ Lead Negotiator:_____

Approved by:_____ Date Approved:_____

CONDUCT THE NEGOTIATION

The following activities are necessary to conduct the negotiation:

11. *Determine who has authority:* If possible, before the negotiation, determine who has the authority to negotiate for each party. At the start of the negotiation, ensure that you know who has that authority, who the lead negotiator is for the other party, and what limits, if any, are placed on the other party's authority.

12. *Prepare the facility:* Most buyers want to conduct the negotiation at their offices to provide them with a sense of control. If you are the seller, try to conduct the negotiation at your location, at a neutral site such as a hotel or conference center, or through a conference call or Net-meeting.

Other key facility considerations include the:

- Size of the room;
- Use of break-out rooms;
- Lighting;
- Tables (size, shape, and arrangement);
- Seating arrangements;
- Use of audiovisual aids;
- Schedule (day and time); and
- Access to telephone, fax, e-mail/Internet, restrooms, food, and drink.

13. *Use an agenda:* A proven best practice of successful negotiators worldwide is creating and using an agenda for the negotiation. Provide the agenda to the other party before the negotiation begins (see Form 3-8). An effective agenda helps a negotiator to:

   - Set the right tone;
   - Control the exchange of information;
   - Keep the focus on the objectives;
   - Manage time; and
   - Obtain the desired results.

Form 3-8. Negotiation Agenda

Contract		
Title		Date
Location		Time
Topics of Action		Time
☐ Introduce team members		_____
☐ Provide overview and discuss purpose of negotiation		_____
☐ Exchange information on key interests and issues		_____
■ Quantity of products		_____
■ Quality of products and services		
■ Past performance		
■ Delivery schedule		
■ Maintenance		
■ Training		
☐ Have a break		_____
☐ Review agreement on all key interests and issues		_____
☐ Agree on detailed terms and conditions		_____
☐ Agree on price		_____
☐ Review and summarize meeting		_____
Date Prepared:_____	Lead Negotiator:_____	

14. *Introduce the team:* Introduce your team members, or have team members make brief self-introductions. Try to establish a common bond with the other party as soon as possible. Chapter 4 provides a much more detailed discussion of planning team-based contract negotiations.

15. *Set the right tone:* After introductions, make a brief statement to express your team strategy to the other party. Set the desired climate for contract negotiation from the start.

16. *Exchange information:* Contract negotiation is all about communication. Be aware that information is exchanged both orally and through body language, visual aids (pictures, diagrams, photographs, or videotapes), and active listening.

17. *Focus on objectives:* Never lose sight of the big picture.

18. *Use strategy, tactics, and countertactics:* Do what you said you were going to do, but be flexible to achieve your objectives. Anticipate the other party's tactics and plan your countertactics. Adjust them as necessary. Chapter 5 provides a comprehensive discussion of contract negotiation strategies, tactics, and countertactics.

19. *Make counteroffers:* A vital part of conducting the negotiation is providing substitute offers, or counteroffers, when the other party does not accept what you are offering. Document all offers and counteroffers to ensure that both parties understand any changes in the terms and conditions.

When offers and counteroffers are done right, they are part art and part science. A seller should know the approximate range (monetary amount) the buyer intends to spend. Plus, a well-prepared seller should know approximately what its competitors are likely to offer and the approximate price. Likewise, well-informed and prepared buyers know what approximate range (monetary amount) the seller is likely to seek. There should be a negotiation zone in which well-prepared buyers and sellers exchange offers and counteroffers (see Table 3-2).

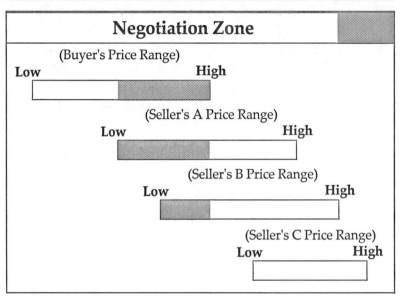

Table 3-2. Negotiation Zone

Given a competitive source business environment, sellers must ensure their initial offer is not so high that they will be eliminated from the competition. However, a seller must also ensure it maintains a healthy profit margin and still has room in the offer to give further price reductions if necessary to capture the business. Clearly, every seller must perform a balancing act between the desire to win business and the need to reduce risks, while maximizing revenue and profit.

As illustrated in the Negotiation Zone (Table 3-2), every buyer has a monetary range it expects to spend for required products or services that extends from low to high based on numerous variables typically set out in the contract's terms and conditions. Further, as depicted in Table 3-2, each seller (A, B, or C) has a monetary range, typically described in its approved business case, within which it can make offers and counteroffers based on its costs, risks, desired profit margin, and preferred terms and conditions.

Once both parties have made their initial offers, the fun really begins. How do you determine how much to move? Do you alter your terms and conditions in conjunction with changes in pricing? Do you offer a different type of pricing arrangement, i.e., firm-fixed price time and materials or cost plus-fixed fee (see Table 3-3, Advantages, Disadvantages & Suitability of Various Contract Types)? Should you refuse to move to force the other party to counteroffer? The answer to all of these questions is—it depends! That is why experienced, highly skilled master contract negotiators are a valuable asset to every organization involved in detailed, complex, and expensive contract negotiations.

Type	Essential Elements and Advantages	Disadvantages	Suitability
Table 3-3. Advantages, Disadvantages, and Suitability of Various Contract Types			
Fixed-Price Contracts (greater risk on seller)			
Firm Fixed Price (FFP)	Reasonably definite design or performance specifications available. Fair and reasonable price can be established at outset. Conditions for use include the following: ■ Adequate competition ■ Prior purchase experience of the same, or similar, supplies or services under competitive conditions. ■ Valid cost or pricing data ■ Realistic estimates of proposed cost. ■ Possible uncertainties in performance can be identified and priced. ■ Sellers willing to accept contract at a level that causes them to take all financial risks ■ Any other reasonable basis for pricing can be used to establish fair and reasonable price.	Price not subject to adjustment regardless of seller performance costs. Places 100% of financial risk on seller. Places least amount of administrative burden on contract manager. Preferred over all other contract types. Used with advertised or negotiated procurements.	Commercial products and commercial services for which reasonable prices can be established.
Fixed Price with Economic Price Adjustment (FP/EPA)	Unstable market or labor conditions during performance period and contingencies that would otherwise be included in contract price can be identified and made the subject of a separate price adjustment clause. Contingencies must be specifically defined in contract. Provides for upward adjustment (with ceiling) in contract price. May provide for downward adjustment of price if escalated element has potential of failing below contract limits. Three general types of EPAs, based on established prices, actual costs of labor or material, and cost indexes of labor or material.	Price can be adjusted on action of an industry-wide contingency that is beyond seller's control. Reduces seller's fixed-price risk. FP/EPA is preferred over any CR-type contract. If contingency manifests, contract administration burden increases. Used with negotiated procurements and, in limited applications, with formal advertising when determined to be feasible. CM must determine if FP/EPA is necessary either to protect seller and buyer against significant fluctuations in labor or material costs or to provide for contract price adjustment in case of changes in seller's established prices.	Commercial products and services for which reasonable prices can be established at time of award.

Table 3-3. Advantages, Disadvantages, and Suitability of Various Contract Types *(continued)*

Type	Essential Elements and Advantages	Disadvantages	Suitability
Fixed Price Incentive (FPI)	Cost uncertainties exist, but there is potential for cost reduction or performance improvement by giving seller a degree of cost responsibility and a positive profit incentive. Profit is earned or lost based on relationship that contract's final negotiated cost bears to total target cost. Contract must contain target cost, target profit, ceiling price, and profit-sharing formula. Two forms of FPI: firm target (FPIF) and successive targets (FPIS). FPIF: Firm target cost, target profit, and profit-sharing formula negotiated into basic contract; profit adjusted at contract completion. FPIS: Initial cost and profit targets negotiated into contract, but final cost target (firm) cannot be negotiated until performance. Contains production point(s) at which either a firm target and final profit formula, or a FFP contract, can be negotiated. Elements that can be incentives: costs, performance, delivery, quality.	Requires adequate seller accounting system. Buyer must determine that FPI is least costly and award of any other type would be impractical. Buyer and seller administrative effort is more extensive than under other fixed-price contract types. Used only with competitive negotiated contracts. Billing prices must be established for interim payment.	Development and production of high-volume, multiyear contracts.
Cost-Reimbursement Contracts (Greatest Risk on Buyer)			
Cost	Appropriate for research and development work, particularly with nonprofit educational institutions or other nonprofit organizations, and for facilities contracts. Allowable costs of contract performance are reimbursed, but no fee is paid.	Application limited due to no fee and by the fact that the buyer is not willing to reimburse seller fully if there is a commercial benefit for the seller. Only nonprofit institutions and organizations are willing (usually) to perform research for which there is no fee (or other tangible benefits)	Research and development; facilities.

Table 3-3. Advantages, Disadvantages, and Suitability of Various Contract Types (*continued*)			
Type	**Essential Elements and Advantages**	**Disadvantages**	**Suitability**
Cost Sharing (CS)	Used when buyer and seller agree to share costs in a research or development project having potential mutual benefits. Because of commercial benefits accruing to the seller, no fee is paid. Seller agrees to absorb a portion of the costs of performance in expectation of compensating benefits to seller's firm or organization. Such benefits might include an enhancement of the seller's capability and expertise or an improvement of its competitive position in the commercial market.	Care must be taken in negotiating cost-share rate so that the cost ratio is proportional to the potential benefit (that is, the party receiving the greatest potential benefit bears the greatest share of the costs).	Research and development that has potential benefits to both the buyer and the seller.
Cost Plus Incentive Fee (CPIF)	Development has a highly probability that is feasible and positive profit incentives for seller management can be negotiated. Performance incentives must be clearly spelled out and objectively measurable. Fee range should be negotiated to give the seller an incentive over various ranges of cost performance. Fee is adjusted by a formula negotiated into the contract in accordance with the relationship that total cost bears to target cost. Contract must contain target cost, target fee, minimum and maximum fees, fee adjustment formula. Fee adjustment is made at completion of contract.	Difficult to negotiate range between the maximum and minimum fees so as to provide an incentive over entire range. Performance must be objectively measurable. Costly to administer; seller must have an adequate accounting system. Used only with negotiated contracts. Appropriate buyer surveillance needed during performance to ensure effective methods and efficient cost controls are used.	Major systems development and other development programs in which it is determined that CPIF is desirable and administratively practical.

Table 3-3. Advantages, Disadvantages, and Suitability of Various Contract Types *(continued)*

Type	Essential Elements and Advantages	Disadvantages	Suitability
Cost Plus Award Fee (CPAF)	Contract completion is feasible, incentives are desired, but performance is not susceptible to finite measurement. Provides for subjective evaluation of seller performance. Seller is evaluated at stated time(s). during performance period. Contract must contain clear and unambiguous evaluation criteria to determine award fee. Award fee is earned for excellence in performance, quality, timeliness, ingenuity, and cost-effectiveness and can be earned in whole or in part. Two separate fee pools can be established in contract: base fee and award fee. Award fee earned by seller is determined by the buyer and is often based on recommendations of an award fee evaluation board.	Buyer's determination of amount of award fee earned by the seller is not subject to disputes clause. CPAF cannot be used to avoid either CPIF or CPFF if either is feasible. Should not be used if the amount of money, period of performance, or expected benefits are insufficient to warrant additional administrative efforts. Very costly to administer. Seller must have an adequate accounting system. Used only with negotiated contracts.	Level-of-effort services that can only be subjectively measured, and contracts for which work would have been accomplished under another contract type if performance objectives could have been expressed as definite milestones, targets, and goals that could have been measured.
Cost Plus Fixed Fee (CPFF)	Level of effort is unknown, and seller's performance cannot be subjectively evaluated. Provides for payment of a fixed fee. Seller receives fixed fee regardless of the actual costs incurred during performance. Can be constructed in two ways: Completion form: Clearly defined task with a definite goal and specific end product. Buyer can order more work without an increase in fee if the contract estimated costs is increased. Term form: Scope of work described in general terms. Seller obligated only for a specific level of effort for stated period of time. Completion form is preferred over term form. Fee is expressed as percentages of estimated cost at time contract is awarded.	Seller has minimum incentive to control costs. Costly to administer. Seller must have an adequate accounting system. Seller assumes no financial risk.	Completion form: Advanced development or technical services contracts. Term form: Research and exploratory development. Used when the level of effort required is known and there is an inability to measure risk.

Type	Essential Elements and Advantages	Disadvantages	Suitability
Table 3-3. Advantages, Disadvantages, and Suitability of Various Contract Types (continued)			
		Time and Materials	
Time and Material (T&M)	Not possible when placing contract to estimate extent or duration of the work, or anticipated cost, with any degree of confidence. Calls for provision of direct labor hours at specified hourly rate and materials at cost (or some other basis specified in contract). The fixed hourly rates include wages, overhead, general and administrative expenses, and profit. Material cost can include, if appropriate, material handling costs. Ceiling price established at time of award.	Used only after determination that no other type will serve purpose. Does not encourage effective cost control. Requires almost constant surveillance by buyer to ensure effective seller management. Ceiling price is required in contract.	Engineering and design services in conjunction with the production of suppliers, engineering design and manufacture, repair, maintenance, and overhaul work to be performed on an as-needed basis.

Form 3-9 provides a simple, yet effective, means of documenting offers and counteroffers exchanged during contract negotiations. Remember, the number of offers and counteroffers exchanged is not as important as the value of the concessions made.

Form 3-9. Offers and Counteroffers Summary

Seller	Buyer
Offer	Counteroffer
Offer	Counteroffer
Offer	Counteroffer
Offer	Counteroffer
Date Prepared:_____	Lead Negotiator:_____

20. *Document the agreement or know when to walk away:* Take time throughout the negotiation to take notes on what was agreed to between the parties. If possible, assign one team member to take minutes. To ensure proper documentation, periodically summarize agreements on all major issues throughout the negotiation. At the end of the negotiation, summarize your agreements both orally and in writing. (See Form 3-10.) If a settlement is not reached, document the areas of agreement and disagreement. If possible, plan a future meeting to resolve differences.

Remember: Do not agree to a bad deal—learn to say, "No thank you," and walk away.

Form 3-10. Negotiation Results Summary

Contract Title	Date of Contract
Parties Involved	Date(s) of Negotiation

Brief Product/Service Description	Location
Agreed-to Price	
Key changes from Approved Proposal	

Date Prepared:_____ Lead Negotiator:_____

DOCUMENT THE NEGOTIATIONS AND FORM THE CONTRACT

The following activities are conducted to document the negotiation and form the contract.

21. *Prepare the negotiation memorandum (minutes or notes):* Document what was discussed during the negotiation. After having the memorandum word processed, spell checked, and edited, have it reviewed by someone within your organization who attended the negotiation and someone who did not. Then determine whether they have a similar understanding.

22. *Send the memorandum to the other party:* As promptly as possible, provide a copy of your documented understanding of the contract negotiation to the other party. First, e-mail or fax it to the other party. Then send an original copy by either overnight or two-day mail. Verify that the other party receives your negotiation memorandum by following up with an e-mail or telephone call, or send it by registered mail, return receipt requested.

23. *Offer to write the contract:* As the seller, offer to draft the agreement so that you can put the issues in your own words. Today, most contracts are developed using electronic databases, which facilitate reviews, changes, and new submissions.

24. *Prepare the contract:* Writing a contract should be a team effort with an experienced contract management professional at the lead. Typically, automated standard organizational forms, modified as needed, are used with standard terms and conditions that were tailored during negotiation. At other times, a contract must be written in full. Ensure that no elements of the contract are missing (see Form 3-11). After the initial draft, obtain all appropriate reviews and approvals, preferably electronically.

Form 3-11. Essential Contract Elements Checklist

Project Name	Prepared by (Print)	Date Prepared
Customer	Telephone/Fax	e-mail

- ☐ Deliverables and prices (provide a listing of deliverables and their prices)
- ☐ Deliverable conformance specifications
- ☐ Requirements in statement of work (determine SOW requirements not listed as deliverables)
- ☐ Delivery requirements (list delivery requirements, deliverable packaging and shipping requirements, and service performance instructions)
- ☐ Deliverable inspection and acceptance
- ☐ Invoice and payment schedule and provisions (include in contract tracking summary)
- ☐ Representations and certifications
- ☐ Other terms and conditions

25. *Prepare negotiation results summary:* Prepare an internal-use-only summary of key negotiation items that have changed since originally proposed. Many organizations have found such a summary to be a valuable tool for explaining changes to senior managers.

26. *Obtain required reviews and approvals:* Depending on your organizational procedures, products, services, and other variables, one or more people may be required to review and approve the proposed contract before signature. Typically, the following departments or staff review a contract: project management, financial, legal, procurement or contract management, and senior management. Increasingly, organizations are using automated systems to draft contracts and transmit them internally for the needed reviews and approvals.

27. *Send the contract to the other party for signature:* Send a copy of the contract to the other party via e-mail or fax, and then follow up with two mailed original copies. With all copies include an appropriate cover letter with a return mail address and time/date suspense for prompt return. Verify receipt of the contract by phone or e-mail. Today, many organizations, as well as the laws of many nations, recognize the validity of electronic signatures.

28. *Provide copies of the contract to affected organizations:* The contract is awarded officially after it is executed, signed by both parties, and delivered to both parties. Ensure that all other affected organizations or parties receive a copy.

29. *Document lessons learned:* Take the time to document everything that went well during the contract negotiation process. Even more important, document what did not go well and why, and what should be done to avoid those problems in the future.

30. *Prepare the contract administration plan:* At the end of the contract negotiation process, follow a proven best practice by having the team that negotiated the contract help the team that is responsible for administering it develop a contract administration plan.

Table 3-4 provides a checklist of proven effective contract negotiation best practices. How many of the actions listed in Table 3-4 do you and your organization both know and do? Remember, knowing what to do is good, but doing it is better!

Chapter 3

Table 3-4 Checklist. Buyer's Contract Negotiation Best Practices

(The Buyer Should:)

☐ Know what you want: lowest price or best value

☐ State your requirements in performance terms and evaluate accordingly

☐ Conduct market research about potential sources before selection

☐ Evaluate potential sources promptly and dispassionately

☐ Follow the evaluation criteria stated in the solicitation: management, technical, and price

☐ Use absolute, minimum, or relative evaluation standards to measure performance as stated in your solicitation

☐ Develop organizational policies to guide and facilitate the source selection process

☐ Use a weighting system to determine which evaluation criteria are most important

☐ Use a screening system to prequalify sources

☐ Obtain independent estimates from consultants or outside experts to assist in source selection

☐ Use past performance as a key aspect of source selection, and verify data accuracy

☐ Conduct price realism analysis

☐ Create a competitive analysis report

☐ Use oral presentations or proposals by sellers to improve and expedite the source selection process

Table 3-4 (cont.) Checklist. Contract Negotiation Best Practices

(The Buyer and Seller Should:)

- ☐ Understand that contract negotiation is a process, usually involving a team effort
- ☐ Select and train highly skilled negotiators to lead the contract negotiation process
- ☐ Know market and industry practices
- ☐ Prepare yourself and your team
- ☐ Know the other party
- ☐ Know the big picture
- ☐ Identify and prioritize objectives
- ☐ Create options—be flexible in your planning
- ☐ Examine alternatives
- ☐ Select your negotiation strategy, tactics, and countertactics
- ☐ Develop a solid and approved team negotiation plan
- ☐ Determine who has the authority to negotiate
- ☐ Prepare the negotiation facility at your location or at a neutral site
- ☐ Use an agenda during contract negotiation
- ☐ Set the right tone at the start of the negotiation
- ☐ Maintain your focus on your objectives
- ☐ Use interim summaries to keep on track
- ☐ Do not be too predictable in your tactics
- ☐ Document your agreement throughout the process
- ☐ Know when to walk away
- ☐ Offer to write the contract
- ☐ Prepare a negotiation results summary
- ☐ Obtain required reviews and approvals
- ☐ Provide copies of the contract to all affected parties
- ☐ Document negotiation lessons learned and best practices
- ☐ Prepare a transition plan for contract administration
- ☐ Understand that everything affects price
- ☐ Understand the Ts and Cs have cost, risk, and value
- ☐ Tailor Ts and Cs to the deal, but understand the financial effects on price and profitability
- ☐ Know what is negotiable and what is not

DESIRED OUTPUTS

■ *Contract:* The output from negotiations and contract formation may be the contract, which is both a document and a relationship between parties.
  Or it may be best to—
■ *Walk away:* Do not agree to a bad deal. No business is better than bad business.

SUMMARY

Contract negotiation and contract formation is vital to the success of buyers and sellers worldwide. When skilled contract negotiators follow a proven process approach, successful business agreements are reached. Through effective contract formation practices, win-win contracts are developed and documented, yielding beneficial results for both parties.

Remember, in the words of Dr. Chester Karrass, author, consultant, and master contract negotiator, "You don't get what you deserve, you get what you have the ability to negotiate." The primary focus of this book is mastering the contract negotiation process, the use of a logical, organized, documented, step-by-step approach to build successful business relationships. The highly effective contract negotiation process discussed in this chapter has been taught to more than 20,000 business professionals worldwide in programs offered by the National Contract Management Association (NCMA), The George Washington University School of Business, The Keller Graduate School of DeVry University, Villanova University On-Line Masters Certificate Program in Contract Management, the University of California at Los Angeles, the U.S. Naval Postgraduate School, to name just a few, with outstanding results. I hope that you will consider using the contract negotiation process, forms, and best practices discussed in this chapter—and throughout this book.

The next chapter will examine more closely the importance of contract planning, especially the advantages and disadvantages of team-based contract negotiations.

QUESTIONS TO CONSIDER

1. Does your organization have a logical, documented, and proven successful contract negotiation process?

2. Do you consistently achieve your desired negotiation results?

3. Has your organization walked away from any potential bad deals in the past year? If so, how many and why?

4. What actions has your organization taken to help develop stronger negotiation skills for your sales managers, project managers, and contract managers?

5. How well do you document and share your negotiation lessons learned?

ENDNOTES

[1] Zartman, I. William, The Negotiation Process, Beverly Hills CA, Sage Publications, 1978.

[2] Ury, William, Getting Past No, New York NY, Bantam Books, 1993.

[3] The following section is a modified extract from World Class Contracting, by Gregory A. Garrett, CCH, Inc. 2003.

[4] For more information about multiple attribute decision-making techniques, consult the following references: Ching-Lai Hwang and Kwangsun Yoon, Multiple Attribute Decision Making Methods and Applications: A State-of-the-Art Survey, Berlin, Srpinger-Verlag, 1981; Paul Goodwin and George Wright, Decision Analysis for Management Judgment, Chichester, England, John Wiley & Sons LTD., 1991; and Thomas Saaty, Decision Making for Leaders: The Analytic Hierarchy Process for Decisions in a Complex World, Pittsburgh PA, RWS Publications, 1995.

Planning Contract Negotiations: People, Tools, and Best Practices

INTRODUCTION

When it comes to negotiating the big deals, if you have no plan, you have no clue, and thus you will most probably lose! As discussed in Chapter 3, The Contract Negotiation Process, there are three distinct and important phases to contract negotiations: planning, conducting, and documenting. While all three phases of the contract negotiation process are important, clearly planning is essential to ensure you achieve ultimate success. The primary focus on this chapter is to discuss the importance of beginning with the end in mind, planning individual vs. team-based contract negotiations, using information technology tools to facilitate negotiations, and understanding the five essential elements of the contract negotiation plan.

Chapter 5 will discuss the details for planning contract negotiation: strategies, tactics, and countertactics. Together, Chapters 4 and 5 will provide you with a wealth of information and best practices to help you improve your skills for planning contract negotiations.

BEGIN WITH THE END IN MIND

The second habit, of Stephen Covey's best-selling book, *7 Habits of Highly Effective People,* is "Begin With the End in Mind." Contract negotiation planning is essentially the embodiment of this simple philosophy. So, what is the desired end? As with so many negotiation questions, the answer is, of course: It depends! But generally what most individuals and organizations need is to build a strong relationship between the parties based upon trust to achieve long-term mutual success. Key to each party's success is their ability to link their organizations' strategy and goals to their respective contract negotiation plans.

BUILDING THE RELATIONSHIP BETWEEN THE PARTIES

In relationship-based cultures, a good relationship is the foundation for all subsequent interactions. Where no relationship exists and parties consider dealing with one another, the principal aim of meetings is to develop a relationship. Remember, a contract is fundamentally a written manifestation of the agreement between the parties. The business assumption is that if there is a strong relationship, a fair and reasonable contract can be negotiated.[1]

In both the public and private sectors, most of the money is exchanged via a relatively few large complex, competitively negotiated performance-based contracts. In order to be successful in forming these few large deals, an established relationship becomes the precondition for conducting the actual contract negotiation. Once there is a relationship, negotiations become episodes in, rather than the aim of, the relationship.[2]

Building a strong professional business relationship is essential to securing the big deals. Contract negotiation planning must be focused on creating deep, knowledge-based trust, reciprocal obligation, and partnership for mutual benefit. Parties contemplating entering such a relationship will likely undertake considerable research and intelligence work regarding one another. Likewise, parties will also be careful to refrain from making a commitment until they have concluded that the other party is a trustworthy partner.[3]

According, to Peter B. Stark, co-author of *The Only Negotiating Guide You'll Ever Need*, in negotiations trust is built up or torn down in cycles. If you are negotiating with a party you trust, your signals will indicate this, and your counterpart will respond with open communication and positive actions that will solidify trust. Of course the opposite is also true.[4]

PLANNING INDIVIDUAL VS. TEAM-BASED CONTRACT NEGOTIATIONS

Some individuals are much more comfortable negotiating a deal by themselves, one on one with the other party. While other individuals are far more comfortable planning and conducting team-based contract negotiations, where each party has their own multi-functional team (e.g., sales, contracts, pricing, technical, program management, and Legal). The decision whether a contract should be negotiated by a single individual or a team should not be based on one's comfort level. Rather, an organization should consider the strengths and weaknesses of both approaches.

Planning, conducting, and documenting a deal as an individual or as a team has both strengths and weaknesses. The following are several of the strengths and weaknesses of individual contract negotiations, followed by several of the strengths and weaknesses of team-based contract negotiations.

Individual contract negotiation strengths:
- Generally, more rapid decision making;.
- No dissention among team members;
- Less game playing when fewer people are involved;
- Negotiations generally conducted more quickly, saving money; and
- Greater sense of accountability for results.

Individual contract negotiation weaknesses:
- No one to help make better, more informed decisions;
- More likely one person could be influenced by emotional tactics or countertactics;
- Lack of sufficient expertise (e.g., technical, financial, legal);
- Single person may lack understanding of the big picture; and
- Individual weaknesses cannot be offset by other team members' strengths.

Team-based contract negotiation strengths:
- Strength in numbers, greater expertise to draw on;
- One person's weakness should not be a major factor;
- Generally, the more people thinking about alternatives, the greater the probability on creating a win-win situation;
- Greater opportunity to effectively use tactics and countertactics to achieve desired results; and

■ If one person becomes ill or unable to continue the negotiation, other team members are available so the deal can be made. Team-based contract negotiation weaknesses:

■ Generally, takes more time and costs more money;

■ Personality conflicts or power struggles within a team may exist and negatively impact negotiation results;

■ If a team can be divided by the other party, it will generally be conquered;

■ Generally, team-based negotiations take more skill to plan and conduct effectively; and

■ Lack of effective planning will lead to conflicts between team members over roles and responsibilities.

In most cases, big deals involving the integration of products (hardware and software) and professional services, often involving multiple parties and multiple functions, will require the use of team-based contract negotiations. Form 4-1 provides a simple but effective checklist of team-based contract negotiation planning best practices.

Form 4-1 Checklist. Team-Based Planning Contract Negotiation Best Practices

☐ Select the right people with the right attitude and right expertise

☐ Select a lead negotiator

☐ Develop a contract negotiation strategy to achieve success

☐ Develop a contract negotiation plan including: the use of tactics & countertactics, desired terms & conditions, list of must-haves, and acceptable price range

☐ Assign roles and responsibilities

☐ Practice together—conduct mock contract negotiations

☐ Select a designated note-taker

☐ Document your contract negotiation plan and ensure all team members execute the plan

INFORMATION TECHNOLOGY TOOLS TO SUPPORT PLANNING CONTRACT NEGOTIATIONS

Increasingly, people are separated by geography, time and, as your organization goes global, language and culture. Information technology tools will help you address these separations and allow you to create a seamless virtual corporate environment that supports the pursuit of new business. Organizations that can create this seamless virtual business environment are the ones who will succeed. Knowing how to leverage their resources on a global basis provides them a tremendous advantage over competitors.   The key to creating this environment is understanding the depth and breadth of information technology tools available and picking the right ones for your organization.

Vendors and applications are constantly changing and evolving to bring more capabilities to the desktop. The intent of this discussion is to focus on the types of tools available, with illustrative examples of each. While numerous specific vendors and applications are cited throughout this discussion, no endorsement or recommendation is being made of any particular vendor or application.

Tools for Planning Contract Negotiations

Technology has made it possible to plan and conduct contract negotiation meetings in a wide variety of mediums which are constantly evolving. While not an exhaustive list, the following are the fundamental types of tools available for meetings, along with the advantages, disadvantages and best applications for each. For many negotiation planning meetings, it is likely you will have a mix of mediums allowing for maximum engagement of all participants. All of the tools mentioned can be used by organizations of all sizes; however, there are security considerations to keep in mind if you use them over the Internet or public phone network.

When considering tools for contract negotiation planning meetings, one also needs to consider the communication needs in terms of the communication flow. As shown in Figure 4-1, communication flows fall into three basic types: broadcast (i.e., one-way send), exchange (i.e., send and receive), and collection (i.e., one-way receive).

Figure 4-1 shows the communication flow for each of the key meetings during the planning phase of contract negotiation.

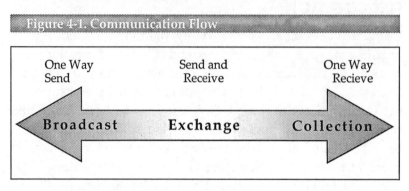

Figure 4-1. Communication Flow

Face-To-Face Meetings: With advances in technology and a continued competitive focus on reducing expenses, face-to-face meetings are often overlooked as a critical tool in negotiating big deals. As you invest in information technology tools, don't naively believe you will (or more importantly should) eliminate face-to-face meetings. Face-to-face meetings are essential to building relationships and developing trust and are an irreplaceable tool for customer meetings, contract negotiations, and discussions with suppliers or partners. Don't be "penny wise and pound foolish" when it comes to investing entirely in technology tools at the exclusion of face-to-face meetings.

Conference Bridges: Voice conference bridges have become the primary alternative to face-to-face meetings. Voice conference calls have the advantage of being easy to use and allow participation from remote locations, thus saving travel expenses and time. Conference bridges are very effective for disseminating information to a large audience, the exchange of information between a small number of speakers, or short meetings. They do have the disadvantage of providing only voice interaction. However, with a little prior planning, presentation materials can be distributed in advance to participants, which significantly increases their effectiveness.

Due to their ease of use and relative affordability, conference bridges are also frequently misused to the detriment of many companies, wasting countless hours of participants' potentially productive time. Conference calls should always have a specific purpose, agenda, and limit. Avoid endless "marathon" or open-ended calls with a large group in favor of multiple shorter calls with fewer participants on each call. This not only saves the time of participants, it will also make each call more focused and productive as you will not lose the attention of participants.

Conference bridges have become so commonplace that many fail to take appropriate precautions to ensure against eavesdropping by unwelcome participants. Always use a conference bridge that provides audible tones when someone joins or leaves the call or that screens participants by name or with an access code, and always take roll. Many conference bridges now offer two access codes, one for participants and one for the host. This not only provides additional security, it also protects against unwanted use of the bridge by someone other than the host. Finally, be sure to change bridge numbers and access codes regularly and only publish them the participants needed for the call.

Collaboration Software: Recent developments have created a number of software collaboration tools, such as Microsoft Net-Meeting, Intel ProShare, and Sun Systems ShowMe. These tools allow for the real-time exchange of visual information using personal computers. Not only can all users see the information being shown (e.g., a presentation, spreadsheet, or document) on their personal computer (PC) screen, if permitted by the host, they can be given control to make changes to the information. These tools are ideal for contract negotiation planning meetings where you want to exchange and edit information, such as strategy sessions, terms-and-conditions development sessions, or possibly a practice or mock contract negotiation. They can also be used effectively for contract negotiation plan review sessions.

Most collaboration software tools also permit simultaneous voice on the same data connection, although the voice quality can be very poor. If you find this to be the case, you can use a collaboration software tool in conjunction with a voice conference bridge. While this does require a separate voice and data connection, it provides the best of both worlds: high quality voice along with interactive sharing of visual information using PCs.

If you have a private data network protected by a firewall, you have some built-in security against eavesdropping by unwelcome participants. Most collaboration software tools either provide or can be used in conjunction with other software applications to provide as much as 128-bit security encryption. While this does make it more difficult for others to eavesdrop, no method is failsafe, so do not share highly proprietary or sensitive information using such tools over public networks or the Internet.

Video Web Conference: Until recently, video conferences required expensive equipment and network infrastructure, thus limiting widespread use. With the introduction of inexpensive PC Web cameras, it is now possible to have a video conference as easy as making a telephone call. Video Web conferencing can be done using many of the collaboration software tools mentioned previously or stand-alone packages. Although the quality of such video conferences often leaves something to be desired, they can be useful for one-on-one meetings and especially in a broadcast mode to give remote participants a greater sense of connection for something like a kickoff meeting. Video conferencing raises the same security considerations as software collaboration tools.

Interactive Chat: The last tool which can be used for meetings is interactive chat software, such Microsoft Windows Messenger, Netscape AOL Instant Messenger, and Yahoo!Messenger. Interactive chat allows you to establish a connection between one or more parties and exchange text or graphics via a virtual bulletin board. While this tool is very useful for short frequent communication between a small number of parties, it can also be used quite effectively as a coaching tool by managers with employees at other locations. On conference calls, you can establish an Instant Messenger connection with a new employee on the same call and use this connection to provide tips or even answer questions. This real-time feedback is invaluable in helping the new employee learn faster, handle problems better, and establish credibility quicker.

TOOLS TO SHARE DOCUMENTS

Traditionally, distributing or mailing documents was the only means to share them with others. Thanks to the advent of modern communications technology, there are a variety of mediums available that permit the near instantaneous sharing of documents with large numbers of individuals. Consequently, there are frequently so many documents being shared from so many sources that team members can be overwhelmed by the volume and find it incomprehensible. One of the biggest challenges in planning contract negotiations is to ensure the right people on your team have access to and use the most current information. In order to overcome this challenge, you are likely to use a mix of tools, such as those described in this section.

E-mail: E-mail has become the most common tool to exchange documents and collect inputs to develop proposals. With your e-mail service, it is possible to establish a team e-mail or broadcast list that can be used by the team to easily share information with everyone. If your e-mail is traveling over a public network or the Internet, be aware that it's not as secure as you may think. Be wise about what to send via e-mail and caution all team members of the same.

Extremely easy to use and nearly universally accessible, e-mail is also one of the most frequently abused tools for sharing documents. Don't constantly broadcast e-mail messages to your team—take the time to write concise, clear, and articulate e-mails. If you are using e-mail to exchange documents, be aware of the size of the files and how long it may take team members to download your e-mail. Compress large files using applications such as WinZip, PKZIP, Stuffit, or Tar, and try to limit the number of times documents are sent and resent by the team.

War Room: A contract negotiation planning workroom, traditionally referred to as a "war room," has tremendous value for companies with a geographical concentration of employees. The term "war room" is a reference to a command center in the military where information on the battle is collected and displayed to support decisions by the battle commander and staff. A war room provides the team a secure (i.e., lockable) dedicated work space where information can be collected and posted for use by the team, promoting team building and creating continuity on large complex deals or deals that may span long periods of time. The use of war rooms to support the capture of large deals continues to be the norm with successful government contractors such as Lockheed-Martin, General Dynamics, Boeing, Raytheon, and SAIC.

Share Point: With new technology, war rooms are being replaced with "virtual war rooms." One common way to do this is by using a server on your company network to establish a file-sharing point accessible to the team. There is a wide range of file-sharing point applications from the simple to the sophisticated, including such applications as Microsoft Share Point, Open Text Live Link, and IBM Lotus QuickPlace.

One of the major considerations in the type of share point you create is who has access to view documents and who has access to edit and add documents. You should make documents readily available to the team; however, you generally do not want them to be changed or overwritten. Most applications allow you to set some users as "read-only" to prevent them from overwriting documents.

There are also considerations of access to information within the contract negotiation team and between teams, so you need to consider how information can be partitioned. For example, not everyone on the team needs access to pricing information, and even fewer should have access to the internal business case information. Most applications allow access permissions to be established for each folder of files and many permit limiting access on a file-by-file basis. Be sure to wisely balance the need for security with the costs—if you establish file-level permissions, someone will have to establish and monitor them as files are created and new team members join the project.

Intranet Website: You can also establish a share point by creating an intranet website to post documents for the team, using applications such as Microsoft FrontPage or HTML. One of the inherent benefits of an intranet website is that only the Web administrator can add or edit documents. There are a variety of ways to limit access.

USING A PROBLEM-SOLVING PROCESS

Using a problem-solving process as a part of planning contract negotiation involves an attempt to understand both one's own needs, values, and objectives and those of the other side. Problem solvers *share* information to discover what their real conflicts are and what they think is important and to facilitate problem-solving efforts. By contrast, competitors *withhold* and *manipulate* information to maximize their own individual gains. Problem-solving contract negotiation is thus a full information perspective of negotiating that calls upon the parties to create and maintain a free, open, and complete flow of information.[5]

If the parties each have full information, they will know what their actual conflicts are. They will know which interests they share and which they do not. They will also know how each of them perceives the situation and what each hopes to accomplish through contract negotiation. If the parties have this information and accurately perceive each other's point of view, they can turn to a collaborative search for solutions that meet the goals and objectives of both sides. When each knows what the other wants, they may see how together they can help each other get what they want, thus forming a win-win contract.[6]

The Contract Negotiation Plan

The most effective contract negotiation plans for both buyers and sellers typically contain five essential elements:
- Selected contract negotiation strategies;
- Selected contract negotiation tactics and countertactics;
- Desired terms and conditions (Ts and Cs);
- List of "must haves"; and
- Selected pricing range.

FIRST ESSENTIAL ELEMENT: SELECTED CONTRACT NEGOTIATION STRATEGIES

Contract negotiators use a number of different approaches to achieve their desired goals. Knowing how to both use and deal with these various contract negotiation strategies is essential for success. Nearly every contract negotiator wants the best deal they can get. Each party's personal and professional self-interest is an obstacle to joint problem-solving,. While, there is nothing wrong with self-interest, as long as it is appropriate and professional, the desired contract negotiation strategy should result in the exchange of mutual benefit, creating a win-win situation. Chapter 5 provides a more detailed discussion of ten proven successful contract negotiation strategies.

SECOND ESSENTIAL ELEMENT: SELECTED CONTRACT NEGOTIATION TACTICS AND COUNTERTACTICS

Strategies alone do not ensure success in contract negotiations. Like most things in life and in business, making a strategy become a reality can be quite a challenge. Unfortunately, there are still many people and organizations, in both the public and private business sectors, which truly care very little, if at all, for the parties they are negotiating against. In addition, there are people who lie, cheat, and steal. Further, even if there are no real ethical problems to be solved, there are often challenges that arise due to differing opinions, facts, interpretations, perceptions, and egos. Thus, it is often both necessary and appropriate to plan to use various tactics and countertactics to deal with the numerous challenges that one may encounter when negotiating large, complex, performance-based contracts. Chapter 5 provides a detailed discussion of the top 50 tactics and related countertactics often used when negotiating complex contracts.

THIRD ESSENTIAL ELEMENT: DESIRED TERMS AND CONDITIONS (TS&CS)

As discussed in Chapter 3, Terms and Conditions (Ts & Cs) are vital to every contract negotiation. Each term and condition in a contract contains a potential risk, has a potential cost, and provides a potential value to one or more parties to the contract. Said more simply, "What the big print giveth, the little print (Ts & Cs) taketh away!"

Most contracts will be in writing. The contract document will contain words, numerals, symbols, and perhaps drawings to describe the relationship that will exist between the contracting parties.

Clauses

A contract consists of a series of statements called *clauses*. The following is a fairly standard contract clause:

Governing Law: Any dispute, controversy, or claim arising out of or in connection with this Agreement, or the breach, termination, or invalidity thereof, shall be finally settled by arbitration based on the laws of the state of New York, United States of America.

This clause is short and easy to understand. But other clauses, especially when the contracting parties are from different legal systems, may be several pages in length and require careful reading to grasp their meanings.

Terms and Conditions (Ts and Cs)

Collectively, clauses form the terms and conditions of the contract, and they define the rights and responsibilities of the parties to the contractual agreement. If called upon to enforce the contract in arbitration or a lawsuit, the arbitrator or court will look to these Ts and Cs in resolving the dispute.

A *term* is simply a part of the contract that addresses a specific subject. In most contracts, terms address payment, delivery, product quality, warranty of goods or services, termination of the agreement, resolution of disputes, and other subjects. Terms are described in clauses. The "Governing Law" clause is a contract term.

A *condition* is a phrase that either activates or suspends a term. A condition that activates a term is called a *condition precedent*; one that suspends a term is called a *condition subsequent*. Understanding the effect of conditions is critical to properly documenting and administering a contract. For example, the following sentence might appear in a "Specifications and Inspections" clause:

Buyer may charge Seller for the cost of an above-normal level of inspection if rejection of the shipment based on the Buyer's normal inspection level endangers production schedules and if the inspected products are necessary to meet production schedules.

In other words, if the buyer rejects the seller's products based on a normal level of inspection, and if that causes those products to be unavailable for production, and if the products in question are necessary to meet a production schedule that will be endangered because of their unavailability, then the seller must pay the buyer the cost of performing inspections made at above-normal levels in order to meet that production schedule.

When experience teaches that certain clauses should always be included in contracts of a given type, those clauses may be pre-printed in standard form. Such preprinted clauses are often called *standard terms and conditions*, which are useful when a business regularly enters many contracts and wants to reduce the administrative costs of its purchasing or sales operation. Standard Ts and Cs eliminate the need to hire an attorney to write a new contract every time a firm wants to buy or sell something.

In addition to reducing the administrative costs of contracting, standard Ts and Cs also reduce the risk of contract ambiguity. Contract managers, project managers, buyers, and sellers can become familiar with standard clauses and their proper interpretation, which will greatly reduce the potential for misunderstandings and disputes.

Certain clauses appear in virtually every kind of contract. Take, for example, the following clause:

ABC Company is not liable for failing to fulfill its obligations due to acts of God, civil or military authority, war, strikes, fire, failure of its suppliers to meet commitments, or other causes beyond its reasonable control.

Clauses of this type are often called *force majeure*, a French term for "major or irresistible force." They appear in nearly all large contracts. Another commonly used clause requires suppliers to:

...comply with all federal, state, and local laws, regulations, rules, and orders. Any provision which is required to be a part of this Agreement by virtue of any such law, regulation, rule, or order is incorporated by reference.

Of course, neither party is familiar with all such provisions, but the idea is to relieve the buyer of any responsibility for the indiscretions of the seller.

Other clauses may give the buyer the right to purchase additional quantities of goods or extend the performance of services at agreed-on prices. Indemnification clauses often require one party to protect the other from certain types of losses, liabilities, judgments, and so forth. The indemnified party is given security of financial reimbursement by the indemnifying party for any loss described in the clause.

A common misunderstanding is that price is separate and distinct from the Ts and Cs, but that is not so. Nearly all Ts and Cs affect price, either increasing or decreasing costs or liabilities to the parties. In world-class companies, senior management ensures that all business managers involved with contracts are aware of and fully understand the costs, risk, and value of Ts and Cs and how they affect price.

APPLYING CONTRACTING PRINCIPLES TO THE NEGOTIATION PLAN AND SELECTION OF Ts AND Cs

Although contracting law in the United States is different from state to state, some basic principles are common to all states. With or without formal legal training, most U.S. business professionals who manage contracts absorb the following principles while doing business. Many principles you may take for granted, however, are the product of the common law developed in the United States and are not valid in civil law countries. When contracting globally, examining your basic assumptions to determine whether your trading partners are operating on the same ones is essential.

Some common law legal principles and concepts are described in the following paragraphs. Differences in civil law are noted below the common law descriptions.

Formation

In common law, to form an enforceable contract, there must be an offer, acceptance, exchange of consideration, competent parties, and legality of purpose.

Offer

An offer must be unequivocal, and it must be intentionally communicated to another party. An offer is presumed revocable unless it specifically states that it is irrevocable. An offer once made will be open for a reasonable period of time and is binding on the offeror unless revoked by the offeror before the other party's acceptance.

Civil law: An offer is usually irrevocable for a reasonable period of time, unless the offer unequivocally states that it is revocable.

Acceptance

Acceptance means agreement to the terms offered. An acceptance must be communicated, and it must be the mirror image of the offer. If the terms change, it is a *counteroffer* that then must be accepted. The UCC changes this mirror image rule by stating that definite and seasonable expression of acceptance that is sent within a reasonable time operates as an acceptance even though it states terms additional to or different from those offered under §2-207(1).

Civil law: Many jurisdictions lack a mirror image rule. Rather, the acceptance must merely be to the significant terms of the offer.

Consideration

For a common law contract to be enforceable, the parties must exchange something of value (consideration). Consideration can be something of monetary value, or it can be a promise to do something not required by law or a promise to refrain from doing something permitted by law.

Competent Parties

Both common and civil law countries require that in order to form (create) an enforceable contract, the party must posses legal capacity to contract, that is, it must be competent. For people, competency generally is tantamount to attaining the so-called legal age. On the other hand, entities such as corporations and partnerships gain legal capacity either by an act of government (issuance of a certificate of incorporation) or by an act of the party itself (execution of the partnership agreement).

Legality of Purpose

Another element in the process of forming an enforceable contract is the requirement that the underlying purpose of the deal be legal (as viewed by the law of the contract). The requirement of legality of purpose is shared by both common and civil law countries.

Contract Privity

One key concept of contract law is contract privity, which is the legal connection or relationship that exists between the contracting parties.[7] Such privity must exist between the plaintiff and defendant with respect to a matter being contested. A major exception to this principle that only the contracting parties can sue each other was created with the enactment of warranty statutes. For example, any person who is in the buyer's family or household may now sue for the breach of a seller's warranty.

Bilateral and Unilateral Contracts

If an offer states that an acceptance is sufficient if the accepting party promises to perform, a *bilateral* contract is created. If the offer states that the only way to accept is by performing, then a *unilateral* contract is created (for example, offering a reward for finding a lost pet).

Civil law: Unilateral contracts are relatively rare in the United States, but are used with some frequency in several civil law jurisdictions.

Executed and Executory Contracts

Executed contracts are contracts that are formed and performed at the same time, such as the purchase of clothing at a department store. *Executory contracts* are contracts that are formed at one time and performed later, such as most commercial contracts.

Statute of Frauds

The *Statute of Frauds* refers to an old English statute designed to alleviate fraudulent claims. It provides that any contract that cannot be fully performed in less than a year and any contract for more the $500 must be in writing to be enforceable.

> *Civil law: Few jurisdictions require that a sale contract be in writing. However, almost all civil law countries require that a sales contract involving real estate be in writing.*

Signature of the Party to Be Charged

For a written contract to be admissible evidence in court, it must have the signature of the party to be charged (the defendant).

> *Civil law: Because a contract does not have to be in writing, few formal rules govern the form of a contract. A written contract transmitted back and forth between the parties may be admitted as evidence of an oral agreement, whether or not there is a signature.*

Actual and Apparent Authority

The difference between actual and apparent authority was defined in Chapter 2 in the section on defining contractual authority. If a principal sets up a situation in which it appears to third parties that an agent has the authority to bind the principal, then the principal is bound by the acts of the agent, despite any agreement between the agent and the principal to the contrary.

Civil law: In parts of Europe and in some Asian countries, corporate law provides for specific officers who are authorized to bind the corporation. The holders of the authorized positions are kept in an official court registry. If a person is not registered to bind the corporation, no action, no matter how deceptive, can serve to bind the corporation.

Waiver

A *waiver* is the voluntary and unilateral relinquishment by some act or conduct of a person of a right that he or she has. In common law countries, any contractual right of a party can be waived explicitly or implicitly by the party benefiting from the right. Similarly, any contractual obligation can be waived explicitly or implicitly by the party to whom the obligation is owed.

Civil law: Like the United States, every sovereign jurisdiction has specific areas sensitive to public policy based on the culture and economy of a nation. Frequently, in areas that touch on public policy, there are statutory rights that cannot be waived in a contract. Each jurisdiction must be examined to determine what, if any, nonwaivable rights the trading partner may have.

Forbearance

Forbearance is an intentional failure of a party to enforce a contract requirement, usually done for an act of immediate or future consideration from the other party. Sometimes forbearance is referred to as a nonwaiver or as a one-time waiver, but not relinquishment, of rights.

Specific Performance vs. Damages

Most contractual disputes are remedied with *damages* (money) to make the aggrieved party "whole." In certain limited circumstances, a party may be forced to actually perform the contract, known as *specific performance.*

Liquidated and Compensatory vs. Punitive Damages

After determining that a party is wronged and is entitled to damages, a determination must be made regarding the appropriate amount of damages. Using the evidence presented by the parties and rules of law, the court will find an exact amount due (*compensatory damages*). In certain situations, parties may agree in advance that if a party is wronged in a specific way, then a specific amount of damages will be due the other party, thereby liquidating the damages in advance. Thus, if the parties include a *liquidated damages* clause in their contract, the court will determine only whether a party was in fact wronged and entitled to damages. Both common law and civil law allow the parties to the contract to agree on future damages. Note, however, that in common law, liquidated run-in damages must have a reasonable relation to the probable actual damages; they cannot be mere penalty. *Punitive damages*, unlike compensatory damages, are those damages awarded to the plaintiff over and above what will barely compensate for his or her loss. Punitive damages are based on public policy considerations of punishing the defendant or setting an example for similar wrongdoers.

Parol Evidence Rule

The best evidence of a written contract is the document itself. If a contract is unambiguous, the court will not allow the introduction of evidence other than the written contract to alter the contract terms.

> *Civil law: The rule does not exist. Oral evidence is usually admissible to vary the contract terms. Some civil courts will even accept oral contract amendments in the face of a clause that states that all amendments must be in writing, provided that someone testifies that both parties agreed to ignore the clause and make an oral amendment.*

The Uniform Commercial Code

As stated previously, despite the fact that each state has its own laws, commercial sales are governed in the United States by a fairly uniform set of rules called the Uniform Commercial Code. The UCC is a model law developed to standardize commercial contracting law among the states. It has been adopted by 49 states (and in significant portions by Louisiana). The UCC comprises articles that deal with specific commercial subject matters, including sales and letters of credit. Article 2 (Sales) governs most trade in goods.

Most of the UCC merely puts into uniform statutory form the common law of contracts. Sometimes however, the UCC has moved the United States more toward civil law concepts. If parties choose U.S. law to govern their contracts, they usually are choosing the UCC. Both the U.S. party and its international business partner should understand the implications. The following sections describe some UCC provisions that are sometimes misunderstood.

Battle of the Forms

In modern business, it has become common for a company to make offers on standardized documents, such as purchase orders, that have numerous Ts and Cs preprinted on the reverse side. Another company would then acknowledge the order on a preprinted form, the reverse of which would include many conditions different from the first form (the battle of the forms). Under common law, the acceptance with the differing terms was not the mirror image of the offer; therefore, no binding contract was formed. In fact, it was a counteroffer. The UCC changed this mirror image rule by stating that a *definite and reasonable expression of acceptance* (which is sent within a reasonable time) *operates as an acceptance* even though it states terms additional to or different from those offered. If the material terms on the faces of the forms match, a contract is formed; any nonmaterial additional terms are added to the terms of the buyer's or seller's form.

FOURTH ESSENTIAL ELEMENT: LIST OF MUST HAVES

In every contract negotiation each party should know what they must have agreed to in order to accept the deal. A proven essential element in contract negotiations for both buyers and sellers is a documented list of "must haves." Plus, a master contract negotiator will also develop a list of items, he or she considers the other party will view as "must haves." Knowing your "must haves" and the other party's "must haves" is indeed essential to success in the world of contract negotiations.

FIFTH ESSENTIAL ELEMENT: SELECTED PRICING RANGE

As discussed in Chapter 3, pricing should be the last item discussed during contract negotiations. Master contract negotiators know everything directly or indirectly affects the price of the deal. Thus, it is vital to each party to agree to all aspects of the deal (products, services, quantity, schedule, detailed Ts and Cs) before discussing the pricing. Likewise, both the buyer and seller should have a predetermined and preapproved pricing range (minimum, target, and maximum) based on the assumption of risk. Generally stated, the greater the assumption of risk one party takes, the greater the reward they should receive if successful in fulfilling the contract requirements.

Checklist of Planning Contract Negotiation Best Practices

Form 4-2 provides a simple yet, highly effective checklist of planning contract negotiation actions, for both buyers and sellers, which can help both parties achieve success.

✓ Form 4-2 Checklist. Planning Contract Negotiation Best Practices

- ☐ Select the right person or people
- ☐ Formulate your selected contract negotiation strategy
- ☐ Identify alternative approaches
- ☐ Select your planned contract negotiation tactics and countertactics
- ☐ Develop your list of "must haves"
- ☐ Develop your selected pricing range
- ☐ Know when to walk away
- ☐ Know the other party's "must haves"
- ☐ Prioritize your interests
- ☐ Prioritize your concessions
- ☐ Understand the risk, cost, and value of your desired Terms and Conditions
- ☐ Prepare for the contract negotiation (people, facility, information technology tools)
- ☐ Select the right location(s) to plan and conduct the negotiations
- ☐ Prepare a negotiation agenda
- ☐ Secure the support of experts
- ☐ Appoint a contract negotiation leader
- ☐ Practice—conduct mock contract negotiations
- ☐ Assign a scribe to document contract negotiations
- ☐ Document your contract negotiation plan
- ☐ Obtain executive review and approval of your negotiation plan

SUMMARY

In this chapter focused on planning contract negotiations, we have discussed the importance of beginning with the end in mind, planning individual vs. team-based contract negotiations, effectively using information technology tools to facilitate planning, and the five essential elements of the contract negotiation plan. Chapter 5 will provide more details for planning contract negotiation strategies, tactics, and countertactics. Together, chapters 4 and 5 provide you with a wealth of information and best practices to help you improve your skills for planning your contract negotiations.

QUESTIONS TO CONSIDER

1. How effectively do you plan your contract negotiations?

2. Do you pre-select contract negotiation strategy, tactics, and countertactics?

3. How effectively do you build a contract negotiation team?

4. Does your organization require a formal documented contract negotiation plan, which must be reviewed and approved prior to the start of contract negotiations?

5. How effectively does your organization limit risk through terms and conditions in your contracts?

6. How well does your organization select or predetermine a pricing range for your contract negotiations?

7. How effectively does your organization use information technology tools to facilitate planning contract negotiations?

ENDNOTES

[1] Goodpaster, Gary, A Guide to Negotiation and Mediation. Transnational Publishers, Inc., New York NY, 1997.

[2] Ibid

[3] Ibid

[4] Stark, Peter B. and Flaherty, Jane, The Only Negotiating Guide You'll Ever Need. Broadway Books, New York NY, 2003.

[5] Ibid Note 1

[6] Ibid Note 1

[7] For example, when a buyer contracts with a seller and the seller contracts with a third party to perform part of the project work, the seller is called the *prime contractor* and the third party is a *subcontractor*. Under ordinary circumstances, privity of contract exists between the buyer and the prime contractor and between the prime contractor and the subcontractor, but not between the buyer and the subcontractor. This principle holds true even though the subcontractor and the buyer have contact with one another on a day-to-day basis during contract performance.

Contract Negotiations Planning: Strategies, Tactics, and Countertactics

INTRODUCTION

Many contract negotiators believe there are only two basic strategies or approaches to conduct contract negotiations: win/lose or win/win. Some contract negotiators consider win/win more of an illusion than a business reality. Some people prefer to describe their contract negotiations as a win/win situation rather than admit they lost. Of course, it is very difficult to determine whether your side won or lost unless your side had an agreed-to negotiation plan with specific performance metrics. As discussed in Chapters 3 and 4, an effective contract negotiation plan should contain your side's negotiation strategy, tactics, possible countertactics, and desired negotiation results.

This chapter focuses on the various strategies, tactics, and countertactics that may be used to achieve success in contract negotiations. Based on extensive research and experience I will discuss the good, the bad, and the ugly aspects of contract negotiation strategies, tactics, and countertactics. While I always recommend taking a highly positive and professional approach to business and building long-term professional relationships, clearly not everyone chooses to practice this philosophy. A master contract negotiator, like a master craftsman, knows all of the various strategies, tactics, and countertactics and when and how to use them to achieve success.

CONTRACT NEGOTIATION PLANNING — TEN SUCCESSFUL STRATEGIES

According to Frank L. Acuff, consultant and author of *How to Negotiate Anything with Anyone Anywhere Around the World*," there are ten strategies that have proven to be highly effective in negotiations throughout the world.

1. *Plan the contract negotiation*—As discussed in detail in Chapters 3 and 4, effective planning is critical to achieve success in contract negotiations. Data gathering, data assessment, and the forming plan, including: strategies, tactics, countertactics, and desired results, are essential to professional contract negotiations.

   Plan the Contract Negotiation: Strategic Guidelines
   - Create a contract negotiation plan that includes strategies, tactics, countertactics, and desired results.
   - Document the contract negotiation plan.
   - Obtain appropriate reviews, agreement, and support of your team members and organization leadership.

2. *Adopt a win/win approach*—In most negotiations, it is in your best interest to create a highly collaborative atmosphere to increase the possibility of achieving a perceived win/win outcome. There are three key strategic guidelines to keep in mind to consistently achieve win/win situations during contract negotiations:

   Win/Win: Strategic Guidelines
   - Do not narrow the negotiation down to one issue!
   - Understand the other side has different interests and needs!
   - Ask questions to try to understand the other side's real needs!

3. *Maintain high aspirations*—It is virtually impossible to achieve more in contract negotiations than what you ask for, or said differently, if you do not ask for it you will not get it. Unfortunately, many individuals have been conditioned not to ask for what they truly want because they are afraid of being perceived as greedy, unreasonable, or just plain silly. Remember the following high-aspiration strategic guidelines.

High Aspiration: Strategic Guidelines
- Do not take away your own power by asking for too little!
- Demonstrate persistence and conviction to achieve high goals!
- Realize if you make high initial demands/offers there is room to negotiate!

4. *Use language that is simple and accessible*—It is important during contract negotiations to communicate clearly and concisely to avoid miscommunication and misunderstandings. Do not speak to impress people or just to hear yourself talk. In the words of Dr. Steven Covey, the author of 7 Habits of Highly Effective People, begin with the end in mind. It is important to know what you want and to articulate your thoughts clearly.

Simple & Accessible Language: Strategic Guidelines
- Avoid the use of clichés, colloquialisms, and slang!
- Avoid the use of excessive technical or legal jargon!
- Do not speak to impress, speak to inform!

5. *Ask lots of questions, then listen with your eyes and ears*—Remember a key part of the art of contract negotiation is seeking to understand the needs and desires of the other side. People convey more by how they say things (i.e., vocal tone, use of pauses, voice inflection) than they do through their spoken words. Many people say things they do not believe; however, most give it away in how they say it. Further, there is a real art to asking the right questions at the right time, in the right way, and of the right person!

Questioning & Listening: Strategic Guidelines
- Seek to understand, by asking lots of questions to the other side.
- Practice and use active listening during contract negotiations.
- Observe how things are said and the other side's nonverbal communications.

6. *Build solid relationships*—Realize it is in your best interests to build a long-term successful business relationship with the other side. Treat the other side as your partner. It is very important to treat your negotiation partner with respect and to seek to build trust. Trust is essential to long-term mutual business success.

Build Solid Relationships: Strategic Guidelines
- Establish challenging but achievable performance-based goals!
- Treat everyone as a partner—with honesty and respect!
- Build trust!

7. *Maintain personal integrity*—Upholding business ethics is vital to the success of every organization involved in buying or selling products or services. Even the appearance of a conflict of interest can damage a person's integrity and compromise the reputation of an entire organization.

Personal Integrity: Strategic Guidelines
- Live by a code of conduct!
- Be a role model for practicing business ethics!
- Manage expectations and honor commitments!

8. *Conserve Concessions*—When you give concessions to the other side, how you give them and the size of the concessions convey a lot of valuable information about your strategy, style, and conviction. Remember, concessions set either a positive or negative tone for the negotiation, plus they establish a precedent for future negotiations with the same party. Master negotiators study the concession patterns of the other side.

Concession: Strategic Guidelines
- Make contingent concessions!
- Vary your concessions' timing and size, do not be too predictable!
- Do not feel you must reciprocate with like concessions to the other side!

9. *Make patience an obsession*—Patience is indeed a virtue, especially in contract negotiations. On the other hand, haste makes waste, especially in contract negotiations. Further, if you want it bad—you will get it bad! Patience or the lack thereof is often linked to negotiators' concession behavior. True master negotiators are very patient people when it comes to negotiating big deals. Apprentice negotiators are often impatient and thus make more and larger concessions in order to bring the deal to closure.

Patience: Strategic Guidelines
- Do not be in a rush—schedule sufficient time to negotiate!
- Be prepared for delay tactics!
- Set a reasonable contract negotiation schedule and propose a settlement deadline!

10. *Be Culturally Literate and Adapt the Contract Negotiation Process to the Host Country Environment*—It is very important to acquire insights into the culture of the other side when negotiating internationally. Cultural awareness or savvy can take many forms.

Cultural Literacy: Strategic Guidelines
- Become culturally aware—obtain training and seek expert assistance as needed!
- Treat everyone with great respect!
- Conduct yourself as a gracious and effective foreigner!
- If you apply them, the preceding ten contract negotiation planning strategies and associated guidelines can help you focus your planning to achieve your desired results.

CONTRACT NEGOTIATION PLANNING: TACTICS & COUNTERTACTICS

There are literally hundreds of tactics and countertactics used in contract negotiations worldwide. I will focus on what I consider to be the top 50 tactics and related countertactics.[1] When considering their use in contract negotiation it is important to understand each tactic and countertactic, know how and when to use each one, and know how and when to effectively counter each.[2] Remember, during contract negotiations you should be focused on building and maintaining a professional business relationship. So use tactics and countertactics appropriately. While I do not advocate the use of some of the following tactics and countertactics, it is important to be aware of all of them because there are many unethical and at times ruthless contract negotiators. In the words of Louis Pasteur, the great scientist and inventor, "chance favors the prepared mind."

 **Contract Negotiations Tactics & Countertactics**

Tactic 1	
Tactic:	"The Full Monty"
Description:	Ask the other party for everything you want and more!
Possible Countertactics:	■ Offer far less than the full monty ■ Offer to provide the full monty, contingent on a multi-year exclusive contract with highly favorable upscope opportunities ■ Walk away ■ Disclose the full monty as unrealistic
Tactic 2	
Tactic	"The Scape-Goat"
Description:	Explain to the other side you completely agree with their requests/demands; however, another key person in your organization will not approve.
Possible Countertactics:	■ Ask to speak to the person in question ■ Who's your boss? ■ Just say no! ■ Not good enough! ■ How much do you have to spend? ■ I don't understand
Tactic 3	
Tactic:	"Say Nothing"
Description:	The less you talk, the better. When your counterpart is a talker, let them talk—they will give you valuable information. Often your talkative counterpart will give more and bigger concessions because of your silence.
Possible Countertactics:	■ Bring in another negotiator ■ Say nothing—silence is golden ■ Disclose the tactic ■ Break-off negotiations; take a break

Contract Negotiations
Tactics & Countertactics (continued)

Tactic 4	
Tactic:	"Just Say No"
Description:	Sometimes the single most effective negotiation tactic is to simply just say no! You can use this at almost any offer or counteroffer made by your counterparts.
Possible Countertactics:	▪ Refuse to accept no ▪ Offer a counter-proposal ▪ Try yes and .... ▪ Escalate
Tactic 5	
Tactic:	"Good Guy/Bad Guy"
Description:	One of your team members pretends to be on the side of your counterpart, while another team member favors your side.
Possible Countertactics:	▪ Play along–have fun ▪ Disclose the tactic ▪ Use the same tactic on the other side
Tactic 6	
Tactic	"Not Good Enough"
Description:	Whenever the other side makes an offer, you simply reply, "not good enough," then pause and allow the other side to make the next response.
Possible Countertactics:	▪ Reply, "So what is good enough?" ▪ Silence ▪ Walk away ▪ Replay your previous offer ▪ Escalate
Tactic 7	
Tactic:	"My Facts Are Better Than Yours"
Description:	Use facts –such as industry benchmarking studies, surveys, standards, or case-studies to lend power and credibility to your point!
Possible Countertactics:	▪ Use your facts –and better sources ▪ Use expert witnesses ▪ Refute their facts ▪ Change the game, move away from this point to another

Contract Negotiations
Tactics & Countertactics (continued)

Tactic 8	
Tactic:	"Attack, Attack, Attack"
Description:	Some contract negotiators will use verbal assaults, including: profane language, profane gestures, personal insults, organizational insults, and emotional attacks, i.e., getting angry, crying, to get you off topic and not thinking clearly.
Possible Countertactics:	■ Know when to walk away ■ Disclose the tactic ■ Strike back ■ Who's your boss? ■ Just say no! ■ Timeout! ■ You can't be serious! ■ Focus on the issue!
Tactic 9	
Tactic:	"Who's Your Boss?"
Description:	Some contract negotiators will seek to escalate any issue in which you disagree with their position to your boss.
Possible Countertactics:	■ Who's your boss? (to the other side) ■ Here's my boss's name, phone number, and e-mail; my boss will tell you the same thing! ■ We can work this out ■ Make a counteroffer ■ Provide a giveaway
Tactic 10	
Tactic:	"Desperate Deals"
Description:	Attempt to get the other side, especially publicly traded companies, to agree to deep discounts in order to report a big deal or recognize revenue before the end of a fiscal quarter or the fiscal year.
Possible Countertactics:	■ Do not make a desperate deal ■ Do not close the deal until the next quarter/fiscal year ■ Do not give a deep discount ■ Provide a giveaway
Tactic 11	
Tactic:	"Stonewall"
Description:	Take a position and do not move! Demonstrate conviction—I shall not move, concede, or alter my position.
Possible Countertactics:	■ Be flexible ■ Make a contingent offer to accept the stonewall in return for something additional. ■ Withdraw or silence ■ Take a break ■ Who's your boss?

Contract Negotiations
Tactics & Countertactics *(continued)*

Tactic 12	
Tactic:	"Playing the Ego"
Description:	If you are negotiating with a person who clearly has an inflated sense of self-worth, then play to their ego through flattery, seeking their advice to solve the problem, and asking if they have the authority to make this deal.
Possible Countertactics:	■ Disclose the tactic ■ Deflate your own ego ■ State your lack of authority ■ Who's your boss? ■ I don't understand

Tactic 13	
Tactic:	"How Much Do You Have to Spend?"
Description:	Many contract negotiators will try to determine the buyer's budget in an attempt to capture all of the available funding.
Possible Countertactics:	■ Variable budget ■ Performance-based budget ■ Budget is contingent on value provided by the contracted products/services ■ Refuse to disclose the budget ■ Split the difference ■ BAFO & BARFO (see Tactic 30) ■ Lack of authority

Tactic 14	
Tactic:	"Lose the Battle, Win the War"
Description:	One party will decide to intentionally allow the other party to obtain a more favorable outcome in one negotiation in order to obtain a better relationship and follow-on opportunities.
Possible Countertactics:	■ Disclose the tactic ■ Every deal is separate ■ No follow-on commitments ■ Who's your boss? ■ Accept

Tactic 15	
Tactic:	"Know When to Walk Away, Know When to Run"
Description:	It is important to know when it is appropriate to walk away. No business is better than bad business!
Possible Countertactics:	■ Pursue the other party ■ Offer an easy concession to bring them back ■ Call a break/recess ■ Escalate

Contract Negotiations
Tactics & Countertactics (continued)

Tactic 16	
Tactic:	"I don't understand"
Description:	Some contract negotiators will repeatedly use the phrase "I don't understand," simply to get the other side to provide more information or to frustrate the other side into making concessions.
Possible Countertactics:	■ Re-explain ■ Suggest the other party should bring in another negotiator who is more knowledgeable ■ Who's your boss? ■ You can't be serious! ■ Know when to walk away ■ Timeout/recess ■ Playing the ego

Tactic 17	
Tactic:	"You Can't Be Serious"
Description:	Some contract negotiators will repeatedly use the phrase "You can't be serious," in an attempt to persuade you that you are being unfair or unreasonable.
Possible Countertactics:	■ Show them the facts ■ They can't be serious ■ Who's your boss? ■ I don't understand!

Tactic 18	
Tactic	"Timeout/Recess"
Description:	Taking a timely break from a contract negotiation can sometimes be the most effective tactic, especially if your team is losing focus or tensions are rising.
Possible Countertactics:	■ We must press on ■ Delay ■ Not right now, just 5 more minutes

Tactic 19	
Tactic:	"The Stealth Offer"
Description:	One party tells the other party that they have another offer from a third party that in fact does not exist.
Possible Countertactics:	■ Let's see it ■ Walk away ■ Who's your boss? ■ Know when to walk away

Contract Negotiations
Tactics & Countertactics (continued)

Tactic 20	
Tactic:	"Here today, gone tomorrow"
Description:	One party makes a time-limited offer, which has a very brief period of effectiveness.
Possible Countertactics:	■ Request more time to review ■ Need more time for higher approvals ■ Reach an agreement ■ Just say no! ■ Know when to walk away ■ Who's your boss? ■ Timeout/rRecess

Tactic 21	
Tactic:	"Low-balling"
Description:	One party makes a ridiculously low offer, which will certainly not be accepted by the other party.
Possible Countertactics:	■ High-balling, a.k.a. the full monty ■ Disclose the tactic ■ Say nothing ■ Accept ■ Just say no!

Tactic 22	
Tactic:	"It's a Competitive World"
Description:	Just the threat of competition can sometimes cause the other party to make concessions.
Possible Countertactics:	■ Defend your position ■ Show them your facts ■ Ask who are your competitors & what are they offering—which is better? ■ Who's your boss?

Tactic 23	
Tactic:	"Delay Actions"
Description:	Often experienced contract negotiators will prey on the impatience of the other party through a variety of delay actions, including: urgent phone call, must attend meeting, big boss needs to talk, family emergency, higher priority deal, etc. They're all designed to make the other party more willing to make compromises.
Possible Countertactics:	■ Who's your boss? ■ Your own delay actions ■ Know when to walk away ■ Timeout/recess ■ Press on ■ Just say no!

Contract Negotiations
Tactics & Countertactics (continued)

Tactic 24	
Tactic:	"The Artificial Deadline"
Description:	Many contract negotiators are known to create artificial deadlines in order to create a sense of urgency in order to drive the other party to make more rapid concessions and to quickly close the deal.
Possible Countertactics:	■ Escalate to verify deadline ■ Offer to accept, with contingencies ■ Refuse the deadline

Tactic 25	
Tactic:	"See if They Flinch"
Description:	Some contract negotiators skillfully observe the other party's reaction to your tactics to determine what tactics or countertactics are appropriate.
Possible Countertactics:	■ Control your nonverbals ■ Display false nonverbals ■ Timeout/recess

Tactic 26	
Tactic:	"Focus on the Issue"
Description:	During contract negotiations do not allow the other party to throw you off track; stay focused on the issues that are of most importance to your organization.
Possible Countertactics:	■ Delay actions ■ Attack, attack, attack ■ Timeout/recess

Tactic 27	
Tactic:	"Split the Difference"
Description:	A common contract negotiation tactic is to have one party offer to split the difference with the other party. In other words, each party agrees to take a 50% share of the difference between their respective offers.
Possible Countertactics:	■ Refuse to split the difference ■ Accept the split, with contingencies ■ Accept the offer ■ Counteroffer

Tactic 28	
Tactic:	"Quid Pro Quo"
Description:	During contract negotiation, any time one party asks the other party for a concession, the latter party in turn seeks a comparable concession.
Possible Countertactics:	■ Refuse to make concession ■ Stonewall ■ Accept

Contract Negotiations
Tactics & Countertactics *(continued)*

Tactic 29	
Tactic:	"Nibbling"
Description:	A common contract negotiation maneuver that is a form of escalation, it typically occurs at the end of the contract negotiation when one party seeks one or more relatively small concessions or additional demands.
Possible Countertactics:	▪ Disclose the tactic ▪ Refuse the nibble ▪ Agree with the nibble ▪ Quid pro quo
Tactic 30	
Tactic:	"BAFO & BARFO"
Description:	The buyer's request for a best and final offer (BAFO). If the buyer considers the final offer not good enough, it then requests a best and really final offer (BARFO).
Possible Countertactics:	▪ Accept the offer ▪ Refuse to play
Tactic 31	
Tactic:	"Red-Herring"
Description:	A common contract negotiation move, providing essentially a false statement to distract attention from other, more important, issues.
Possible Countertactics:	▪ Disclose the tactic ▪ Show your facts ▪ Timeout/recess
Tactic 32	
Tactic:	"The Power of Nice"
Description:	Some contract negotiators will display friendliness, goodwill, and positive attitude to gain an advantage with the other party.
Possible Countertactics:	▪ Disclose the tactic ▪ [same as be nice too?] ▪ Attack, attack, attack, ▪ Be nice too
Tactic 33	
Tactic:	"Lack of Authority"
Description:	The contract negotiator without authority can use the situation to advantage to explore the other side's positions and even obtain concessions without making any real commitments.
Possible Countertactics:	▪ Verify authority upfront ▪ Who's your boss? ▪ You can't be serious!

Contract Negotiations
Tactics & Countertactics (continued)

Tactic 34	
Tactic:	"Bring in the Big Dog"
Description:	During contract negotiations, one party may decide to influence the other party by bringing in a person of high-level position, great expertise/stature, great wealth, celebrity status, etc., which may influence the other party.
Possible Countertactics:	▪ Disclose the tactic ▪ Bring in your own big dog with a different view point ▪ Who's your boss?

Tactic 35	
Tactic:	"Principle-Centered"
Description:	A contract negotiation approach that appeals to moral values or principles, which can be highly persuasive to the other party.
Possible Countertactics:	▪ Disclose the tactic ▪ Show your facts ▪ Accept ▪ Just say no!

Tactic 36	
Tactic:	"The Follow-on Deal"
Description:	A common contract negotiation tactic in which the buyer offers to tie the results of this deal directly to the seller's chance of obtaining a future deal.
Possible Countertactics:	▪ Accept the offer, with contingencies ▪ Accept the offer ▪ Reject the offer ▪ Not good enough!

Tactic 37	
Tactic:	"Re-Open Negotiation"
Description:	After the completion of contract negotiation, one party demands to re-open negotiation to undo one or more issues previously agreed to in order to gain leverage.
Possible Countertactics:	▪ Refuse to re-open negotiation ▪ Quid pro quo ▪ Disclose the tactic

Tactic 38	
Tactic:	"Bluffing"
Description:	Bluffing is a form of pretense or deception, often used to hide a weakness during contract negotiations.
Possible Countertactics:	▪ Disclose the tactic ▪ Show your facts ▪ Who's your boss? ▪ You can't be serious!

Contract Negotiations
Tactics & Countertactics (continued)

Tactic 39	
Tactic:	"Failure to Fully Disclose"
Description:	Rather than lie or provide false information, some contract negotiators often fail to provide all of the available information.
Possible Countertactics:	■ Disclose the tactic ■ Know the facts ■ Know the rules of the game ■ Who's your boss?

Tactic 40	
Tactic:	"Use of False Facts"
Description:	Knowingly provide false information and present it as a proven fact.
Possible Countertactics:	■ Disclose the tactic ■ Know the facts ■ Escalate

Tactic 41	
Tactic:	"Loaded Questions"
Description:	Some contract negotiators use loaded questions, which are questions that a party usually can't answer and that have a message more important than the information they seek.
Possible Countertactics:	■ Disclose the tactic ■ Refuse to answer ■ Use your facts

Tactic 42	
Tactic:	"Open Questions"
Description:	A common contract negotiation tactic is the use of open questions. Open questions invite long, relatively undirected answers, usually intended to gather as much information as possible.
Possible Countertactics:	■ I don't understand ■ Disclose the tactic ■ Refuse to answer ■ Use a loaded question ■ Answer briefly

Tactic 43	
Tactic:	"Rhetorical Questions"
Description:	Rhetorical questions are questions that expect no answer but also attempt to create a new meaning or to persuade one's thinking
Possible Countertactics:	■ Disclose the tactic ■ Return a rhetorical question ■ Use a loaded question ■ Say nothing

Contract Negotiations
Tactics & Countertactics (continued)

Tactic 44	
Tactic:	"Yes or No Questions"
Description:	Experienced contract negotiators will often use yes or no questions to control the discussion.
Possible Countertactics:	■ Disclose the tactic ■ Use an open-ended question as a response ■ Refuse to answer ■ Redirect the question

Tactic 45	
Tactic:	"Redirected Questions"
Description:	During contract negotiations, if you choose not to respond to a direct question, you can redirect or transfer the question back to the person who asked the question or to another party involved in the contract negotiation.
Possible Countertactics:	■ Refuse to answer ■ Answer the question ■ Redirect the question ■ Disclose the tactic

Tactic 46	
Tactic:	"Role Reversal"
Description:	Changing from bad guy to good guy can make the other side believe you truly understand their side, which will likely create a more collaborative environment.
Possible Countertactics:	■ Disclose the tactic ■ Play along

Tactic 47	
Tactic:	"Divide and Conquer"
Description:	When involved in team-based contract negotiations with the other side, seek to divide their team, then pull aside key team members from the other side to try to win them over one at a time.
Possible Countertactics:	■ Do not allow your team to be divided ■ Disclose the tactic ■ Divide and conquer their team

Tactic 48	
Tactic:	"Stalemate/Deadlock"
Description:	When both parties are frustrated by their inability to make progress, they no longer see any point in talking any further.
Possible Countertactics:	■ Offer to make a concession ■ Who's your boss? ■ You can't be serious!

Contract Negotiations
Tactics & Countertactics *(continued)*

Tactic 49	
Tactic:	"Stay in the Game"
Description:	During contract negotiations, when dealing with difficult people it is important to find a way to stay in the game. Remember, you cannot win if you're not in the game.
Possible Countertactics:	■ Timeouts/recess ■ Show your facts ■ Counteroffer ■ Agree
Tactic 50	
Tactic:	"Say yes, and ..."
Description:	A common and highly effective contract negotiation tactic is to agree with the other side on an issue, then say "and ..." so you can get something you want as well.
Possible Countertactics:	■ Refuse the and ... ■ Accept the and ... ■ Counteroffer ■ Who's your boss? ■ Split the difference!

SUMMARY

This chapter has focused on the importance of contract negotiation planning. Specifically, it offers 10 highly successful contract negotiation strategies, 30 proven strategic guidelines, and 50 of the most effective contract negotiation tactics and related countertactics. Of course, in contract negotiation planning, knowing is good, but doing is better!

QUESTIONS TO CONSIDER

1. What contract negotiation strategies does your organization typically employ?

2. How well does your organization plan your contract negotiation strategies, tactics, and countertactics?

3. Does your organization conduct mock contract negotiations to prepare for negotiating big deals?

4. How many of the 50 contract negotiation tactics does your organization typically use when negotiating a big deal?

ENDNOTES

[1] Stark, Peter B. and Jane Flaherty, The Only Negotiating Guide You'll Ever Need, Broadway Books, New York NY, 2003.

[2] Goodpaster, Gary, A Guide to Negotiation and Mediation, Transnational Publishers Inc., New York NY, 1997.

Conducting Contract Negotiations: Building Relationships and Successful Outcomes

INTRODUCTION

As discussed in Chapter 3, the contract negotiation process is composed of three phases: planning, conducting, and documenting. Chapters 4 and 5 examined in detail the planning phase of the contract negotiation process, which is vital to achieving success. However, the best-laid plan may fail if it is not properly executed. Master contract negotiators strive to develop an excellent contract negotiation plan, then successfully execute the plan. Master contract negotiators understand that applying strategies, tactics, and countertactics through effective communications is key to achieving a win-win situation in contract negotiations. This chapter is focused on providing proven effective best practices, for both buyers and sellers, to build mutually successful outcomes when conducting contract negotiations. Specifically, this chapter will address the key questions and best practices pertaining to conducting contract negotiations: when, who, how, where, and what. This chapter will conclude with a brief discussion of the importance and best practices of price analysis.

CONDUCTING CONTRACT NEGOTIATIONS: WHEN?

One of the most basic, but most important, lessons to learn is when contract negotiation begins. Some people will tell you contract negotiation officially begins after the exchange of formal proposals and related pricing information. Others may tell you contract negotiation does not begin until after the buyer has completed its post-bid fact finding. I contend contract negotiation begins at first contact, with the first communications concerning a possible opportunity between the buyer and seller.

First contact may occur at any level of an organization or between one or more functional areas. Sometimes contract negotiations begin when senior executives within the buyer and seller organizations have a meeting or conference call. Sometimes first contact occurs when the buyer's technical or operational people conduct some market research and contact their technical counterparts in their respective industries. Sometimes first contact occurs by means of a seller's advertising in the media or the publication of articles or technical papers in professional magazines or journals.

The first time a buyer or seller communicates to the other party regarding a potential product, service, or integrated solution, that buyer or seller begins to set expectations with the other party. As soon as one or both parties begin to form and set expectations regarding the capabilities of potential products, services, or solutions, the contract negotiation game has begun. So, what is important to remember and share within your organization is that everyone who interfaces between buyer and seller should realize that what they say, do, and do not do sends a message to the other party, thereby creating expectations that form the initial basis for contract negotiations.

CONDUCTING CONTRACT NEGOTIATIONS: WHO?

One of the key aspects of conducting contract negotiations is deciding if one person is going to conduct the negotiation for your organization or if a team of people is required. If a contract negotiation team is going to be formed, then numerous critical questions should be addressed.

Form 6-1 provides a checklist of critical questions that should be addressed before the start of contract negotiations. The skills needed to be successful in contract negotiations are discussed in detail in Chapter 2. The answers to most of the questions posed in Form 6-1 usually depend on the unique aspects of a particular business situation, including: size, monetary amount, level of complexity, overall assessment of risk, urgency of requirement, the scope of work (product and services mix), and the skills of the people in your organization. The key to success in contract negotiation is understanding the importance of the four Ps: people, process, performance, and price—in that order! Too many organizations care too much about job titles and level or seniority and not enough about the real skills or competencies required to be consistently successful in contract negotiations.

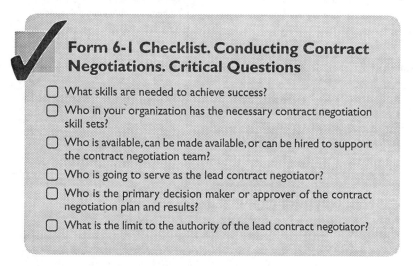

Form 6-1 Checklist. Conducting Contract Negotiations. Critical Questions

☐ What skills are needed to achieve success?

☐ Who in your organization has the necessary contract negotiation skill sets?

☐ Who is available, can be made available, or can be hired to support the contract negotiation team?

☐ Who is going to serve as the lead contract negotiator?

☐ Who is the primary decision maker or approver of the contract negotiation plan and results?

☐ What is the limit to the authority of the lead contract negotiator?

CONDUCTING CONTRACT NEGOTIATIONS: HOW?

With the numerous advances in communication technologies, there are several methods or means to conduct contract negotiations. It is vital to determine which method, including: face-to-face, teleconference, video conference, Netmeeting, or some combination of these, is most appropriate for your contract negotiation situation.

Form 6-2 provides a simple, yet valuable summary of the advantages and disadvantages of the most common contract negotiation methods.

Form 6-2. Contract Negotiations Methods — How?

Methods	Possible Advantages	Possible Disadvantages
Face-to-Face Contract Negotiations	■ Able to use the power of nonverbals ■ Better opportunity to build a business relationship	■ Harder to say no! ■ Nonverbals can be read by the other party ■ Travel and lodging expenses ■ Time away from the office
Teleconference Contract Negotiations	■ No travel and lodging expenses ■ No time away from the office ■ Usually requires less time ■ Easier to give bad news or say no!	■ Less able to read or use the power of nonverbals ■ More impersonal ■ Harder to build a business relationship
Videoconference Contract Negotiations	■ No travel and lodging expenses ■ No time away from the office ■ Able to use some power of nonverbals	■ Less able to read or use the power of nonverbals ■ Harder to build a business relationship
NetMeeting Contract Negotiations	■ No travel and lodging expenses ■ No time away from the office ■ Able to share data real time ■ Able to use some power of nonverbals ■ Easier to say no!	■ More prone to technical difficulties ■ Less able to read or use power of nonverbals

CONDUCTING CONTRACT NEGOTIATIONS: WHERE?

The general rules regarding the location of where a face-to-face contract negotiation should be conducted are the following:
- Most buyers want to negotiate at their offices;
- Conducting contract negotiations at your office is best;
- Conducting contract negotiations at a neutral site is good; and
- Conducting contract negotiations at their office is worst.

Factors to take consider in selecting and preparing a contract negotiation location include:
- Appropriate size of room(s);
- Use of breakout rooms;
- Adequate lighting;
- Use of audio/visual/computer aids;
- Selected seating arrangements;
- Access to Internet;
- Access to fax;

- Access to restrooms;
- Access to smoking;
- Selected schedule (date and time);
- Access to lodging; and
- Access to airport/train/taxi.

CONDUCTING CONTRACT NEGOTIATIONS: WHAT?

In this section, we will discuss the following topics relevant to conducting contract negotiations:
- Use an agenda;
- Checklist of best practices for conducting contract negotiations;
- Checklist of typical contract negotiation issues;
- Checklist of best practices for verbal exchange of information;
- Nonverbal Communication – key points;
- Active listening best practices;
- Common mistakes to avoid; and
- Conducting contract negotiations do's and don'ts.

USE AN AGENDA

What is or is not communicated during the course of contract negotiations is vital to achieve success. One of the proven most effective tools of contract negotiations is the use of an agenda. An agenda can be used as a tool to:
- Introduce team members;
- Set the right tone;
- Control the exchange of information;
- Keep focus on objectives;
- Manage time;
- Obtain desired results; and
- Review and summarize areas/items of agreement.

CHECKLIST OF BEST PRACTICES FOR CONDUCTING CONTRACT NEGOTIATIONS

Form 6-3 provides a checklist of proven effective best practices for conducting contract negotiations.

Form 6-3 Checklist. Best Practices for Conducting Contract Negotiations

☐ Ensure you have the right people on your team

☐ At the beginning of negotiations, determine the negotiation authority of your counterpart

☐ Identify any behind-the-scene decision makers

☐ Have a person taking detailed notes/minutes

☐ Assess your counterpart's negotiating style

☐ Determine which tactics the other party is using

☐ Select and use appropriate countertactics

☐ Set the right tone

☐ Treat the other party with respect

☐ Use an agenda

☐ Act professionally and ethically

☐ Execute your contract negotiation plan

☐ Control your emotions

☐ Focus on joint problem-solving

☐ Clearly communicate your needs

☐ Seek to understand

☐ Know when to call a recess

☐ Use interim summaries

☐ Know when to make concessions

CHECKLIST OF TYPICAL CONTRACT NEGOTIATION ISSUES

Form 6-4 provides a checklist of typical contract negotiation issues for both buyers and sellers.

Form 6-4. Checklist of Typical Contract Negotiation Issues	
Buyer Issues	**Seller Issues**
■ Aggressive delivery schedule	■ Realistic delivery schedule
■ Quality	■ Quality
■ Products	■ Products
■ Services	■ Services
■ Quantity	■ Quantity
■ Approval of subcontractors	■ Management of subcontractors
■ Getting what we want	■ Buyer micromanagement
■ Acceptance	■ Acceptance criteria
■ Maintenance	■ Cost, timing
■ Training	■ Value-added services
■ Warranties	■ Risk, cost, value
■ Choice of law	■ Desired: choice of law
■ Changes	■ Change management process
■ Forum for disputes	■ Disputes process
■ Payment	■ Method of payment
■ Reputation of seller	■ Progress payments
■ Past experience	■ Advance payments
■ Past performance	■ Cost reimbursement
	■ Reputation in the industry and with the buyer
	■ Company improvement actions taken

CHECKLIST OF BEST PRACTICES FOR VERBAL EXCHANGE OF INFORMATION

Form 6-5 provides of checklist of proven effective best practices for the verbal exchange of information during contract negotiations.

Form 6-5 Checklist. Best Practices for Verbal Exchange of Information

- ☐ Agree wherever you can
  - ☐ Agree without conceding
  - ☐ Accumulate yeses
  - ☐ Tune in to their point of view
- ☐ Build a working relationship
  - ☐ Express your views - without provoking
  - ☐ Don't say "But," say "Yes ... and "
  - ☐ Acknowledge differences with optimism
- ☐ Ask problem-solving questions
- ☐ Obtain information in order to reach an agreement
- ☐ Word questions clearly and concisely
- ☐ Avoid using deliberately ambiguous or controversial questions
- ☐ Be careful of your tone of voice and the rods you use
- ☐ Ask questions in a normal conversational tone, without being accusatory
- ☐ Ask "Why?", "Why not?", "What if?", "What do you think?"

NONVERBAL COMMUNICATION – KEY POINTS

It is important to remember that everyone communicates more nonverbally than verbally. Master contract negotiators know how to control their own nonverbals and how to read and interpret the nonverbals of others. Many people are experienced at saying one thing and meaning another- lying! It is far more difficult to control all of your nonverbals when lying.

Many novice contract negotiators say one thing and mean another, but, they often easily giveaway their lack of sincerity via their nonverbals. Master contract negotiators know how to read and interpret the following nonverbals either individually or in groups or clusters.

- Facial expressions
- Eye contact/movement/position
- Head movement/position

- Arms and hands movement/position
- Body and legs movement/position
- Voice – tone, pauses, volume, and inflection
- Breathing – rate and depth

While some intermediate level contract negotiators can control some of their nonverbals, most can not effective control all of their nonverbals, which often occur in a cluster or group of movements. Master contract negotiators realize you must read the whole person's nonverbals, which usually communicate the person's real feelings. Likewise, master contract negotiator's know it is best to conduct major negotiations of important deals in a face-to-face manner to maximize the opportunity to read and interpret the nonverbals of the other side. Like highly–skilled poker players, master contract negotiators enjoy playing the game, especially the art and science of reading and interpreting the nonverbals of their opponents.

Active Listening:
Seven Best Practices[1]

- **Take time.** If you feel that someone is troubled or needs to talk, listen with attention. It is not a waste of time. If you can help that person clear his or her mind, you will also clarify later communication between the two of you.

- **Be understanding.** If the speaker becomes extremely emotional, let it pass until it is exhausted. Show you understand and that you feel the subject is important. Remember, the judo expert does not oppose force but steps aside and lets it pass.

- **Limit your verbal reactions.** While the speaker continues to talk, confine yourself to what has been called a series of "eloquent and encouraging grunts": "Hmmm," "Oh," or "I see." If the speaker pauses, say nothing. A nod or other nonverbal form of feedback may encourage him or her to continue.

- **Do not attempt to evaluate what has been said.** Remember, there are no absolutes, especially in an emotional situation.

- **Do not give guidance, even if asked to do so.** The speaker is searching for his or her own creative solution.

- **In retrospect, analyze the information you have received in different ways.** Shift levels vertically (different positions) and horizontally (different points of view) to see how it might apply to your own problems and growth. And remember, you can learn as much, if not more, from "losers" as from "winners." This is what makes these terms so meaningless to a good listener.

- **Silence is the listener's strength and skill.**

Conducting Contract Negotiations: Common Mistakes to Avoid

- Power-oriented mistakes
  - Underestimating your strength
  - Assuming the other party knows your weaknesses
  - Worrying about status and who gets the credit or blame
  - Being intimidated by:
    - Quantitative data—challenge it
    - Irrationality—denounce it openly
  - Revealing your position to early
  - Discussing your problems or potential losses if you fail
- Concession-oriented mistakes:
  - Beginning at your minimum acceptable position
  - Assuming you really know what the other party wants
  - Aspiring to a marginal level of achievement
  - Throwing away the first offer
  - If you give, making sure you get a concession
  - Agreeing that the issue is beyond compromise, due to principle
  - Making big concessions first
  - Feeling guilty about accepting a concession
  - Tracking the number of concessions
  - Forgetting the agenda and listing issues at hand.

Conducting Contract Negotiations: Do's and Don'ts

Don't

- Don't make concessions without getting something in return
- Don't try to drive to hard a bargain
- Don't try to be well liked or popular during contract negotiations
- Don't permit more than one person on your team to talk at one time
- Don't disagree among yourselves at the table
- Don't bluff unless you are prepared to have your bluff called
- Don't lose sight of the big picture
- Don't try to know all the answers yourself; use the team
- Don't go into any meeting unprepared
- Don't talk to people across the table as though they were inferior

Do

- Keep your contract negotiation strategy clearly in mind at all times
- Negotiate in such a manner that concessions or minor points will lead to agreement on more important points
- Summarize agreements
- Have your contract negotiation strategy planned in advance
- Be discriminating; accept a good offer; don't feel you always have to reduce the price
- Fight hard on the important points—win the war, not the battles; don't start fights you have no chance of winning or that, even if you do win, are not worth the fight
- Remember that you usually are in at least as good a negotiating position as the other party
- Be courteous and considerate; do what you say you will; have integrity
- Know when to talk and when to listen; stop talking when you've made your point, won your case, and reached agreement
- Remember that negotiation is a two-way street and that pre-negotiation preparation is the most important attribute of a successful negotiation

CONDUCTING CONTRACT NEGOTIATIONS: PRICE ANALYSIS BEST PRACTICES[2]

Price analysis is the process of examining and evaluating a proposed price to determine if it is fair and reasonable without evaluating its separate cost elements and proposed profit. Price analysis always involves some form of comparison with other prices. Adequate price competition is normally considered one of the best bases for price analysis.

Price analysis may involve a number of comparisons. The comparison process is typically described using five steps:
- Select prices for comparison:
  - Competitive proposal prices;
  - Catalog prices;
  - Historical prices;
  - Price estimates based on parametric analysis; or
  - Independent Company Estimates;
- Identify factors that affect comparability;
- Determine the effect of identified factors;
- Adjust prices selected for comparison; and
- Compare adjusted prices.

SELECT PRICES FOR COMPARISON

The types of comparisons used typically depend on the estimated dollar value of the contract. Evidence of price reasonableness might include previous prices paid for same or similar items purchased competitively or knowledge of the supply or service gained from published price catalogs, newspapers, and other sources of market information. If you believe the quoted price is unreasonable, it will be necessary to solicit additional quotes.

Competitive Proposal Prices

Price competition is generally considered to be one of the best bases for price analysis. Competitive prices are offers received from sellers under conditions of adequate price competition. Adequate price competition exists when two or more responsible sellers, competing independently, submit priced offers that satisfy the expressed requirement. The award will be made to a responsible seller whose proposal offers either the greatest value or the lowest evaluated price and you have not found that the price of the otherwise successful seller is unreasonable.

When comparing competitive offers, never use an offer from a seller that you have determined is not responsible. Never use a nonresponsive bid. Also, never use a price from a proposal that is technically outside the competitive range. Although price competition is considered to be one of the best bases for price analysis, you should normally place less reliance on competition when you find the solicitation was made under conditions that unreasonably denied one or more known and qualified sellers an opportunity to compete. In assessing reasonableness, you need to make sure that the offers are comparable.

Catalog Prices

Catalog prices are prices taken from a catalog, price list, schedule, or other verifiable and established record that is regularly maintained by a manufacturer or vendor and is published or otherwise available for customer inspection.

Historical Prices

Historical prices are prior prices paid by the buyer for the same or similar items. Important factors to think about when considering historical price analysis are whether the product or service have been purchased before (by your office or another office within the company), what the historical price was and whether it can be obtained, and whether the historical price was fair and reasonable (make sure the circumstances are the comparable).

Price Estimates Based on Parametric Analysis

Parametric analysis uses cost estimating relationships, often referred to as pricing yardsticks. They are formulas for estimating prices based on the relationship of past prices with a product's physical or performance characteristics (e.g., dollars per pound, dollars per horsepower, or dollars per square foot). When considering a yardstick for price analysis, it is important to determine whether the yardstick has been widely accepted in the marketplace (do both buyers and sellers agree on the validity and reasonableness of the values obtained by a particular yardstick), whether the yardstick has been properly developed (the developer of the yardstick should be able to produce data and calculations used in developing the estimate), and whether the yardstick is accurate (some yardsticks provide rough estimates and not precise prices).

Independent Company Estimates

Independent company estimates are made by the buyer itself. The most common estimate is the material requisition where a blind estimate is made of the approximate price of the item. A value analysis estimate is another type of buyer estimate. This analysis takes into account the apparent value of one proposed item over another. While the prices may not be comparable, the value of the items to the company may be.

Individuals familiar with the product or service and its use should perform these estimates independent of the requisition and solicitation process. They should determine what the product must do, what the total costs related to purchasing the product or service are, identify other ways in which the function can be performed, and document the total costs related to purchasing an alternative produce or service.

IDENTIFYING FACTORS THAT AFFECT COMPARABILITY

When comparing prices you must attempt to account for any factors that affect comparability. The following factors affect many price analysis comparisons:
- Market conditions;
- Quantity or size;
- Geographic location;
- Extent of competition; and
- Technology.

Market Conditions

The passage of time usually is accompanied by changes in supply, demand, technology, product designs, pricing strategies, laws and regulations that affect supplier costs, and other such factors. As a general rule, select the most recent prices available. The less recent the price, the greater the likelihood and impact of differences in market conditions. However, do not select a price for comparison merely because it is the most recent—look instead for prices that were established under similar market conditions.

Quantity or Size

Variations in quantity can have a significant impact on unit price. Economies of scale do not always apply. For example, increases in order size beyond a certain point may tax the seller's capacity and result in higher prices.

Geographic Location

Geography can have a range of effects on comparability. In major urban centers, you will be able to rely on data from within that geographic region; in more remote, less urban areas, you must often get data from beyond the immediate area. When you must compare prices across geographic boundaries, take the following steps to enhance comparability:

- Check the extent of competition;
- Determine the extent to which variations in the price of labor must be neutralized;
- Check the freight requirements and accompanying costs; and
- Identify geographic anomalies or trends (for example, many items are more expensive in one region than in another).

Extent of Competition

When comparing one price with another, assess the competitive environment shaping the prices. For example, you can compare last year's competitive price with a current offer for the same item. However, if last year's procurement was made without competition—based on urgency, for example—it may not be a good price with which to compare the current offer.

Technology

Prices from declining industries can rise because the technologies don't keep pace with rising costs. However, technological advances have been made so fast that a comparison of prices separated by a single year must account for these advances. Engineering or design changes must also be taken into account. This means you must identify new or modified features and estimate their effect on price.

DETERMINING THE EFFECT OF IDENTIFIED FACTORS

Once you have identified the factors that may affect comparability, you must determine the effect on each specific comparison with the offered price. Questions to keep in mind are:

- What factors affect this specific comparison?
- How do these factors affect the comparison?
- Does this comparison, even with its limitations, contribute to the price analysis?

ADJUSTING THE PRICES SELECTED FOR COMPARISON

If you have a price analysis comparison base that does not require adjustment, use it. If you must make an adjustment, try to make the adjustment as objectively as possible. Remember, in order to establish price comparability you must:

- Identify and document price-related differences, taking into account the factors affecting comparability; and
- Factor out price-related differences.

Restoring comparability by establishing a common basis for comparison requires that you assign a monetary value to each identified difference. The cost of terms and conditions peculiar to certain contracts is hard to estimate, so exercise discretion. The challenge is to use the available information and to estimate the price that should be paid. If you cannot objectively adjust the prices for the factor involved, you may need to make a subjective adjustment, such as when estimating the effect on price of unique contract terms and conditions.

COMPARING ADJUSTED PRICES

After adjusting prices for comparison, determine the weight to give each price comparison. Then establish a should-pay price. If the should-pay price departs significantly from the apparently successful offer, analyze and document any differences.

SUMMARY

This chapter has provided proven effective best practices, for both buyers and sellers, when conducting complex contract negotiations. Specifically, this chapter has addressed the key questions and best practices pertaining to conducting contract negotiations: when, who, how, where, and what. Plus, the chapter has provided a brief discussion of the importance and best practices of price analysis, recognizing there are various price analysis techniques for conducting contract negotiations. Remember, the key to conducting contract negotiations is to stay focused on building a strong relationship with the other party and creating a mutually successful deal.

 QUESTIONS TO CONSIDER

1. How well does your organization conduct contract negotiations?

2. How often is your organization actually able to negotiate and obtain agreement on all of the key terms and conditions included in your negotiation plan?

3. How does your organization select a lead contract negotiator?

4. Does your organization document your contract negotiation best practices?

5. Which price analysis techniques does your organization typically use?

6. How well does your organization build strong business relationships while conducting contract negotiations?

ENDNOTES

---

[1] This section is a modified excerpt from the Contract Pricing Reference Guide, jointly issued by the U.S. Federal Acquisition Institute and the Air Force Institute of Technology.

[2] Ibid

Forming and Documenting the Right Performance-Based Contract

INTRODUCTION

Performance-based contracts (PBCs) have been used successfully to buy and sell products, services, or integrated solutions in both the public and private business sectors for many years. The critical aspect of PBCs is customer requirements. The buying organization must: determine its needs, be able to communicate its needs in terms of performance-based requirements, and be able to create challenging yet realistic performance-based metrics to hold its suppliers accountable. Typically, PBCs contain the following five critical components:

- Performance work statement (PWS), a.k.a. performance-based statement of work (SOW);
- Quality assurance surveillance plan (QASP);
- Performance-based metrics;
- Contractual incentives (positive or negative); and
- The right pricing arrangement (type of contract).

The buying organization should develop these critical components in partnership with its suppliers. This chapter focuses on using the results from the contract negotiation phase to form and document the right PBC. The chapter discusses the five critical components PBCs in detail.

FIRST CRITICAL COMPONENT: PERFORMANCE WORK STATEMENT (PWS)

Although a PBC does not direct how the work is to be accomplished, which should be determined by a supplier with specialized business knowledge, the PWS should provide a mix of measurable objective and subjective performance requirements.

There are important reasons to expend the time and effort to analyze the work to be performed. This is the beginning of the effort to specifically identify needs. It becomes evident as development of the PWS and the quality assurance surveillance plan progresses why participants should include the output desired, and why functional area representatives should at this time eliminate vague, confusing, or incomplete requirements. This is an excellent opportunity for the functional managers to ask if particular services are required.

All tasks required of the supplier should be analyzed for clarity and simplicity to ensure the seller will understand the requirements. This will improve supplier performance and reduce friction between the buyer and the seller. Sellers generally use higher costs to hedge against perceived contracting risks. If the buyer eliminates questionable or ambiguous requirements, the seller's concern about risks is reduced and so are costs.

Once it has developed a specific list of desired capabilities, the buyer should specify performance requirements for each of the tasks identified as required outputs. A PWS can serve as a powerful tool to inform the seller of the buyer's needs while allowing the seller the flexibility to be innovative, creative, and not bound by detailed product or service specifications.

SECOND CRITICAL COMPONENT: QUALITY ASSURANCE SURVEILLANCE PLAN (QASP)

The QASP establishes the plan that will be followed to ensure the buyer receives the performance it is paying for. The information developed by this plan provides objective evidence of acceptable performance and also provides the means whereby deductions may properly be taken for unacceptable performance. In order to accomplish this goal, the QASP should be carefully planned. The make-up and depth of the QASP depend on the size and complexity of the contract. Generally the QASP will contain:

- A statement of the plan's purpose;
- The name, specific authority, and responsibility of the technical representative, or quality assurance evaluator, including alternates;

- Instructions on how to utilize the plan;
- A surveillance schedule;
- The surveillance methods that will be used;
- Appropriate documentation for each method (e.g., schedules, checklists, reports);
- The performance requirements summary;
- Sampling guides for each task to be sampled; and
- Deduction and incentive formulas as appropriate.

Properly written, the QASP can be an excellent communications tool. In fact, it is a good idea to discuss it with the seller so that all surveillance methods are understood. The QASP should be included in the solicitation to reinforce the buyer's emphasis on the quality assurance aspects of the PBC process.[1]

The PWS and QASP should be prepared together and read together during surveillance. The goal of these documents is to clearly state the buyer's requirements and how the buyer will determine acceptable and unacceptable performance.

THIRD CRITICAL COMPONENT: PERFORMANCE-BASED METRICS

Figure 7-1 lists many of the key performance areas and related metrics commonly used in complex contracts to buy or selling products, services, or integrated business solutions. No one performance area or metric is more important than the others. In fact, most buying organizations are developing a balanced scorecard composed of numerous metrics designed to evaluate their performance and the performance of their suppliers. Every organization should decide which performance areas and related metrics are most appropriate for its business and related contracts.

Figure 7-1. Perfromance-Based Metrics

Customer and Supplier Key Performance Areas	Checklist of Customer & Supplier Key Performance Metrics

Financial	☐ Return on investment (ROI)
	☐ On budget (planned expenses vs. actual expenses)
	☐ Cost reduction (current costs vs. future costs)
	   ☐ Implementation costs
	   ☐ Operations costs
	   ☐ Maintenance costs
	   ☐ Support costs
	☐ Return on assets (ROA)
	☐ Net present value (NPV)
	☐ Cost performance index (CPI)
	☐ Revenue generated (annual and quarterly)
	☐ Days of sales outstanding (DSO)
	☐ Revenue or expense to headcount
	☐ Inventory turns

Schedule	☐ # of milestones on time
	☐ On-time-delivery % (mutually agreed-to date)
	☐ # of days cycle time (drder to delivery)
	☐ Earned value method
	   ☐ Budgeted Cost of Work Schedule (BCWS)
	   ☐ Budgeted Cost of Work Performed (BCWP)
	☐ Schedule performance index (SPI)

Technical	☐ Capacity volume ☐ Operating time/usage ☐ Capabilities/features ☐ Speed ☐ # of product failures/outages
Quality	☐ Mean time between failures (MTBF) ☐ Mean time to repair (MTTR) ☐ # of complaints ☐ # of defects

From: Managing Complex Outsourced Projects, by Gregory A. Garrett, CCH Incorporated, 2004.

FOURTH CRITICAL COMPONENT: CONTRACTUAL INCENTIVES

The care with which the PBC is developed and the direct relationship between the PWS and the QASP create a vastly improved understanding between the buyer and seller. The contractual incentives selected by the buyer should accomplish the same goal. Incentives can emphasize areas where superior performance is desired and where inadequate performance is particularly undesirable. Consequently, incentives may be positive, negative, or both. Deductions represent the value of tasks not preformed satisfactorily.

The mutual understanding of positive and negative performance incentives is established in the solicitation and may be discussed during source selection. Incentives reflect reasonable value to the buyer; they should not be provided to attain the specified minimum requirements of the contract. Incentives to be innovative and perform in a highly satisfactory manner must be built into the entire PBC process. Discussion with the seller to change values for deductions should be conducted with careful analysis so that incentives are effective for their intended purpose. A more detailed discussion of contractual incentives is provided later in this chapter, as part of the discussion of the various pricing arrangements used to form a PBC.

FIFTH CRITICAL COMPONENT: THE RIGHT PRICING ARRANGEMENT[1]

The pricing arrangement or contract type will impact the PBC process significantly. When deciding which type of contract to use, the buyer should ask:

- Can the buyer properly describe the requirements in a performance-based statement of work?
- Can sellers accurately estimate the cost to perform the contract with the information provided in the solicitation?

Procurement planning is necessary to ensure sufficient workload data is available to accurately describe tasks in the PWS. This task is easier if the contract is replacing a previous contract for the same product or services. If there is adequate data to develop an effective performance work statement, a quality assurance surveillance plan, and appropriate performance metrics, then in most cases a fixed-price contract should be selected. However, there are many factors that must be considered when selecting the right pricing arrangement to ensure the seller is properly motivated to achieve mission success.

Both buyers and sellers must be aware of the many types of contract pricing arrangements available in order to choose the right type for each situation. Over time, three general pricing arrangement categories have evolved: fixed-price, cost-reimbursement (CR), and time-and-materials (T&M). These categories and the contract types within each category are described along with information on determining contract price and using pricing arrangements to balance the risk between contracting parties. In today's complex business world, a solid understanding of contract pricing options is essential for meeting business objectives.

Assessing Requirements to Determine Costs

Contract cost is determined by the contract requirements, which fall into two main categories: technical and administrative.

Technical Requirements

The solicitation PWS should contain technical requirements that describe what the buyer wants to buy in terms of desired performance results or outputs rendered by the seller. The seller's costs will be determined by the consumption of resources—labor, capital, and money—necessary to provide products and services that meet these technical requirements.

Administrative Requirements

Contract clauses describe other terms and conditions that will require the seller to consume resources, although the Ts and Cs relate only indirectly to the technical requirements. The following clause excerpt provides such an example:

> *Company-Furnished Property*
> *... orders from ABC Company shall be held at the Seller's risk and shall be kept insured by the Seller at the Seller's expense while in Seller's custody and control in an amount equal to the replacement cost thereof, with loss payable to ABC Company.*

The insurance requirement will cost money, but it is only indirectly related to the technical requirements of the project. Contracts contain many such administrative requirements.

Pricing Contracts

Contract pricing begins with determining the cost of performing the contract. To determine contract cost, a business professional who manages contracts must thoroughly analyze a prospective buyer's solicitation and develop a work breakdown structure based on the technical and administrative performance requirements. Next, he or she decides how the work will be implemented—that is, the order in which it will be performed and the methods and procedures that will be used to accomplish it. Based on these plans, the business professional estimates performance costs so that a price can be proposed. After the company has agreed on a contract price, it will be obligated to complete the work at that price unless a different arrangement can be negotiated.

To estimate performance costs, the following questions must be answered: What resources (labor, capital, money) will be needed to do the work? In what quantities will they be needed? When will they be needed? How much will those resources cost in the marketplace?

Estimating techniques do not necessarily require developing detailed answers to those questions. Parametric estimates, for instance, are used at a very high level and do not involve the type of analysis implied by the four questions. Nevertheless, some level of response to those questions is implicit in every cost estimate.

Uncertainty and Risk in Contract Pricing

The business professional's cost estimate will be a judgment, that is, a prediction about the future, rather than a fact. When the project manager says, "I estimate that the contract will cost $500,000 to complete," that statement really means, "I *predict* that when I have completed the project according to the specifications, statement of work, and other contract terms and conditions, I will have consumed $500,000 worth of labor, capital, and money."

The problem with this prediction, as with all predictions, is that no one will know whether it is true until all the events have occurred. Predictions are based largely on history; they assume that cause-and-effect relationships in the future will be similar to those in the past. However, people frequently have an incorrect or incomplete understanding of the past. In addition, they may carry out even the best-laid plans imperfectly because of error or unexpected events. All these factors can cause the future to materialize differently than predicted.

Thus, the business professional's estimate may be incorrect. If it is too high, the company's proposal may not be competitive. If it is too low, the contract price may not be high enough to cover the project costs, and the company will suffer a financial loss.

However sound the cost estimate, the contract *price* must be negotiated. Every negotiated price is a compromise between the extremes of optimistic and pessimistic predictions about future costs. The range between these two extremes is called the *range of possible costs*. The compromise results from negotiation between a risk-avoiding buyer and a risk-avoiding seller.

The risk-avoiding buyer wants to minimize the risk of agreeing to a higher price than necessary to cover the seller's costs plus a reasonable profit. Thus, the buyer tends to push the price toward the more optimistic end of the range of possible costs. The risk-avoiding seller wants to avoid the risk of agreeing to a price that may not cover its actual performance costs or allow a reasonable profit. Thus, the seller tends to push the price toward the more pessimistic end of the range of possible costs.

The consequence of uncertainty about the future is risk, or the possibility of injury. A seller who undertakes a contractual obligation to complete a project for a fixed price but has estimated too low will suffer financial loss, unless it can shift the excess costs to the buyer or avoid them altogether. The effort made to avoid the injury will be proportional to its magnitude and related to its cause and direction.

Developing Pricing Arrangements

Over the years some standard pricing arrangements have evolved. These arrangements fall into three categories: *fixed-price, cost-reimbursement,* and *time-and-materials* contracts (the Project Management Institute also designates unit-price contracts as a separate category). These contract categories have developed as practical responses to cost risk, and they have become fairly standard formal arrangements. Incentives can be added to any of the contract types in these three categories and are discussed in detail later in this chapter. Figure 7-2 lists several common contract types in these categories.

These pricing arrangements, however, are manifested in the specific terms and conditions of contracts, that is, in the contract clauses. No standard clauses for their implementation exist. Therefore, the contracting parties must write clauses that describe their specific agreement.

Figure 7-2. Contract Categories and Types		
	Fixed-Price	**Cost-Reimbursement Or Unit Price**	**Time-and-Materials**
Types of Contracts	Firm-fixed-price Fixed-price with economic price adjustment Fixed-price incentive	Cost-reimbursement Cost-plus-a-percentage-of-cost Cost-plus-fixed fee Cost-plus-incentive fee Cost-plus-award fee	Time-and-materials Unit price

Fixed-Price Category

Fixed-price contracts are the standard business pricing arrangement. The two basic types of fixed-price contracts are *firm-fixed-price (FFP)* and *fixed-price with economic price adjustment (FP/EPA)*. Firm-fixed-price contracts are further divided into *lump-sum* and *unit-price* arrangements.

Firm-Fixed-Price Contracts

The simplest and most common business pricing arrangement is the FFP contract. The seller agrees to supply specified goods or deliverables in a specified quantity or to render a specified service or level of effort (LOE) in return for a specified price, either a lump sum or a unit price. The price is fixed, that is, not subject to change based on the seller's actual cost experience. However, it may be subject to change if the parties modify the contract. This pricing arrangement is used for the sale of commercial goods and services.

Some companies include a complex clause in their FFP contracts. Such a clause may read in part as follows:

> *Prices and Taxes*
> *The price of Products shall be ABC Company's published list prices on the date ABC Company accepts your order less any applicable discount. If ABC Company announces a price increase for Equipment, or Software licensed for a one-time fee, after it accepts your order but before shipment, ABC Company shall invoice you at the increased price only if delivery occurs more than 120 days after the effective date of the price increase. If ABC Company announces a price increase for Services, Rentals, or Software licensed for a periodic fee, the price increase shall apply to billing periods beginning after its effective date.*

Note that this clause was written by the seller, not the buyer, and reflects the seller's point of view and concerns. Nevertheless, the pricing arrangement it describes is firm-fixed-price, because the contract price will not be subject to adjustment based on ABC Company's actual performance costs.

Clauses such as "Prices and Taxes" frequently form part of a document known as a *universal agreement*. Such a document is not a contract; it is a precontract agreement that merely communicates any agreed-to Ts and Cs that will apply when the buyer places an order. After the seller accepts an order, the company's published or announced list prices become the basis for the contract price according to the terms of the universal agreement. This agreement is discussed later in this chapter in "Purchase Agreements."

FFP contracts are appropriate for most commercial transactions when cost uncertainty is within commercially acceptable limits. Those limits depend on the industry and the market.

Fixed-Price with Economic Price Adjustment

Fixed-price contracts sometimes include various clauses that provide for adjusting prices based on specified contingencies. The clauses may provide for upward or downward adjustments, or both. Economic price adjustments are usually limited to factors beyond the seller's immediate control, such as market forces.

This pricing arrangement is not firm-fixed-price, because the contract provides for a price adjustment based on the seller's actual performance costs. Thus, the seller is protected from the risk of certain labor or material cost increases. The EPA clause can provide for price increases based on the seller's costs but not on the seller's decision to increase the prices of its products or services. Thus, there can be a significant difference between this clause and the "Prices and Taxes" clause discussed previously.

The shift of risk to the buyer creates greater buyer intrusion into the affairs of the seller. This intrusion typically takes the form of an audit provision at the end of the clause, particularly when the buyer is a government.

EPA clauses are appropriate in times of market instability, when great uncertainty exists regarding labor and material costs. The risk of cost fluctuations is more balanced between the parties than would be the case under an FFP contract.

Cost-Reimbursement Category

Cost-reimbursement contracts usually include an estimate of project cost, a provision for reimbursing the seller's expenses, and a provision for paying a fee as profit. Normally, CR contracts also include a limitation on the buyer's cost liability.

A common perception is that CR contracts are to be avoided. However, if uncertainty about costs is great enough, a buyer may be unable to find a seller willing to accept a fixed price, even with adjustment clauses, or a seller may insist on extraordinary contingencies within that price. In the latter case, the buyer may find the demands unreasonable. Such high levels of cost uncertainty are often found in research and development, large-scale construction, and systems integration projects. In such circumstances, the best solution may be a CR contract—but only if the buyer is confident that the seller has a highly accurate and reliable cost accounting system.

The parties to a CR contract will find themselves confronting some challenging issues, especially concerning the definition, measurement, allocation, and confirmation of costs. First, the parties must agree on a definition for acceptable cost. For instance, the buyer may decide that the cost of air travel should be limited to the price of a coach or business-class ticket and should not include a first-class ticket. The buyer will specify other cost limitations, and the parties will negotiate until they agree on what constitutes a reimbursable cost.

Next, the parties must decide who will measure costs and what accounting rules will be used to do so. For example, several depreciation techniques are in use, some of which would be less advantageous to the buyer than others. Which technique will the buyer consider acceptable? How will labor costs be calculated? Will standard costs be acceptable, or must the seller determine and invoice actual costs? What methods of allocating overhead will be acceptable to the buyer? How will the buyer know that the seller's reimbursement invoices are accurate? Will the buyer have the right to obtain an independent audit? If the buyer is also a competitor of the seller, should the seller be willing to open its books to the buyer?

If these issues remain unsettled, the buyer is accepting the risk of having to reimburse costs it may later find to be unreasonable. This issue is the central problem with cost-reimbursement contracting, and it has never been resolved entirely.

Clearly, the CR contract presents the parties with difficulties they would not face under a fixed-price contract. The parties must define costs and establish acceptable procedures for cost measurement and allocation, the buyer takes on greater cost risk and must incur greater administrative costs to protect its interests, and the seller faces greater intrusion by the buyer into its affairs. Nevertheless, many contracting parties have found a CR contract to be a better arrangement than a fixed-price contract for undertakings with high cost uncertainty.

Types of CR contracts include *cost, cost-sharing, cost-plus-a-percentage-of-cost (CPPC)*, and *cost-plus-fixed fee (CPFF)*.

Cost Contracts

The cost contract is the simplest type of CR contract. Governments commonly use this type when contracting with universities and nonprofit organizations for research projects. The contract provides for reimbursing contractually allowable costs, with no allowance given for profit.

Cost-Sharing Contracts

The cost-sharing contract provides for only partial reimbursement of the seller's costs. The parties share the cost liability, with no allowance for profit. The cost-sharing contract is appropriate when the seller will enjoy some benefit from the results of the project and that benefit is sufficient to encourage the seller to undertake the work for only a portion of its costs and without a fee.

Cost-Plus-a-Percentage-of-Cost Contracts

The CPPC contract provides for the seller to receive reimbursement for its costs and a profit component, called a *fee*, equal to some predetermined percentage of its actual costs. Thus, as costs go up, so does profit. This arrangement is a poor one from the buyer's standpoint; it provides no incentive to control costs, because the fee gets bigger as the costs go up. This type of contract was used extensively by the U.S. government during World War I but has since been made illegal for U.S. government contracts, for good reason. It is still occasionally used for construction projects and some service contracts in the private sector.

The rationale for this pricing arrangement was probably "the bigger the job, the bigger the fee," that is, as the job grows, so should the fee. This arrangement is similar to a professional fee, such as an attorney's fee, which grows as the professional puts more time into the project. This arrangement may have developed as a response to the cost-growth phenomenon in projects that were initially ill defined. As a seller proceeded with the work, the buyer's needs became better defined and grew, until the seller felt that the fees initially agreed to were not enough for the expanded scope of work.

Cost-Plus-Fixed Fee Contracts

Cost-plus-fixed fee is the most common type of CR contract. As with other CR contracts, the seller is reimbursed for its costs, but the contract also provides for payment of a fixed fee that does not change in response to the seller's actual cost experience. The seller is paid the fixed fee on successful completion of the contract, whether its actual costs were higher or lower than the estimated costs.

If the seller completes the work for less than the estimated cost, it receives the entire fixed fee. If the seller incurs the estimated cost without completing the work and if the buyer decides not to pay for the cost overrun necessary for completion, the seller receives a portion of the fixed fee that is equal to the percentage of work completed. If the buyer decides to pay the cost overrun, the seller must complete the work without any increase in the fixed fee. The only adjustment to the fee would be a result of cost growth, when the buyer requires the seller to do more work than initially specified.

This type of contract is on the opposite end of the spectrum from the FFP contract, because cost risk rests entirely on the shoulders of the buyer. Under a CR contract, a buyer might have to reimburse the seller for the entire estimated cost and part of the fee but have nothing to show for it but bits and pieces of the work.

CLASSIFICATION OF CONTRACT INCENTIVES

The fundamental purpose of contract incentives is to motivate desired performance in one or more specific areas. Contract incentives are generally classified as either objectively based and evaluated or subjectively based and evaluated. Further, both classifications of contract incentives are typically categorized as either positive incentives (rewards—get more money) or negative incentives (penalties—get less money) or some combination thereof.

Incentives that use predetermined formula-based methods to calculate the amount of incentive, either positive or negative, in one or more designated areas are objectively based and evaluated. Facts and actual events are used as a basis for determination—individual judgment and opinions are not considered in evaluating performance.

Objectively based and evaluated contract incentives commonly include the following designated performance areas:

- Cost performance;
- Schedule or delivery performance; and
- Quality performance.

Subjectively based and evaluated contract incentives are incentives that use individual judgment, opinions, and informed impressions as the basis for determining the amount of incentive, either positive or negative, in one or more designated areas. These incentives can and often do contain some objective aspects or factors. However, subjective contract incentives are ultimately determined by one or more individuals making a decision based on their experience, knowledge, and the available information—a total judgment.

Subjectively based and evaluated contract incentives typically include the following:

- Award fees; and
- Other special incentives.

Figure 7-3 summarizes the link between rewards and penalties and contract incentives as described in the following paragraphs.

Figure 7-3. Contract Incentives

Types of Incentives	Positive (Rewards)	No Reward or Penalty	Negative (Penalties)
Objective incentives			
Cost Performance	Under Budget	On Budget	Over Budget
Schedule or delivery performance	Early Delivery	On-time delivery	Late Delivery
Quality performance	Exceed requirements	Achieve Contract Requirements	Do not achieve requirements
Subjective incentives			
Award fee Other special incentives	Exceed requirements	Achieve Award fee Plan	Do not achieve requirements

OBJECTIVE INCENTIVES

Incentives Based on Cost Performance

Cost is the most commonly chosen performance variable. For fixed-price (cost) incentive contracts, the parties negotiate a *target cost* and a *target profit* (which equals the *target price*), and a *sharing formula* for cost overruns and cost underruns. They also negotiate a *ceiling price*, which is the buyer's maximum dollar liability. When performance is complete, they determine the final actual costs and apply the sharing formula to any overrun or underrun. Applying the sharing formula determines the seller's final profit, if any.

Consider an example in which the parties agree to the following arrangement:

Target cost: $10,000,000
Target profit: $850,000
Target price: $10,850,000
Sharing formula: 70/30 (buyer 70 percent, seller 30 percent)
Ceiling price: $11,500,000

Assume that the seller completes the work at an actual cost of $10,050,000, overrunning the target cost by $50,000. The seller's share of the overrun is 30 percent of $50,000, which is $15,000. The target profit will be reduced by that amount ($850,000 – 15,000 = $835,000). The seller will then receive the $10,050,000 cost of performance plus an earned profit of $835,000. Thus, the price to the buyer will be $10,885,000, which is $615,000 below the ceiling price. The $35,000 increase over the target price of $10,850,000 represents the buyer's 70 percent share of the cost overrun.

Had the seller overrun the target cost by $100,000, raising the actual cost to $10,100,000, the seller's share of the overrun would have been 30 percent, or $30,000. That amount would have reduced the seller's profit to $820,000.

Basically, at some point before reaching the ceiling price, the sharing arrangement effectively changes to 0/100, with the seller assuming 100 percent of the cost risk. This effect is implicit in fixed-price incentive arrangements because of the ceiling price and is not an explicit element of the formula. The point at which sharing changes to 0/100 is called the *point of total assumption (PTA),* which represents a cost figure. Indeed, the PTA is often appropriately referred to as the *high-cost estimate.* The PTA can be determined by applying the following formula:

$$\text{PTA} = \left(\frac{\text{Ceiling price - Target price}}{\text{Buyer Share Ratio}} \right) + \text{Target Cost}$$

In the event of an underrun, the seller would enjoy greater profit. If the final cost is $9,000,000 (a $1,000,000 underrun), the seller's share of the underrun is 30 percent, which is $300,000.

The price to the buyer would include the $9,000,000 cost and the $850,000 target profit plus the seller's $300,000 underrun share (total profit of $1,150,000). Thus, $9,000,000 actual cost plus $1,150,000 actual profit equals $10,150,000 actual price, reflecting precisely the buyer's 70 percent share of the $1,000,000 underrun ($10,850,000 target price − 70 percent of the $1,000,000 underrun ($700,000) = $10,150,000).

Incentives Based on Schedule or Delivery Performance

For many years, construction, aerospace, and numerous service industries have used schedule or delivery performance incentives to motivate sellers to provide either early or on-time delivery of products and services.

Liquidated damages is a negative incentive (penalty) for late delivery. Typically, a liquidated damages clause stated in the contract terms and conditions designates how much money one party, usually the seller, must pay the other party, usually the buyer, for not meeting the contract schedule. Often the amount of liquidated damages payable is specified as an amount of money for a specific period of time (day, week, month). A key aspect of liquidated damages is that the penalty is to be based on the amount of damages incurred. Liquidated damages are compensable in nature, not excessive or punitive.

A proven best practice for buyers is to require negative incentives (or penalties) for late delivery and late schedule performance. Likewise, a proven best practice for sellers is to limit their liability on liquidated damages by agreeing to a cap, or maximum amount, and seeking positive incentives (or rewards) for early delivery and early schedule performance.

Incentives Based on Quality Performance

Quality performance incentives is one of the most common topics in government and commercial contracting. Surveys in both government and industry have revealed widespread service contracting problems, including deficient statements of work, poor contract administration, performance delays, and quality shortcomings.

When a contract is based on performance, all aspects of the contract are structured around the purpose of the work to be performed rather than the manner in which it is to be done. The buyer seeks to elicit the best performance the seller has to offer, at a reasonable price or cost, by stating its objectives and giving sellers both latitude in determining how to achieve them and incentives for achieving them. In source selection, for example, the buyer might publish a draft solicitation for comment, use quality-related evaluation factors, or both. The statement of work will provide performance standards rather than spelling out what the seller is to do. The contract normally contains a plan for quality assurance surveillance. And the contract typically includes positive and negative performance incentives.

Few people disagree with the concept that buyers, who collectively spend billions of dollars on services annually, should look to the performance-based approach, focusing more on results and less on detailed requirements. However, implementing performance-based contracting (using cost, schedule, and/or quality performance variables) is far easier said than done. The sound use of performance incentives is key to the success of the performance-based contracting approach.

Problems with Applying Objective Incentives

Objective-incentive schemes have some merit, but they also involve some serious practical problems. First, they assume a level of buyer and seller competence that may not exist. Second, they assume effects that may not occur. Third, they create serious challenges for contract administration.

To negotiate objective incentives intelligently, the parties must have some knowledge of the range of possible costs for a project. They also must have some knowledge of the likely causes and probabilities of different cost outcomes. If both parties do not have sufficient information on these issues, they will not be able to structure an effective incentive formula.

It is important that the parties share their information. If one party has superior knowledge that it does not share with the other, it will be able to skew the formula in its favor during negotiation.

If that happens, the whole point of the arrangement, which is to equitably balance the risks of performance, will be lost. The buyer is usually at a disadvantage with respect to the seller in this regard.

An objective incentive assumes that the seller can effect a performance outcome along the entire range of the independent variables. However, that may not be the case. For instance, the seller may actually exercise control over only a short sector of the range of possible costs. Some possible cost outcomes may be entirely outside the seller's control because of factors such as market performance. In reality, the seller's project manager may have little control over important factors, such as overhead costs, that may determine the cost outcome. In addition, short-term companywide factors, especially those involving overhead, may make it more advantageous for the seller to incur additional cost rather than earn additional profit on some contracts..

In addition, objective cost incentives are complicated and costly to administer, with all the cost definition, measurement, allocation, and confirmation problems of CR contracts. The parties must be particularly careful to segregate the target cost effects of cost growth from those of cost overruns; otherwise, they may lose money for the wrong reasons. As a practical matter, segregating such costs is often quite difficult.

When using other performance incentives, the parties may find themselves disputing the causes of various performance outcomes. The seller may argue that schedule delays are a result of the buyer's actions. Quality problems, such as poor reliability, may have been caused by improper buyer operation rather than seller performance. The causes of performance failures may be difficult to determine.

One reason for using objective incentive contracts is to reduce the deleterious effects of risk on the behavior of the parties. Thus, if a pricing arrangement increases the likelihood of trouble, it should not be used. The decision to apply objective incentives should be made only after careful analysis.

Best Practices: 15 Actions to Improve Your Use of Contract Incentives

■ Think creatively: creativity is a critical aspect in the success of performance-based incentive contracting;

■ Avoid rewarding sellers for simply meeting contract requirements;

■ Recognize that developing clear, concise, objectively measurable performance incentives will be a challenge, and plan accordingly;

■ Create a proper balance of objective incentives: cost, schedule, and quality performance;

■ Ensure that performance incentives focus the seller's efforts on the buyer's desired objectives;

■ Make all forms of performance incentives challenging yet attainable;

■ Ensure that incentives motivate quality control and that the results of the seller's quality control efforts can be measured;

■ Consider tying on-time delivery to cost and or quality performance criteria;

■ Recognize that not everything can be measured objectively—consider using a combination of objectively measured standards and subjectively determined incentives;

■ Encourage open communication and ongoing involvement with potential sellers in developing the performance-based SOW and the incentive plan, both before and after issuing the formal request for proposals;

■ Consider including socioeconomic incentives (non-SOW-related) in the incentive plan;

■ Use clear, objective formulas for determining performance incentives;

■ Use a combination of positive and negative incentives;

■ Include incentives for discounts based on early payments; and

■ Ensure that all incentives, both positive and negative, have limits.

SUBJECTIVE INCENTIVES

Award Fee Plans

In an award fee plan, the parties negotiate an estimated cost, just as for CPFF contracts. Then they negotiate an agreement on the amount of money to be included in an *award fee pool*. Finally, they agree on a set of criteria and procedures to be applied by the buyer in determining how well the seller has performed and how much fee the seller has earned. In some cases, the parties also negotiate a *base fee*, which is a fixed fee that the seller will earn no matter how its performance is evaluated.

The contract performance period is then divided into equal *award fee periods*. A part of the award fee pool is allocated to each period proportionate to the percentage of the work scheduled to be completed. All this information is included in the award fee plan, which becomes part of the contract. In some cases, the contract allows the buyer to change the award fee plan unilaterally before the start of a new award fee period.

During each award fee period, the buyer observes and documents the seller's performance achievements or failures. At the end of each period, the buyer evaluates the seller's performance according to the award fee plan and decides how much fee to award from the portion allocated to that period. Under some contracts, the seller has an opportunity to present its own evaluation of its performance and a specific request for an award fee. The buyer then informs the seller how much of the available award fee it has earned and how its performance could be improved during subsequent award fee periods. This arrangement invariably involves subjectivity on the buyer's part—precisely how much depends on how the award fee plan is written.

Pros and Cons of the Award Fee Arrangement

The cost-plus-award fee (CPAF) contract is a cost-reimbursement contract, with all its requirements for cost definition, measurement, allocation, and confirmation. For the buyer, the CPAF contract requires the additional administrative investment associated with observing, documenting, and evaluating seller performance. However, this disadvantage may sometimes be overemphasized, because the buyer should already be performing many of these activities under a CR contract.

The disadvantages for the buyer are offset by the extraordinary power it obtains from the ability to make subjective determinations about how much fee the seller has earned. The buyer may have difficulty establishing objective criteria for satisfactory service performance.

The power of subjective fee determination tends to make sellers extraordinarily responsive to the buyer's demands. However, the buyer must be careful, because that very responsiveness can be the cause of cost overruns and unintended cost growth.

The buyer's advantages are almost entirely disadvantages from the viewpoint of the seller, because the seller will have placed itself within the buyer's power to an exceptional degree. Subjectivity can cross the line and become arbitrariness. The seller may find itself dealing with a buyer that is impossible to please or that believes that the seller cannot earn all the award fee because no one can achieve "perfect" performance.

Other Special Incentives

There is a growing recognition by buyers and sellers worldwide, in both the public and private sectors, that contract incentives can be expanded and that they are indeed valuable tools to motivate the desired performance. Increasingly, when outsourcing, buyers are motivating sellers to subcontract with local companies, often with special rewards for subcontracting with designated small businesses.

Likewise, many sellers are providing buyers with special incentives for early payment, such as product or services discounts or additional specified services at no change.

INCENTIVE CONTRACTS

Cost-Plus-Incentive Fee Contracts

Cost-plus-incentive fee (CPIF) contracts allow sharing of cost overruns or underruns through a predetermined formula for fee adjustments that apply to incentives for cost category contracts. Within the basic concept of the buyer's paying all costs for a cost contract, the limits for a CPIF contract become those of maximum and minimum fees.

The necessary elements for a CPIF contract are maximum fee, minimum fee, target cost, target fee, and share ratio(s).

Fixed-Price Incentive Contracts

In an FPI contract, seller profit is linked to another aspect of performance: cost, schedule, quality, or a combination of all three. The objective is to give the seller a monetary incentive to optimize cost performance.

Fixed-price incentive contracts may be useful for initial production of complex new products or systems, although the parties may have difficulty agreeing on labor and material costs for such projects because of a lack of production experience. However, the cost uncertainty may not be great enough to warrant use of a CR contract.

Cost-Plus-Award Fee Contracts

Cost-plus-award fee contracts include subjective incentives, in which the profit a seller earns depends on how well the seller satisfies a buyer's subjective desires. This type of contract has been used for a long time in both government and commercial contracts worldwide. Based on its contracting experience during World War I, the U.S. Army Corps of Engineers developed an evaluated fee contract for use in construction during the early 1930s. The U.S. National Aeronautics and Space Administration has used CPAF contracts to procure services since the 1950s. Other U.S. government agencies, including the Department of Energy and the Department of Defense, have also used these contracts extensively. A small but growing number of commercial companies now use award fees to motivate their suppliers to achieve exceptional performance.

Cost-plus-award fee contracts are used primarily to procure services, particularly those that involve an ongoing, long-term relationship between buyer and seller, such as maintenance and systems engineering support. Objective criteria for determining the acceptability of the performance of such services are inherently difficult to establish. The award fee arrangement is particularly well suited to such circumstances, at least from the buyer's point of view. However, this type of contract also is used to procure architecture and engineering, research and development, hardware and software systems design and development, construction, and many other services.

TIME-AND-MATERIALS (T&M) CATEGORY

In T&M contracts, the parties negotiate hourly rates for specified types of labor and agree that the seller will be reimbursed for parts and materials at cost. Each hourly rate includes labor costs, overhead, and profit. The seller performs the work, documenting the types and quantities of labor used and the costs for parts and materials. When the work is finished, the seller bills the buyer for the number of labor hours at the agreed-on hourly rates and for the costs of materials and parts.

T&M contracts are most often used to procure equipment repair and maintenance services when the cost to repair or overhaul a piece of equipment is uncertain. However, these contracts are also used to procure other support services.

Although T&M contracts appear to be straightforward, they may create some difficulties. This type of contract must be negotiated carefully, because each hourly rate includes a component for overhead costs, which include both *fixed* and *variable costs*. Fixed costs are the costs that will be incurred during a given period of operation, despite the number of work hours performed. To recover its fixed costs, the seller must estimate how many hours will be sold during the contract performance period and allocate a share to each hour. If the parties overestimate how many hours will be sold during the period of performance, the seller will not recover all its fixed costs. If the parties underestimate how many hours will be sold, the seller will enjoy a windfall profit.

Although the hourly labor rates are fixed, the number of hours delivered and the cost of materials and parts are not. Therefore, the buyer faces the problems of confirming the number of hours delivered and the cost of materials claimed by the seller. These problems are not as great as those under CR contracts, but they are not insignificant.

OTHER PRICING METHODS

In addition to the variety of pricing arrangements already discussed, buyers and sellers use other kinds of agreements to deal with uncertainty and reduce the administrative costs of contracting. These include *purchase agreements, memorandums of understanding (MOUs),* and *letters of intent (LOIs).*

Purchase Agreements

When two parties expect to deal with one another repeatedly for the purchase and sale of goods and services, they may decide to enter into a long-term purchase agreement. Rather than negotiating a new contract for every transaction, the parties agree to the terms and conditions that will apply to any transaction between them of a specified type. This arrangement reduces the time required to obtain products and services once a purchase order is released by the buyer to the seller.

Commercially, these purchase agreements are known by a variety of names, including: frame contracts, universal agreements, and general purchase agreements. Within the U.S. federal government, these more flexible purchase agreements have several names, including: Blanket Purchase Agreement (BPA) and Indefinite Delivery Indefinite Quantity (IDIQ) contracts.

The critical business aspect is to select the appropriate pricing arrangement or combination of pricing arrangements for the contractual situation, carefully considering the following factors:
- Technical difficulty;
- Urgency of requirements;
- Administrative costs for both parties;
- Accuracy of seller's cost estimating and cost accounting systems;
- Product/service/solution maturity; and
- Overall risk assessment (e.g., technical, schedule, cost, quality).

PERFORMANCE-BASED CONTRACTING: SUMMARY

In this chapter, we have discussed the five critical components to forming and documenting a berformance-based contract (PBC) for use in either the public or private business sector. The five critical components of a successful PBC are:
- Performance wWork statement (PWS);
- Quality assurance surveillance plan (QASP);
- Performance-based metrics;
- Contractual incentives; and
- The right pricing arrangement(s).

In addition, the U.S. federal government has developed a detailed guide specifically for acquiring professional services using PBCs, called "The Seven Steps to Performance-Based Services Acquisition." For a full version go to: www.acqnet.gov/library/OFPP/BestPractices/pbsc. The executive summary of this guide is reproduced in Appendix A of this book.

QUESTIONS TO CONSIDER

1. How well does your organization understand, agree to, and document your customer's requirements?

2. How effectively does your organization translate customer requirements into performance-based contracts?

3. Which performance-based metrics does your organization typically use in your business to evaluate and measure performance?

4. How effectively does your organization use contractual incentives to motivate your suppliers to improve performance?

5. Which pricing arrangements does your organization use most frequently for contracts to buy or sell products and services?

ENDNOTES

[1] Jones, Gerard, Mickaliger, Michael, and Joseph Witzgtall, Performance Sunrise: Blending Contract Management with Project Management, NCMA, Contract Management Magazine, April 2004.

U.S. Federal Government Contract Negotiations— Best Practices

INTRODUCTION

As the largest buyer of products and services in the world, the U.S. federal government and its numerous and diverse departments and agencies are unique and possess tremendous buying power. The federal government is able to obtain exceptional economic order quantity discounts when it practices collective purchasing practices. The federal government also uses its purchasing practices to implement social and economic policies. These demanding socio-economic requirements can be stringent and are unique to government contracting.

Nearly all federal government departments and agencies are required to follow the Federal Acquisition Regulation (FAR), which was issued in 1984. Each of the major departments and agencies have additional or supplemental purchasing requirements contained in their respective FAR supplements. The largest departments and agencies (Department of Defense (DOD), Department of Homeland Security (DHS), Department of Energy (DOE), General Services Administration (GSA), and National Aeronautics and Space Agency (NASA)) have the most demanding requirements. The overall intent of most FAR requirements is to ensure the federal government receives quality products, services, and solutions from honest and ethical business partners. However, some federal requirements are designed solely to implement specific socio-economic policies that Congress has legislated into law. Many of these policy-driven requirements flow down to all levels of subcontractors.

The additional costs and specialized knowledge an organization must possess to comply with the federal government's complex acquisition process and numerous unique requirements make it a real challenge for both large businesses and small businesses to penetrate the federal government marketplace. Before your organization negotiates a deal with one or more federal government departments or agencies, your organization must learn and be able to practice the rules of the game set out in the FAR and numerous supplemental regulations, policies, procedures, and guidelines. Most companies, based upon my experience incur significant additional costs ranging from 5% to 30% compared to the costs of similar commercial transactions in order to comply with the federal government's complex and time-consuming acquisition process.

The Competition In Contracting Act (CICA) of 1984 encourages federal government departments and agencies to maximize the use of competitiont to ensure they get the best deal, usually at the lowest reasonable price. As a result, most companies that choose to do business with the federal government typically incur not only higher costs for conducting business but also lower profit margins. Yet many companies do choose to do business with the federal departments and agencies, largely because they have a lot of money to spend, they are for the most part fair and ethical buyers, and they do pay their bills on-time—which is a beautiful thing!

PLANNING CONTRACT NEGOTIATION— BEST PRACTICES

The following discussion provides a brief summary of some of the proven effective best practices for preparing or planning for contract negotiations with a federal government department or agency. While each department or agency is specialized in terms of the products or services it provides, all departments and agencies require and follow many common products, services, and buying practices. Best practices for planning contract negotiations with the federal government include:

- Understanding how to influence federal government buying appropriately and ethically;

- Having an acceptable cost estimating and accounting system;
- Understanding the legal framework of federal government contracts;
- Understanding the Truth in Negotiation Act (TINA); and
- Knowing the key federal government acquisition thresholds.

Understand How to Influence Federal Government Buyers Appropriately and Ethically

Yes, it is possible to influence federal government buyers appropriately and ethically. The following is a brief checklist of do's and don'ts when influencing federal government buyers to purchase your company's products, services, or solutions.

Do's

- Create a government liasion office within your company;
- Hire a registered lobbyist(s);
- Join professional advocacy groups such as the Professional Services Council (PSC);
- Participate in joint U.S. government/industry professional associations (e.g., the National Contract Management Association (NCMA), the Project Management Institute (PMI), the Association of Proposal Management Professionals (APMP), the Software Engineering Institute (SEI), the National Defense Industry Association (NDIA), the Air Force Association (AFA));
- Write articles on the latest technologies, products, services, solutions, or proven best practices and have them published in professional magazines or journals, such as: *Government Executive Magazine, Contract Management Magazine, PM Network Magazine, PM Journal, Harvard Business Review, Fast Company Magazine, Fortune Magazine, Forbes Magazine*, and *MIT Technology Journal*;
- Provide professional presentations by your company's top business leaders at joint U.S. government/industry conferences and trade shows, including: FOSE, e-Government, NCMA World Congress, PMI Annual Conference, Project World Conferences, Bi-Annual DOD Procurement Conference, General Services Administration (GSA) Annual Conference, and Small Business Administration (SBA)-sponsored conferences/tradeshows;
- Serve as board members of professional associations or charitable associations along with U.S. government agency leaders;
- Execute existing contracts and projects flawlessly to develop an outstanding track record of superior performance on both commercial and federal government contracts;

- Develop a robust base of U.S. small businesses that your company uses on all U.S. government prime contracts—especially small businesses owned by disadvantaged individuals, women, and veterans and businesses such as Hub-Zone businesses that receive preferential treatment;

- Establish strategic alliances and/or teaming arrangements with numerous major U.S. government prime contractors and systems integrators: e.g., Lockheed Martin, General Dynamics, Boeing, CACI, Northrop Grumman, SAIC, EDS, and Raytheon;

- Create a board of advisors that includes active and retired business leaders from the U.S. government and industry; and

- Hire people who have formerly served in senior positions in the U.S. government and military, carefully observing all the rules of the Procurement Integrity Act and other ethical hiring laws and practices.

Don'ts

- Offer a job to a senior U.S. government procurement official who is actively involved in any procurement with or related to your company;

- Offer bribes, kickbacks, or other inappropriate gratuities to U.S. government employees;

- Illegally obtain procurement planning solicitation or budgetary information from a U.S. government employee;

- Illegally obtain confidential information about a competitor's bid proposal regarding a potential U.S. government contract;

- Make false statements to the government during the negotiation process;

- Fail to certify the accuracy and completeness of your cost and pricing information on large U.S. government contracts as required; or

- Make false claims to the U.S. government;

HAVE AN ACCEPTABLE COST ESTIMATING AND ACCOUNTING SYSTEM

The primary goal of an acceptable cost estimating and accounting system is to ensure that costs are appropriately, equitably, and consistently estimated then allocated to all final cost objectives (i.e., individual contracts, jobs, or products). The Federal Acquisition Regulation (FAR) essentially requires a company to maintain, and consistently apply, any generally accepted accounting method that is adequate, efficient, reliable, and equitable, but not necessarily exact and specific, and not biased against the government. The government does not require companies to adopt separate or necessarily complex accounting systems. Consequently, contractors are free to develop and use the type of cost estimating and accounting system most appropriate for their businesses. However, consistent application is vital.

Although the use and design of certain specific cost estimating accounting records and practices may vary from company to company, at a minimum, the record-keeping system for all companies doing business with the government must include a general ledger, a job-cost ledger, labor distribution records, time records, subsidiary journals, a chart of accounts, and financial statements.[1]

To determine whether a company's accounting system is acceptable, a government auditor generally will go through a checklist, asking questions similar to those found in the accounting system questionnaire (see Figure 8-1).

Figure 8-1.
Government Auditor Accounting System Questionnaire

	Yes	No
Is the system in accord with Generally Accepted Accounting Principles (GAAP)?	☐	☐
Will the system be able to identify and segregate direct costs from indirect costs and allocate these costs equitably to specific contracts on a consistent basis?	☐	☐
Is the system that accumulates costs integrated with, and reconcilable to, the general ledger?	☐	☐
Do the timekeeping and labor distribution systems appropriately identify direct and indirect labor charges to intermediate and final cost objectives?	☐	☐
Will the system be able to determine the cost of work performed at interim points (at least monthly) because of routine posting of costs to the books of account?	☐	☐
Will the system be able to identify and segregate unallowable costs as required by FAR Part 31 and any contract terms?	☐	☐
If required by the contract, will the system be able to identify costs by contract line item or by unit?	☐	☐
Will the system be able to segregate preproduction costs from production costs?	☐	☐
Is the system capable of provided the necessary information required by FAR 52.232-20, Limitation of Cost (Also -21 and -22), or FAR 52.216-16, Incentive Price Revision-Firm Target?	☐	☐
Is the system able to provide the necessary data for recovery of costs, using progress payments?	☐	☐
Is the accounting system designed? Are the records maintained in such a manner, that adequate, reliable data is developed for use in pricing follow-on contracts?	☐	☐
Is the accounting system currently in full operation?	☐	☐

From: "Beyond an 'Adequate' Accounting System," by Jeffrey A. Lubeck, CM Magazine, May 2004.

Accounting information can, and should, be used in more ways than merely to produce financial statements and job-cost reports. Only after identifying activities that are important to your business and beginning to measure them can you encourage the rest of your team to support your goals. A business that provides clear expectations and real-time performance feedback can be managed on a real-time basis and, therefore, has greater control over its destiny.[2]

ADEQUATE COST ESTIMATING

Developing a sound cost estimate requires a coordinated effort by a team of qualified company personnel who understand how to extract and price requirements presented in the government's request for proposal (RFP). At a minimum, the team should consist of a program manager, technical contract manager, accounting/finance manager, and a senior executive responsible for final review and submission of the proposal to the buyer. Depending on the company's size, the magnitude of the proposal, and the types of costs being estimated, the estimating team also may include representatives of purchasing, budgeting, human resources, and other operations.

All personnel with any responsibility for preparing a proposal should be well versed in the guidelines contained in the Federal Acquisition Regulation (especially FAR 15.4 – Contract Pricing). All team members should have adequate experience and knowledge of the particular requirements of the pricing function to which they have been assigned. Responsible contractor personnel should know where to obtain the most relevant and current data and be aware of the turnaround time allowed for submission of the proposal.[3]

A proposal preparation system that entrusts one person with the sole authority for translating the RFP into requirements, pricing those requirements, and reviewing and submitting the final proposal is an accident waiting to happen. Omission of key personnel in the estimating process can result in cost and delivery projections that do not consider current and future business decisions and company plans. In other words, the proposal may not realistically represent the company's ability to deliver the product or services within the estimated cost or required delivery timelines.

Including personnel who are familiar with various components of business operations will reduce the risk that a proposal will be overstated or understated. Even in small companies with few employees, in which officials wear several hats of responsibility, it is just as important that the estimating system involve at least two or three qualified persons to better ensure an accurately priced final product.

Finally, a forward-pricing proposal should minimize the use of judgmental estimates and maximize the use of factual data, when such data are available and relevant. Developing extensive priced requirements with judgmental estimates does not provide the visibility required by the government to evaluate the reasonableness of a proposal. Judgmental estimates add time to the government audit and cost analysis and sometimes result in adverse audit opinions because of a lack of verifiable data. The typical cost elements in Figure 8-2 are examples of verifiable proposal supporting data.[4]

Figure 8-2. Examples of Verifiable Proposal Supporting Data

Direct labor hours:	Labor-hour history of the same or similar projects Company or industry standards
Bill of direct materials:	Material panning documents Engineering blueprints
Direct labor rates:	Labor cost history for the same or similar project Average labor rates from payroll data Market wage or salary survey information
Direct materials:	Purchase history of same or similar items Vendor quotations Vendor catalogues
Indirect rate:	Historical annual indirect rates Budgetary/provisional rates

From: "Is Your Estimating System Asking for Trouble?," by Darryl L. Walker, CM Magazine, May 2004.

In selecting the proposal resources for developing and pricing RFP requirements, the contractor must be careful to use the most current, accurate, and complete information, especially if the submission of cost or pricing data is required. This means selecting the data most relevant to the proposal being prepared and ensuring that the source information is as current as possible. Even if the proposal is not specifically subject to the Truth in Negotiations Act, companies have an obligation to prepare reasonable estimates and, in that pursuit, should rely on up-to-date, relevant, and accurate data when possible.

It goes without saying that estimating techniques must be relevant to the specific RFP requirements. Contractor techniques should be consistent among all bid proposals, except in cases in which those techniques clearly will not produce the most accurate cost estimate for the RFP's scope of work.[5]

COST PROPOSAL PACKAGE: INFORMATION REQUIRED FOR PRIME CONTRACTS

A prime contract cost proposal requiring cost or pricing data must follow the format shown in FAR 15.408, Table 15-2. This information may be helpful in assessing the adequacy of a subcontractor's proposal.

1. First Page of Proposal—Table 15-2, Item I. A lists 11 separate informational requirements:
   a. Solicitation/contract no.
   b. Offeror name and address
   c. Contact point and phone number
   d. Name of contract administration office
   e. Type of contract option (i.e. new contract, change order, letter contract, etc.)
   f. Date of submission
   g. Name, title and signature of authorized representative
   h. Proposed cost, fee and total
   i. What government property is required
   j. Cost accounting standards
      i. Whether organization is subject to CAS
      ii. Whether disclosure statement is submitted and determined adequate
      iii. Any notifications of material noncompliance with CAS or disclosure statement and whether proposal is consistent with CAS and disclosed practices—no need to disclose "technical" noncompliances
   k. Statement that proposal reflects estimated/actual costs and that contracting officer/authorized representatives have access to records
2. Summary of Cost and Detailed Support–Table 15-2, Items I. C-G, II and III
3. Disclosure Narrative—Table 15-2, Items C–G
   a. Helps protect against defective pricing allegations
   b. Describes the basis of estimates
      i. Specific discussion by cost category (direct materials, direct labor, other direct costs, overhead, etc.)
      ii. Discusses assumptions made and the rationale such as judgmental factors, applied and mathematical or other methods used in the estimate

       iii. Method used in projecting from known data

       iv. Includes the nature and amount of contingencies in the proposed price

   c. Discloses significant cost or pricing data in narrative form

       i. Discusses key data used in cost estimating

       ii. Discloses cost date not used in cost estimating and states why it was not used

4. Disclosure Index—Table 15-2, Item I. B

   a. Helps protect against defective pricing claims by listing all available cost or pricing data, or other information accompanying the proposal or identified in the proposal, appropriately referenced

   b. Index should specifically identify all reports and documents. Should include:

       i. Specific report name and/or number

       ii. Date of most recent report

       iii. Physical location of data

   c. Includes items such as:

       i. General ledger

       ii. Payroll register

       iii. Vendor invoice

       iv. A/P history, etc.

   d. Future addition and/or revisions up to the date of agreement on price must be annotated on a supplemental index.

UNDERSTAND THE LEGAL FRAMEWORK OF FEDERAL GOVERNMENT CONTRACTS

The actual power of the federal government to enter into contracts is not specifically enumerated in the Constitution. Instead, it is implied in order for the government to sustain itself as a political entity. Because the federal system in our country is based on the principle of separation of powers, power is shared by all three branches of the federal government. Basically, Congress passes laws, appropriates money, and raises revenues; the President signs or vetoes legislation, appoints executive department heads, and manages the system; and the judicial branch judges the constitutionality of the laws, based on its interpretation of the Constitution.

The Federal Acquisition Regulation (FAR) is the product of laws passed by Congress to provide guidance for federal government contract negotiators. The FAR is the primary regulation used by federal executive agencies that use appropriated funds for the acquisition of supplies and services. The FAR system, which was established to codify and publish uniform policies and procedures for acquisition by all executive agencies, was developed in accordance with the Office of Federal Procurement Policy Act of 1974, as amended by Public Law 96-83. The FAR is issued under the joint authority of the General Services Administration (GSA) Administrator, the Secretary of Defense, and the National Aeronautics and Space Administration (NASA) Administrator.

The purpose of the FAR is to provide uniformity in the federal acquisition process. Prior to the issuance of the FAR, each agency followed its own regulations. For example, the Department of Defense (DOD) had the Armed Services Procurement Regulation (ASPR), which was superseded by the Defense Acquisition Regulation (DAR). On April 1, 1984, the FAR replaced these individual agency regulations, including the Federal Procurement Regulations System, the DAR, and the NASA Procurement Regulation. Agency regulations that unnecessarily repeat, paraphrase, or otherwise restate the FAR are specifically prohibited.[6] However, agencies are permitted to develop individual agency supplements to the FAR to address their unique contracting needs. Major differences still exist, however, in the individual agencies' interpretation and implementation of the FAR.

Each federal agency has evolved over time to satisfy its own specific mission. In addition to federal agencies, there are departments and offices with their own missions, most of which are responsible to the executive branch (the President). Each agency with contracting authority is authorized to issue and maintain its own regulations that further implement the FAR. Some of the more prominent agencies that issue supplements are NASA, GSA, the Department of State, the Department of Energy, the DOD, the Department of Homeland Security, the Department of Transportation, and the Department of Commerce. Whether the procurement is for supplies or services, specific agency regulations will reflect the conditions unique to the agency and should be familiar to those dealing with that agency.[7]

FAR PART 15

FAR Part 15, Contracting by Negotiation, "prescribes policies and procedures governing competitive and noncompetitive negotiated acquisitions. A contract awarded using other than sealedbidding procedures is a negotiated contract." This part of the FAR prescribes the procedures to be used when the method of contracting is negotiation. With the passage of CICA, Congress emphasized a new standard—competition versus the formal advertising method of procurement. Previously, Congress had been oriented to using formal advertising procedures to ensure that the government received the lowest, "fair and reasonable" prices. While negotiation was recognized as a method of procurement during World War II, its use was strictly controlled and required approval. In 1948 and 1949 respectively, Congress passed two major procurement statutes in the Armed Services Procurement Act (ASPA) and the Federal Property and Administrative Services Act (FPASA). These statutes required formal advertising, unless certain statutory exceptions could be cited for the use of negotiation. The passage of CICA in 1984 eliminated the mandate for the use of sealed bidding, and it also changed terminology from "formal advertising" to "sealed bidding." However, a major shift in focus also took place with the recognition that the use of competitive proposals was a viable form of full and open competition. Thus, a new standard was born. It still emphasized a preference for sealed bidding when appropriate but also recognized negotiations and discussions as a form of achieving competition.[8]

FAR Subpart 15.405, Price Negotiation, describes what many consider to be the heart of negotiation. Note, however, that this subpart deals with the issue of price negotiations as a byproduct of technical understanding. In other words, before one can negotiate price, there must first be an understanding of the technical requirements and contractual terms and conditions. To attempt to negotiate price in isolation of technical requirements, terms, and conditions is shortsighted and may significantly reduce the likelihood of achieving an effective contractual agreement.

FAR Subpart 15.404-4, Profit, provides guidance for determining profit using a structured approach. This subpart applies to price negotiation based on cost analysis, prescribing policies for an agency's development and use of a structured approach for determining the profit or fee prenegotiation objective. In general, the government considers profit to be that portion of the prenegotiation objective representing the potential remuneration that contractors may receive for contract performance over and above allowable costs. Because this perspective is somewhat different from considering profit as net income, the negotiation parties need to be aware of the methods or structured approach (i.e., DOD's Weighted Guidelines Method) when preparing to negotiate this important element of their objectives.

Department of Defense—Weighted Guidelines

The Department of Defense structured approach to profit/fee analysis is known as the Weighted Guidelines. These guidelines are implemented using DD Form 1547. DD Form 1547, Record of Weighted Guidelines Application, provides the structure of profit/fee objectives and reporting the amount negotiated. Several organizations have developed computerized versions of the form to assure accurate calculation and reporting. The most widely circulated software is the Air Force Material Command WGM (Weighted Guidance Method), currently marketed by the National Contract Management Association.

DD Form 1547 is divided into nine sections, as listed below (and described in further detail in the Contract Pricing Reference Guide, Volume III, Chapter 12.3):

- Identification information;
- Contractor effort cost category;
- Performance risk;
- Contract type risk;
- Working capital adjustment;
- Facilities capital employed;
- Total profit objective;
- Negotiation summary; and
- Contracting officer approval.

In lieu of the Weighted Guidelines method, contracting officers may use an alternative structured approach for the following:
- Architect-engineering contracts;
- Construction contracts;
- Termination settlements;
- Contracts smaller than $500,000; and
- Contracts primarily for delivery of materials from subcontractors.

Finally, FAR Subpart 15.5 covers the notification process and procedures for handling mistakes made during this entire process.[9]

UNDERSTAND THE TRUTH IN NEGOTIATIONS ACT (TINA)

Congress enacted the Truth in Negotiations Act (TINA) as Public Law 87-653 (10 U.S.C. 2306) in December, 1962. The TINA has been viewed as one of the most significant pieces of procurement legislation. The original act covered only contracts entered into by DOD and NASA. Civilian agencies subsequently adopted the same statutory provisions under their own regulations. The statutory disparity between the various government agencies was addressed by CICA, which required that the TINA apply to all government contracts. This remedy has significantly decreased the number of disputes brought before the various boards of contract appeals.

The TINA requires prime contractors and subcontractors to submit and certify to the government the data related to the basis of estimated contract costs. The objective is to provide the government with all necessary and relevant information to be able to negotiate a fair and reasonable price for a contract. The TINA requires that such information be "current, accurate, and complete" at the time such an agreement is reached by the negotiating parties.[10]

The TINA requires contractors to disclose factual data that prudent buyers and sellers would reasonably expect to significantly affect the contract price negotiation. Typical data that is disclosed under the TINA include the following:
- Historical costs, such as material costs, labor hours expanded, labor rates paid, or labor union settlements;
- "Make or buy" program decisions;
- Subcontractor and vendor quotations;

- Learning curve projections; and
- Other business base projections.

Although the TINA requires disclosure of these types of information to the government, the contractor is not required to rely on this data in developing its proposal. A contractor is not constrained in exercising its best judgment in developing the estimated cost of a contract. The key to compliance with the TINA is disclosure of relevant factual data. If current, accurate, and complete cost or pricing data has been disclosed, then it is assumed that the government or prime contractor negotiators have the necessary information to reach an informed agreement and a fair and reasonable contract price.[11]

In order to ensure that contractors are providing data in compliance with the TINA, contractors are required to certify that such disclosures are accurate (i.e., current, accurate, and complete) for contracts or modifications to existing contracts with a value greater than certain dollar thresholds). Exceptions to disclosure and certification are provided in the following cases:

- The contract price is based on adequate price competition;
- An established catalogue or market price exists, and the item is sold in substantial quantities to the general public;
- The prices are set by law or regulation; or
- It is an exceptional case. Such cases must be approved after agency head determinations.

Of course, the government negotiator must likewise spend considerable time analyzing and using such information in negotiating the best deal for the government. Accordingly, after the final "handshake," but before signing the certification, the contractor generally performs a final review to be sure that all of the cost and pricing data that may affect the final, agreed-to price has been disclosed.

If the certified cost or pricing data is not current, accurate, or complete on the effective date of the certificate, the government is entitled to a downward adjustment to the contract price. Such a situation is known as "defective pricing" under the TINA. In addition to an adjustment to the contract price (if warranted), the contractor may be subject to further investigation for fraud, and, in cases where fraud is determined, criminal penalties may be imposed.

TINA DOCUMENTATION REQUIREMENTS

Common sense would dictate that any business person would "document" the results of a business negotiation. For government negotiators, the regulations require extensive and specific documentation. The FAR requires government contracting officers to establish and document written prenegotiation objectives prior to entering negotiations in accordance with FAR 15.406-1.

■ A record of significant events in the acquisition;
■ A list of attendees at the briefing;
■ The current acquisition situation;
■ The previous price history;
■ A synopsis of offers submitted or received;
■ The analytical methods used to establish price objectives;
■ The delivery objectives;
■ The negotiation plan; and
■ Signature blocks for the signature(s) of the approving official(s).

For a completed contract negotiation, the government contracting officer shall use a Price Negotiation Memorandum (PNM), in accordance with FAR 15.406-3. Understanding the many federal regulations that are a part of the negotiation process is a major step towards improving the resulting agreements for the buying and selling of products and services for the American public, although having such knowledge is not in itself enough to ensure optimal negotiations. After all, negotiation involves interacting with other people, making it a dynamic and challenging process.

UNDERSTAND THE KEY FEDERAL GOVERNMENT ACQUISITION THRESHOLDS

The following Federal Acquisition Regulation (FAR) dollar thresholds are subject to change.[12]

Figure 8-3. Federal Acquisition Regulation (FAR) Dollar Thresholds			
Authority	**Current**	**Temp. Emergency Procurement Authority Funds Obligated by DOD 12/28/2002–9/30/2003**	**Homeland Security Act Solicitations Issued by Federal Agencies 1/24/2003–11/24/2003**
Micro-purchase Threshold (Construction)	$2,500 ($2,000)	$15,000 ($2,000)	$7,500 ($2,000)
Simplified Acquisition Threshold	$100,000	For "contingency" Inside U.S. = $250,000	For "contingency opns" Inside U.S. = $200,000
Purchase Outside Of U.S. for Contingency or Peacekeeping/ Humanitarian Opns	$200,000	To support defense against terrorism or chemical/biological attack in contingency Outside U.S. = $500,000	To support defense against, recovery from terrorism or chem/bio/ nuclear/radiological attack contingency Outside U.S. = $300,000
Commercial Item Rules	Use Part 12 of Coml Items; use 13.5 SAP for coml. items to $5M	Treat buys for biotechnology and biotechnology services as commercial items	Treat buys to support defense against, recovery from terrorism or chem/ bio/nuclear/radiological attack as coml. items; use FAR 13.5 SAP UNLIMITED $
Small Business Set-Aside (FAR 19.502)	$2,500– $100,000	$15,000–$100,000	$7,500–$100,000 For "contingency opns" Inside U.S. $7,500– $200,000
Very Small Business Pilot Program (FAR 19.903)	$2,500–$50,000	$15,000–$50,000	$7,500–$50,000
Dollar limit on Sole Source 8(a) (FAR 19.805)	$5M NAICS Mfg. And $3M other NAICS		Eliminated dollar limits on sole source 8(a) acquisitions and HUBZone sole source for buys to support defense against, recovery from terrorism or chem/bio/nuclear/ radiological attack
HUBZone	$5M NAICS Mfg. and $3M other NAICS		
Buy-American Act Clause (FAR 52.225-51)	Apply to solicitations and contracts over $2,500	Apply to solicitations and contracts over $15,000	Apply to solicitations and contracts over $7,500

CONDUCTING CONTRACT NEGOTIATIONS— BEST PRACTICES

The following is a summary of some proven effective best practices and do's and don'ts of negotiation for best value and using oral presentations with a federal government department or agency. The section also includes a summary of seven best practices to win a General Services Administration (GSA) Federal Supply Schedule Contract.

Negotiating for Best Value

The term "best value" can have several meanings, depending on one's particular perspective. FAR Subpart 2.1 defines best value as the expected outcome of an acquisition that, in the Governments estimation provides the greatest overall benefit in response to the requirement. Best value is usually associated with the source selection process, per FAR 15.101. However, the concept can also be applied to other situations.

In all situations, best value is a tool for the buyer and seller to establish a proper balance between factors such as price, quality, technical and performance. Best value applies to products and services already developed, as opposed to value engineering (also referred to as value analysis), which examines tradeoffs during the design process.

Perhaps it would be more helpful to define best value in terms of what it is and what it is not. It is a disciplined, balanced approach, an assessment of tradeoffs between price and performance, a team effort, an evaluation of qualitative and quantitative factors, and an integrated risk assessment. Best value is not price cutting, uncompensated overtime, accounting gimmicks, specials, one-time discounts, the shifting of all price and performance risk to the contractor, or an excuse not to define requirements properly.[13]

For our purposes, best value is a determination of which offer presents the best tradeoff between price and performance, where quality is considered an integral performance factor, see FAR 15.101-1. The bestvalue decision can be made using a variety of qualitative and quantitative management tools.

Relation of Best Value to Contract Negotiations

Best-value contracting is intrinsically tied to the process of contract negotiations for several reasons. First of all, to be successful, negotiations must focus on some specific quantifiable objective. Best value offers a meaningful objective to each negotiation party. In addition, contract negotiation typically requires tradeoffs among a variety of interrelated factors. Using best-value techniques helps contract management professionals assess the impact of these tradeoffs to ensure a successful negotiation session. These techniques also help determine the range of values, e.g., cost, production, quality requirements, life-cycle cost, where tradeoffs can be made while preserving the optimal balance between price, performance, and quality. Lastly, best value establishes realistic negotiation objectives up front. For example, best-value contracting techniques can discourage the use of unrealistic initial negotiation positions by contractors seeking to win a contract with practices such as uncompensated overtime or unrealistically low initial prices.

To be successful, best-value contracting must be an integral part of the acquisition strategy planning process; this means early planning must occur. Best-value contracting also requires a team effort among various disciplines such as engineering, accounting, legal, manufacturing, and contracts, to clearly identify all acquisition requirements and determine the optimum tradeoffs among various factors.

Tradeoffs in Sole-Source Negotiation Situations

Tradeoffs in making a best-value decision should always consider the objectives of both the buyer and seller, which was discussed previously. Tradeoffs may have to be revisited as negotiations progress, since the needs of the buyer and seller will be revealed (usually incrementally) during the course of negotiations.

The level of analysis in a best-value tradeoff decision depends on the complexity of the particular procurement. Low-technology procurements usually require a simple, straightforward tradeoff approach, since price is normally the primary factor. However, high-technology procurements usually require more sophisticated tradeoff analysis tools, because price is usually secondary to technical and quality concerns.[14]

Due to the many types of contracting situations, there is no single preferred way to determine best value. Rather, a combination of techniques should be used, preferably integrating quantitative and qualitative factors. The use of a team approach helps with making the necessary tradeoffs rationally (see Figure 8-4).

Figure 8-4. Sample: Best Value Proposal Evaluation Process

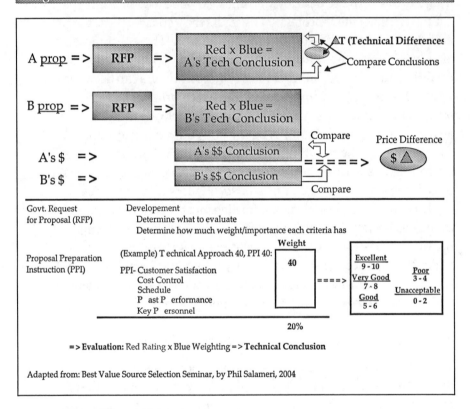

=> Evaluation: Red Rating x Blue Weighting => Technical Conclusion

Adapted from: Best Value Source Selection Seminar, by Phil Salameri, 2004

The Evolution of Best-Value Negotiation

The practice of best-value contracting has continued to grow in importance over the past decade. First of all, the federal regulatory environment has continually evolved, gradually allowing for increased best-value contracting techniques. Government contractors have responded to these changes by offering best-value pricing as a part of an overall value-based cost and technical approach. This has helped make government contractors more efficient and competitive. In addition, the items and services to be purchased have continued to become more technical and complex, e.g., sophisticated consulting, advanced hardware, software, and professional services. This has often made quality and past performance factors more important than price-related factors. Also, the emphasis on making best-value purchasing decisions will increase as the government refines its attempts to obtain more value for its money. Finally, the continual improvement in the professional qualifications and credentials of both government and industry acquisition workforce personnel has fostered the use of best value on both sides.

The commercial sector has long used best-value contracting techniques as a means of remaining competitive and profitable. The federal government has not had the same degree of flexibility to employ best–value techniques because it must comply with various requirements that have no material bearing on the business aspects of the contract but are mandated by law to be included in all federal acquisitions as a matter of public policy. As a result, best-value implementation has not achieved its full potential in the government-contracting arena.[15]

✔ Form 8-1 Checklist. Best Value Negotiation "Dos"

Do:

- ☐ Develop or obtain proven best-value contracting tools.
- ☐ Select best-value measurement tools that are easy to understand and use.
- ☐ Ensure quality factors do not become secondary to cost issues, except for noncomplex acquisitions.
- ☐ Consider using automation tools for best-value decision support during source selection.
- ☐ Tailor best-value measurement tools to specific procurement situations, realizing that complexity increases with the size and scope of the acquisition.
- ☐ Use a contract type that fairly allocates risks.
- ☐ Provide contract incentives for superior (quality) performance.

Continue on Next Page

Continue from Last Page

☐ Implement guidance throughout the agency or company.

☐ Continue to improve techniques.

☐ Make each best-value decision a team effort between contracts, engineering, production, quality assurance, and other related offices.

☐ Ensure a best-value approach supports the overall negotiation strategy.

☐ Realize the best-value approach works only if you know what you're buying. This means all relevant price and performance-related issues need to be researched.

☐ Document the rationale for best-value decisions

☐ Allow flexibility for tradeoffs.

From: Negotiating a Quality Contract, NCMA, 1992.

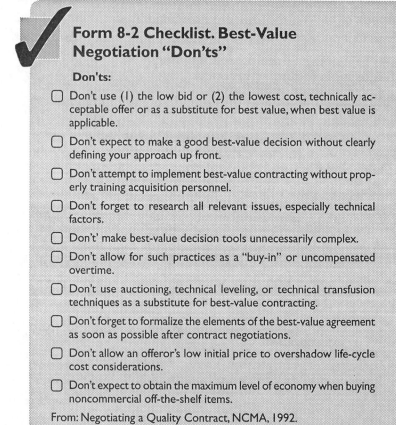

Form 8-2 Checklist. Best-Value Negotiation "Don'ts"

Don'ts:

☐ Don't use (1) the low bid or (2) the lowest cost, technically acceptable offer or as a substitute for best value, when best value is applicable.

☐ Don't expect to make a good best-value decision without clearly defining your approach up front.

☐ Don't attempt to implement best-value contracting without properly training acquisition personnel.

☐ Don't forget to research all relevant issues, especially technical factors.

☐ Don't' make best-value decision tools unnecessarily complex.

☐ Don't allow for such practices as a "buy-in" or uncompensated overtime.

☐ Don't use auctioning, technical leveling, or technical transfusion techniques as a substitute for best-value contracting.

☐ Don't forget to formalize the elements of the best-value agreement as soon as possible after contract negotiations.

☐ Don't allow an offeror's low initial price to overshadow life-cycle cost considerations.

☐ Don't expect to obtain the maximum level of economy when buying noncommercial off-the-shelf items.

From: Negotiating a Quality Contract, NCMA, 1992.

Use the Power of Oral Presentations

The fight to win and keep government contracts is an intense and unforgiving business. Competition for contracts will only grow, especially as the federal government increases funding to wage the war on terror and recapitalize the armed forces. In fact, it is estimated that those seeking Department of Defense contracts will collectively increase their Bid & Proposal budgets by over $100 billion over the next five years.[16] To compete effectively, contractors must use every resource they can find to successfully win contracts. *Competition will be formidable.*

A New Type of Proposal

When a Request for Proposal (RFP) is announced, those seeking the contract typically prepare a large, comprehensive written proposal. However, preparing a single written proposal involves a long and costly process. What's more, reliable studies have shown that, due to the complexity of today's proposals, selection board members generally do not understand 75 percent of what they read in the proposal.[17] Because of the challenges associated with written proposals, government agencies are placing more emphasis on untraditional methods for awarding contracts.

While a comprehensive written proposal is still often expected, an additional method, the oral presentation, is quickly becoming a standard feature of the evaluation process. In fact, a General Services Administration executive recently estimated that over 70 percent of solicitations for $10 million or more will have orals requirements, with the orals counting an average of 40 percent of the evaluation.[18] The Department of Energy has issued a statement encouraging the widespread practice of orals. And oral proposals are in line with the revised methods advocated in the new Federal Acquisition Regulation Part 15 guidelines.[19] Orals requirements are now the norm in government contracting.

In contrast to written proposals, oral proposals more effectively convey the contractor's technical approach, management experience, and past performance. Orals reduce procurement lead time and administrative costs for both government and industry. Most important, orals help the selection board create a relationship with the potential contractor, providing a clearer picture of the contractor's adaptability, competence, and responsiveness. The selection board is able to evaluate the key members of the potential contractor and gain deeper insights into the proposed technical and management approach.[20]

Oral Presentations Matter

The bottom line for business development is that the orals part of the evaluation process matters and will probably determine the outcome of the entire contract. In response to the importance of the oral proposal, organizations have begun to invest in orals coaching to effectively prepare the orals team.

Organizations realize that the orals team represents the company and can project a positive or negative image based on the perceived cohesiveness and competency of the team. Thus, contractors who want to win contracts engage an orals coach. As a general rule, teams who have an orals coach win more contracts than teams without such guidance. Some contractors choose an internal orals coach to direct their proposal team. Though this may reduce costs in the short term, an internal coach usually lacks experience, objectivity, and full expertise in the oral proposal process.

Today, more organizations hire external orals coaches. These external coaches have extensive experience, understand what it takes to win contracts, and have a proven track record of teaching effective presentation skills. They know how to direct the intense orals coaching process of selecting team members, developing individual presentation skills, creating a cohesive team, highlighting discriminators, and continually practicing until the presentation is flawless.[21]

Know How to Win a GSA
Federal Supply Schedule Contract

The General Services Administration (GSA), through its Federal Supply Service (FSS) administers the Federal Supply Schedules Program, also known as the GSA Schedules or the Multiple Award Schedules (MAS) Program. The MAS Program is a unique method of contracting under which GSA awards contracts with common terms and conditions to multiple companies supplying comparable services and products, at varying prices. The MAS Program incorporates over 10,000 contracts for millions of commercial products and services.

According to Mr. Tom Reid, President, Certified Contracting Solutions, LLC, there are seven best practices for winning a GSA Federal Supply Schedule Contract:

- Obtain a Dun and Bradstreet reference check;
- Identify the schedule that covers your commodity or service;
- Obtain a copy of the Federal Supply Service's (FSS) solicitation for the product or service (most of the schedules are continuously open);
- Complete all information (including your administrative proposal, technical proposal, price proposal, and representations and certifications) and be sure your price is in the competitive range;
- Submit your offer with examples of commercial prices you have charged and references from satisfied customers;
- Be sure you are financially sound and be prepared to demonstrate it; and
- Be ready to negotiate your best and final offer with FSS.

Upon receipt of your proposal, GSA will review the submission to make sure that it meets all of the criteria defined in the RFP for the proper submission. It will then make a determination that your company meets the responsibility criteria specified in the Federal Acquisition Regulation (FAR) Part 9. Assuming that the company meets these standards, GSA will examine the following to determine if your price is fair and reasonable:

- Overall soundness of your company's pricing;
- Your company's commercial selling practices;
- The state of the current marketplace; and
- Industry trends.

GSA also evaluates a company's internal compensation practices to ensure its people are compensated fairly and appropriately, that the company has the ability to attract and retain quality workers, and that its compensation levels demonstrate an understanding of the work to be performed. GSA will negotiate a price that is equal to or better than the best price given by your company to your commercial customers under comparable terms and conditions. Following the requirements of FAR, GSA will determine that the contract prices are fair and reasonable.

After Award

Further , Tom Reid states: "Once a GSA schedule contract is awarded, be ready to market your product or service to the federal government and comply with the many contract clauses, reports, and amendments. You will need to track the following:

- Each quarter GSA requires an on-line report to be filed for all orders received under the contract. At this time, the 1% industrial funding fee must be submitted to GSA electronically.
- While many procurement actions are advertised for schedule holders only, most success in marketing comes from direct marketing to contracting officers who buy the goods or services you offer.
- Buyers are still required to follow the ordering procedures contained in FAR Part 8. This usually involves a limited form of competition.
- GSA actively manages its schedule contracts. Most schedules are modified several times throughout each year. Failure to acknowledge each amendment can cause your schedule to become inactive.
- All GSA schedules are required to be listed in GSA Advantage, an on-line catalog of all GSA schedules and the goods or products offered by each schedule holder. As your offerings change, you will be required to update your Advantage listing. Depending on the frequency of these changes, this effort may be substantial.
- Listing your offerings in GSA Advantage results in the public disclosure of your pricing. Some commercial entities object to this disclosure, but it is a "cost of doing business" with the government in the MAS Program.
- Each schedule holder must maintain at least $25,000 in annual sales on its schedule. Failure to do so may result in GSA canceling your schedule.
- Each GSA RFP consists of several hundred pages. Most of these pages become part of the final contract document and contain

numerous unique clauses. Each of these clauses must be read and understood.

■ In following a common government practice, each contract contains numerous clauses that are "incorporated by reference." Each of these clauses must be located, read, and understood as well.

■ Where Blanket Purchase Agreement opportunities exist, these agreements will be negotiated separately with particular agencies.

■ Often subcontracting opportunities are available to schedule holders. Occasionally this results in the creation of Team Agreements with prime contractors.

■ Schedule holders are required to accept government credit cards."

The above list is not intended to scare you off but to make sure you have a realistic expectation of what is required in obtaining and holding a GSA FSS Schedule.

DOCUMENTING CONTRACT NEGOTIATIONS— BEST PRACTICES

The following summarizes two proven effective best practices for documenting contract negotiations and forming a contract with a federal government department or agency. More specifically, the key aspects of developing a Price Negotiation Memorandum (PNM) and forming a contract using the Uniform Contract Format (UCF) are discussed.

Use of a Price Negotiation Memorandum (PNM)

After the parties reach final agreement, it must be documented for internal management. In addition to apprising management of the results of the negotiations, the negotiation memorandum also becomes part of the permanent negotiation file of the party that generated it. The head of the negotiation team (usually the contracting representative) prepares the internal negotiation memorandum. The government refers to this document as the Price Negotiation Memorandum (PNM), pursuant to FAR 15.406-3. Documentation of the actual negotiation must be adequate so that anyone who picks up the file can understand what was agreed to. The following is a list of topics to be addressed in the typical negotiation memorandum:

- **Subject.** This section, together with the introductory summary, should offer a complete overview of the negotiations. This includes basic data on the other party, such as name, address, and point of contact. It also includes basic data on the specific action, such as the solicitation, contract, or modification number and a brief description of the project.
- **Introductory summary.** This section details the contract type and the negotiation action (e.g., modification, new contract, sole source). It also lists the party's objectives and what was actually negotiated. For price, this involves making a comparative list.
- **Particulars.** This section provides specific information, such as who was in attendance (names, titles, telephone numbers, e-mail addresses) on what dates, and what is being bought (description and quantities).
- **Procurement situation.** This lists factors that influenced the procurement (schedule, urgency) and subsequently impacted the final price.
- **Negotiation summary.** This details price exchanges between the parties, listed in columns for comparison. It can be broken down by major elements of cost and profit.

Some negotiations are accomplished on a bottom-line basis. The negotiation memorandum, however, calls for major elements of cost to be segregated. To accomplish this, it is sometimes necessary to "back into" the breakdown. In order to explain such details, the number columns are accompanied by descriptive paragraphs. Thus, the negotiation memorandum should offer a reconstruction of all significant considerations and agreements. The negotiation summary section should be as detailed as necessary to convey all information about the negotiations.

It is not unusual for the buyer's and the seller's negotiation memorandum to differ significantly from one another. Because two different thought processes can yield the same compromise, one party's internal memorandum may not be consistent with the other party's. This is usually not realized by either side because typically neither side sees the other's memorandum. Many negotiations are completed with a compromise at the bottom line. Consequently, the seller may write that it reduced hours to reach agreement, while the buyer may write that the proposed hours were agreed to but that the overhead and profit were reduced. The internal memorandums reflect the thinking of that party in accepting the agreement.

Use of the Uniform Contract Format (UCF)

In accordance with FAR 14.201-1, the Uniform Contract Format (UCF), the standard format used by the government to purchase most supplies and services, provides a common architecture to organize the solicitation (and resultant contract). It is applicable to both sealed bidding and negotiated methods of contracting. The UCF is optional for acquisitions of the following:

- Construction
- Shipbuilding;
- Subsistence items;
- Contracts requiring special forms;
- Firm-fixed-price or fixed-price with economic price adjustment acquisitions that use the simplified contract format (FAR 14.201-9); and
- Agency-exempted contracts.

A format familiar to all enables the reader to focus on content rather than form and facilitates communication between the parties. While the format is uniform, it is also flexible, permitting the contracting officer some latitude in structuring the document. Since sections A through J of the solicitation will ultimately become the contract, investments of time and effort during the solicitation phase will pay handsome dividends during contract performance phase. The UCF is divided into four parts comprising thirteen sections as shown in Figure 8-5.

Figure 8-5 Uniform Contract Format

The Federal Acquisition Regulation prescribes a uniform format for RFPs and IFBs, consisting of sections A through M

Part I — The Schedule
Section A. Solicitation/Contract Form
Section B. Supplies or Services and Prices
Section C. Description/Specifications
Section D. Packaging and Marking
Section E. Inspection and Acceptance
Section F. Deliveries or Performance
Section G. Contract Administration Data
Section H. Special Contract Requirements

Part II — Contract Clauses
Section I. Contract Clauses

Part III — List of Documents, Exhibits and Other Attachments
Section J. List of documents, exhibits, and other attachments

Part IV — Representations and Instructions
Section K. Representations, Certifications, and other Statements of bidders
Section L. Instructions, Conditions, and Notices to bidders
Section M. Evaluation Factors for Award

Section A. Solicitation/Contract Form

Standard Form (SF) 33, used for most requirements, is divided into three main parts: solicitation, offer, and award. The government contracting officer completes the solicitation section before releasing the document. It contains information concerning where and when offers should be submitted as well as a table of contents that applies the UCF to this procurement. The offer section, completed by the contractor and returned as part of its offer, constitutes a legally binding offer in the process of contract formation. The award section is completed by the government contracting officer after the source selection decision has been made. Some agencies use the Standard Form 1447. Delivery of the document to the contractor or its authorized agent represents an executed contract.

Section B. Supplies or Services and Prices

Section B is a brief description of the contract deliverables by line item. The FAR lists no specific structure for this section; however, DOD, GSA, the Department of Energy, and other agencies have specific formats for their agency requirements. Under DOD's structure, for example, contract line item numbers (CLIN) consist of four numeric digits and are numbered sequentially. Section B lists nomenclature, quantity, unit of issue, unit price, and total amount for each CLIN (see Figure 8-6).

Figure 8-6

Item No.	Supplies/services	Quantity	Units	Unit Price	Amount
0001	Personal Computer	15	EA	$500.00	$7,500.00

Identifying requirements at the highest (system) level may not communicate all of the information required for contract performance or administration. In those cases, subline items are used to (1) provide more information and (2) permit separate delivery date, place and/or payment for components of the requirement. Informational subline items provide a further breakdown of the CLIN and are identified by a two-digit numeric suffix (see Figure 8-7). Subline items are not separately priced for invoicing purposes nor are they to be delivered separately.

Figure 8-7

Item No.	Supplies/services	Quantity	Units	Unit Price	Amount
0001 0000101 0000102	Personal Computer Keyboard Monitor	15	EA	$500.00	$7,500.00

Section C. Description/Specification

Section C is a companion section to Section B and provides more detailed information about the deliverable items identified. Again, the FAR requires no specific structure for this section. Section C addresses what the seller is required to do during performance of the contract.

If the objective of the contract is services or research and development, Section C will contain a Statement of Work (SOW) that describes tasks to be performed. Section C can sometimes be a hybrid because the work requires both supplies and services.

If data is required to be delivered under the contract, they must be specified as well. If many data deliverables are specified, requirements may be grouped together and listed as an exhibit in

Section J in a format similar to DOD's Contract Data Requirements List (CDRL) (DD Form 1423).

Section D. Packaging and Marking

Packaging and marking requirements are designed to prevent deterioration and damage during shipping and storage. The contractor may simply be required to preserve, pack, and mark all items in accordance with standard commercial practice, or more stringent requirements could be specified if the supplies may be subjected to a more hostile environment.

Section E. Inspection and Acceptance

In addition to inspection and acceptance criteria, this section also specifies any quality assurance and reliability requirements. Government contracts involve any of three general levels of quality control-based guidance in FAR Part 46.

Section F. Deliveries or Performance

Section F specifies the time, place, and method of delivery or performance. For supplies, the delivery schedule is usually stated in terms of a calendar date or a specified period after the contract has been awarded. It also lists the place of delivery, usually stated as f.o.b. origin or f.o.b. destination. For services, Section F specifies the period of performance.

Section G. Contract Administration Data

This section supplements the administrative information contained in Section A and may include the following:
- Name and address of the contracting officer, contracting officer's technical representative, transportation office, and contract administration officer;
- Accounting and appropriation data including how to account for multiple funded requirements;
- Procedure for preparing invoices and where they should be submitted; and
- Payment address of the seller.

Section H. Special Contract Requirements

This section is reserved for contract clauses specifically tailored for each contract (e.g., warranty) and for agency-unique clauses. Policies concerning placement of clauses in Section H vary among agencies and even among buying offices within an agency. Special requirements that may be found in Section H include:

- Government furnished property or facilities;
- Options;
- Technical data;
- Payment of incentive fee;
- Key personnel;
- Limitation of government obligation;
- Savings clause;
- Foreign sources;
- Total system performance responsibility;
- Organizational conflict of interest; and
- Multiyear funding.

Government personnel have several hundred clauses and provisions in FAR 52 to choose from in drafting Section H. Obviously, not every clause will be appropriate for every solicitation. Every clause included in this section (and in section I) must be there for a reason—either it is required by regulation or it is necessary for the administration of the contract. Solicitations and contracts often contain clauses that have been included because of habit or standard operating procedure, without regard to their applicability. Unneeded clauses add to contract cost and have the potential of raising objections from contractors.

Section I. Contract Clauses

Clauses required by law or regulation are contained in this section and are commonly referred to as the boilerplate. Most clauses are incorporated by reference by citing the clause number, title, date, and regulation source. Clauses are incorporated in full text if:

- The seller is required to complete it;
- A deviation is required;
- The FAR specifically requires full text;
- The clause is published below head of agency level;

- The chief of the contracting office directs; or
- The clause is based on a FAR or agency regulation but will not be used verbatim.

Section J. List of Attachments

This section is used for requirements that do not fit into any of the other sections. The FAR provides little guidance on format or content for attachments, although it does direct the contracting officer to provide a listing of the title, date, and number of pages for any document attached. Some agencies use this section to append lengthy statements of work or specifications. Items that may be found in Section J include:

- Work breakdown structure;
- System specification;
- Engineering drawings;
- Contract data requirements list (CDRL);
- Contract security classification specification;
- Government furnished property;
- Base support list; and
- Test plan.

Section K. Representations, Certifications, and Other Statements of Bidders

The solicitation provisions listed in Section K are used to assist the contracting officer in determining the eligibility of the offeror for award. The matrices in FAR Subpart 52.3 guide the contracting officer in selecting appropriate provisions. Some provisions relate to compliance with law or regulation (e.g., Affirmative Action Compliance, Clean Air and Water Certification); others relate to the status of the seller (e.g., Small Business Concern Representation); others relate to contract formation (e.g., Period of Acceptance Offers); and still others relate to contract performance (e.g., Buy American Certificate). After award, the contracting officer retains the completed Section K, although it is incorporated into the contract by reference.

Contracting officers generally accept self-certification by the seller unless there is reason to challenge it or it is challenged by another contractor. In addition to being ineligible for award, contractors may be prosecuted for false statements.

Section L. Instructions, Conditions, and Notices to Bidders

This section provides information to potential offerors to help them prepare proposals. Matrices contained in FAR Subpart 52.3 provide guidance to the contracting officer on selecting solicitation provisions.

In complex acquisitions, this section may include very detailed proposal preparation instructions to facilitate the evaluation. The government may, for example, specify the number of volumes, their organizational structure and content, page limitations, or any other required features of the proposal.

Section M. Evaluation Factors for Award

In this section, the government identifies the criteria, including significant subcriteria, that will be sued to select the winning contractor.

In sealed bidding, award is made to the lowest responsive and responsible bidder. The criteria are limited to price and price-related factors. Price-related factors may include:

- Costs or delays resulting from differences in inspection, location of supplies, and transportation;
- Changes to the solicitation requested by a bidder (so long as it is not grounds for rejection of the bid);
- Costs or savings that could result from making multiple awards;
- Federal, state, and local taxes; and
- Application of Buy American Act or other prohibition on foreign purchases.

In negotiated procurements, the government selects and weights evaluation criteria to reflect their relative importance. Typical criteria include technical, management, and cost. If no relative order is explicitly stated, the evaluation criteria should be tailored to each acquisition.Cost or price must always be a criterion. Award may be made to the lowest priced, technically acceptable offer or to the offer that represents the "best value" to the government, depending on the objectives of each procurement. Best-value analysis is typically used for research and development contracts and cost-reimbursement contracts where cost is not the deciding factor in the selection decision.[22]

SUMMARY

In this chapter, we have discussed the following ten best practices:

Planning Contract Negotiations
1. Understand how to influence federal government buying appropriately and ethically;
2. Have an acceptable cost estimating and accounting system;
3. Understand the legal Framework of federal government contracts;
4. Understand the Truth In Negotiations Act (TINA);
5. Know the key federal government acquisition thresholds;

Conducting Contract Negotiations
6. Negotiating for best value;
7. Use the power of oral presentations;
8. Know how to win a GSA federal supply schedule contract;

Documenting Contract Negotiations
9. Use of a price negotiation memorandum (PNM); and
10. Use of the Uniform Contract Format (UCF).

In the next chapter, we will briefly discuss some of the proven effective best practices when negotiating commercial (nongovernment) contracts within the United States.

QUESTIONS TO CONSIDER

1. Do you understand how to influence U.S. Federal Government buying appropriately and ethically?

2. Does your organization/company have an acceptable cost estimating and accounting system?

3. Do you understand the legal framework of federal government contracts?

4. Do you understand the requirements of the Truth In Negotiations Act?

5. Does your company use the power of oral presentations to win more business?

6. How well does your organization develop Price Negotiation Memorandums (PNMs)?

ENDNOTES

[1] The Armed Services Pricing Manual, Vol. I, 1996.
[2] Lubeck, Jeffrey A., Beyond an Adequate Accounting System, *Contract Management Magazine,* NCMA, May 2004.
[3] *Ibid.*
[4] Walker, Darryl, L., Is Your Estimating System Asking for Trouble, *Contract Management Magazine,* NCMA, May 2004.
[5] *Ibid.*
[6] Hernandez, Richard J. and Delane F. Moeller, Negotiating a Quality Contract, NCMA, 1992.
[7] *Ibid.*
[8] *Ibid.*
[9] Nash, Ralph C., Jr. and John Cibinic, Formation of Government Contracts 3d, Washington, D.C., CCH Incorporated, 1998.
[10] *Ibid.*
[11] *Ibid* Note 6.
[12] The Federal Acquisition Regulation, CCH Incorporated, July 2004.
[13] *Ibid* Note 9.
[14] *Ibid* Note 6.
[15] *Ibid* Note 6.

[16] DeVore, C. & Moler, T., US Department of Defense B&P Expenditures on the Rise, *Proposal Management*, 11-12, Fall/Winter 2002.

[17] *Ibid.*

[18] http://www.orgcom.com/newsletter/newsletter2.html. retrieved on Oct. 27, 2003.

[19] Kausal, B.A., Thoughts on Oral Proposals, *Program Manager*, 22-27, Sept./Oct. 1998.

[20] Newsletter from Steward Systems, Inc., 2004.

[21] *Ibid.*

[22] *Ibid* Note 6.

Commercial Contract Negotiations— Correcting Misconceptions and Applying Best Practices

INTRODUCTION

In the highly competitive U.S. commercial marketplace, most companies must try to hold down the cost of getting goods and services to market while still ensuring quality, on-time delivery, and customer satisfaction. World-class companies continually benchmark, internally and externally, to discover innovative and proven practices that can offer better results. Prominent among these practices are effective means of contract management, especially excellent contract negotiation skills.

Similarly, federal, state, and local governments are seeking ways to provide more to their constituents with less. The federal government is reexamining its own, often highly regulated, processes for buying and selling. All sectors of government are therefore looking to the private sector or commercial marketplace for streamlined contract management models to do business better, faster, and cheaper.

To help organizations in pursuing these goals, this chapter explains some common misconceptions about U.S. commercial contract management and provides a summary of of the most important commercial best practices for planning, conducting, and documenting contract negotiations.

CORRECTING MISCONCEPTIONS

- *Misconception:* Commercial contracting differs so radically from federal government contracting that parallels cannot be drawn.

■ *Reality:* Commercial and government contracting share many common skills, including contract negotiations, processes, phases, functions, procedures, and challenges. Many differences are rapidly diminishing, so even greater similarities will emerge in the coming years.

■ *Misconception:* The Uniform Commercial Code (UCC) is a clear, precise document that uniformly and specifically governs all commercial transactions throughout the United States.

■ *Reality:* On most points, the UCC's guidance is anything but clear and precise. It does not attempt to provide the type of detailed, step-by-step guidance provided by the Federal Acquisition Regulation system, nor does it prescribe contract clauses. Numerous UCC articles are vague and subject to interpretation. Furthermore, the UCC's articles come into play only when a contractual dispute arises and the matter must be arbitrated or settled in the courts.

Developed and adopted in the 1950s and 1960s, the UCC was intended only to provide broad guidance on conducting commerce within the United States. Moreover, as a product of its times, the UCC primarily addresses the commercial transactions that were most prevalent when it was introduced—transactions for the sale of manufactured goods—as opposed to the more complex procurements of services and systems that prevail today. Many individual states have adopted their own modifications to the UCC, which complicates the situation, because the rules applied in a legal proceeding in one state may differ from those applied in another.

■ *Misconception:* All private-sector or commercial companies use the same, or similar, standard terms and conditions in their contracts for goods and services.

■ *Reality:* No set of standard terms and conditions exists for U.S. commercial contracts. Each company develops its own standard terms and conditions and then tailors them to meet the requirements of specific contract negotiations or business arrangements.

■ *Misconception:* Commercial contracts do not require any contract documentation.

■ *Reality:* Per UCC Article 2, commercial contracts in the United States for the sale of goods valued at more than US $500 must be written. However, many countries do not require contracts between companies within their boundaries to be written. Thus, oral contracts are binding and, indeed, quite common in many countries, including Mexico, Brazil, Argentina, France, South Korea, Ukraine, and Chile. As more multinational contracts are negotiated and formed, ongoing contract documentation—modifications, invoices, meeting notes, payments, and correspondence—is increasingly critical and the maintenance of such documentation increasingly practiced.

■ *Misconception:* Contract managers tend to be highly trained, highly experienced, excellent contract negotiators, and professionally certified.

■ *Reality:* It depends! Although many contract managers fit this description, most have little experience, have received little or no professional training or continuing education in contract management, are not master contract negotiators, and are not certified by a recognized professional association or accredited university. Although thousands are certified in either purchasing management or contract management, many more are not. Many companies hire only well-trained, experienced, certified contract managers, often because they do not want to invest in training a person in the basics. Many other companies have internal training programs for contract management personnel, but those programs are frequently taught by company managers who are not experienced instructors and who teach primarily the company's own practices. Some companies use the training programs of organizations such as the National Contract Management Association, the Institute for Supply Management, the American Management Association, or various institutions of higher learning. Yet, most of these educational programs are limited, because they focus on the buyer's, as opposed to the seller's side of the contracting equation. Most of these educational programs only offer very basic training in negotiations, often not specific to contract negotiations. Increasingly, however, companies are recognizing the value of well-trained, professionally certified managers in contracting and in accounting, engineering, project management, and numerous other related professions.

USING U.S. COMMERCIAL BEST PRACTICES TO IMPROVE NEGOTIATION RESULTS

Use a contract management and negotiation methodology: Every company should have a logical, organized, yet flexible process by which it buys and sells goods and services. An effective contract management methodology thoroughly addresses the entire buying and selling process. It sets forth all steps required and clearly defines the roles and responsibilities of everyone involved. Some companies have such a process in place to detail the roles and responsibilities of employees in all stages of an acquisition, from sales through negotiation, contract formation through project management and contract administration; to set forth all the steps required; and to clearly define the roles and responsibilities of everyone involved.

Commit to a contract management professional development program: As business transactions become increasingly customized and complex, more organizations are recognizing that successful contract management, including contract negotiation, requires trained, experienced, professional personnel, not simply clerks. Villanova University, Regis University, The George Washington University, and other universities have established a professional development program composed of continuing education training leading to a master's certificate in commercial contract management.

Establish a list of prequalified suppliers: Many private-sector companies are taking this proactive approach, widely practiced among government agencies. Potential suppliers are screened in advance to determine which are qualified for subsequent contract negotiation opportunities. Buying lead time is thus reduced.

Take advantage of electronic commerce or electronic data interchange: Many private-sector entities, like many federal government agencies, use electronic means of issuing solicitations, submitting bids and proposals, forming contracts, awarding contracts, exchanging contract correspondence, submitting invoices, and receiving payments. Many large manufacturers and retailers, in fact, are requiring that their suppliers institute an electronic data interchange to reduce cycle time, cut costs, increase productivity, and improve customer service.

Use corporate credit cards: More companies are using credit cards to simplify relatively small-scale or routine purchases. Most establish clear controls, including dollar thresholds, limited access, and specific purchasing guidelines. Cycle times, internal documentation, and overhead costs are all being lowered through this practice. The need to spend time negotiating deals for small purchases of commercially available off-the-shelf items is eliminated.

Adopt value-based pricing when sensible: Value-based pricing, sometimes called customer-based pricing, is top down rather than cost based. Instead of pricing products and services by estimating the cost to manufacture or provide them and then adding a desired margin, value-based pricing focuses on the customer's needs and the benefits the customer expects to reap. In other words, it offers a sound business rationale for charging more for the same products and service, thereby increasing profitability. Success in practicing value-based pricing is often closely linked to an individual's contract negotiation skills.

Use universal sales agreements: Such agreements—in the form of distributor agreements, supply agreements, master agreements, framework agreements, basic ordering agreements, and more—are widely used in commercial contracting. They greatly reduce administrative time, effort, and paperwork by establishing a mutually agreed-on set of terms and conditions that will apply to all business transactions made pursuant to the agreement. Universal sales agreements allow contract negotiators to get deals set up faster and then focus on tailoring the terms and conditions (Ts and Cs) to the specific purchase order as needed.

Conduct risk versus opportunity assessment: Nothing is more profitable than a good bid/no-bid decision. The ability to make informed bid/no-bid decisions, intelligently weighing risk against opportunity, is critical in today's highly competitive marketplace. Many companies have developed sophisticated tools that help their managers identify and quantify both risk and opportunity. Remember, risk must either be limited by the Ts and Cs or be priced into the contract.

Simplify standard contract terms and conditions: Too many companies use standard Ts and Cs that are needlessly wordy, overly legalistic, and difficult to understand. More companies are realizing that such Ts and Cs are viewed negatively by the other party and constitute obstacles to successful business deals. Some are attacking the problem head-on by rewriting their standard Ts and Cs in language that is clear, concise, and easy for all parties involved to understand. Master contract negotiators understand the power, value, and risk associated with Ts and Cs.

Permit oral presentation of proposals: This time-saving practice is increasingly used by purchasing organizations worldwide. Most establish a few presentation guidelines and state them expressly in their solicitations to ensure that all competing sellers use the same rules. Master contract negotiators understand the value of oral presentations and when to use them.

Employ highly skilled contract negotiators: For many years, companies have realized the value of developing and maintaining a team or group of master contract negotiators to negotiate the megadeals for their organizations.

Conduct mock contract negotiations: Many headaches can be avoided and a lot of money saved by conducting mock contract negotiations internally before the actual negotiations. The primary purpose of conducting mock contract negotiations is to be fully prepared for the actual contract negotiations with the other party. Mock contract negotiations may be face-to-face meetings or they may be videoconferences, teleconferences, net-meetings, or a combination of these venues.

Adopt a uniform solicitation, proposal, and contract format: The logical, organized approach of issuing all solicitations in a common format, requiring that proposals follow the same format, and awarding contracts that use the format has been used by the federal government for many years. Although only a few private-sector entities use this practice, it greatly simplifies the source selection and proposal evaluation process and facilitates contract management for both parties.

Develop and maintain a negotiation best-practices and lessons-learned database: Corporations are increasingly realizing the value of maintaining a database containing comprehensive information—both current and historical—about customers, suppliers, contract negotiation plans, negotiation results, and actual contracts. The database, ideally in electronic form, must be user friendly and accessible to all appropriate personnel. Few companies pursue this practice and even fewer pursue it well, primarily because of the initial and continuing investment in cost, time, and effort. Yet that investment can pale in comparison with the benefits of significant cost avoidance, increased customer satisfaction, and more successful long-term business relationships.

SUMMARY

The learning process is a two-way street. As illustrated by several items in the discussion of best practices, those responsible for contract negotiation in the commercial realm are benefiting by adopting practices long used by government, just as government contract managers are benefiting from adopting commercial best practices.

What matters most is that the senior leadership of an organization realizes the value of contract negotiation as a critical aspect of integrated business management. For sellers, it is not enough to have good sales managers and quality products and services—an organization must have professional contract negotiators to successfully manage the entire contract negotiation process. For buyers, it is not enough to know what they need to purchase—organizations must have a process to ensure that they effectively communicate their needs, select the right source, negotiate a successful contract, and obtain quality products and services. The contract negotiation process and the more than 400 best practices described in this book will contribute to more effective business management only when adopted with foresight and implemented with commitment by everyone.

Teamwork is the essential element of business success. In today's highly complex commercial world of integrated products (hardware and software), services, and business solutions, it takes a highly talented, focused, and multi-functional team to deliver results, with buyers and sellers working together as business partners.

QUESTIONS TO CONSIDER

1 How many of the best practices discussed in this chapter does your organization routinely practice?

2 What other commercial best practices does your organization practice?

3 How well educated and trained are your organization's contract managers, sales managers, and/or purchasing managers in commercial contracting/negotiation best practices?

Multinational/Global Contract Negotiation— Best Practices

INTRODUCTION

Clearly, negotiating contracts outside the borders of the United States has numerous unique political, cultural, socio-economic, and technological aspects. This chapter focuses on the following key points:

- Globalization—What is It?
- Global Thinking
- Multinational Trade Organizations and Agreements
- Global Marketing and Sales
- What it Takes to Win Business Globally
- Negotiating Around the World - Best Practices Scorecard
- 20 Best Practices - When Using an Interpreter
- 15 Best Practices for Cross-Cultural Negotiations

GLOBALIZATION—WHAT IS IT?

Globalization can be defined in several ways, depending on the level you choose to focus on. You can speak of globalization of the entire world, a single country, a specific industry, a specific company or even a particular line of business or function within a company. At the worldwide level, globalization refers to the growing economic interdependence among countries as reflected in increasing cross-border flows of goods, services, capital, and know-how. At the level of a specific country, globalization refers to the extent of the linkages between a country's economy and the rest of the world. At the level of specific industry, globalization refers to the degree to which a company's competitive position within an industry in one country is interdependent on its position in another country.

Clearly, since the terrible terrorist attacks of September 11, 2001, on the United States, the entire world has been forced to reevaluate how the complex process of globalization will continue to evolve. In fact, most organizations and companies are continually evaluating the changing characteristics that shape the global business environment.

GLOBAL THINKING

In order to make globalization work, you must practice global thinking. There are three critical dimensions to global thinking:
- Understand global sources of demand!
- Understand global sources of supply!
- Understand global marketing, sales, and execution!
- Or said differently, know the following better than your competitors:
  - How to market to worldwide buyers;
  - How to source more efficiently; and
  - How to sell, manufacture, and distribute more effectively.

Global Sources of Demand—IBM, Toys R Us, and NCR are three very different companies with very different products and services, yet they all have successfully mastered global thinking and the art of globalization. All three understand the multinational demands for their respective products and services, especially in developed countries with higher per capita income.

Toys R Us for example has learned the opportunities and challenges one must face in the $6 Billion Japanese toy market. Likewise, NCR has made considerable international investments in Europe, Japan, and South America to penetrate the multi-billion dollar automated teller machine, optical scanner, and computer cash register markets. IBM likewise realizes the tremendous global demand of businesses both large and small to outsource computer support services.

Global Sources of Supply—The Limited is regarded as one of the world's most successful apparel retailers. While all of The Limited's retail outlets are located inside the United States, it successfully established global sourcing practices. The process of product design to shipment of garments to individual stores takes less than 60 days, which is a dramatically reduced cycle time compared to its competitors. In addition, superior global supply-chain management allows The Limited to have its garments designed by numerous companies throughout Europe, produced in Asian and other countries by local manufacturers, and shipped via global logistics networks to Columbus, Ohio, where they are distributed to thousands of retail outlets including The Limited Express, Victoria's Secret, Abercrombie and Fitch, Lerner, and Henri Bendel.

Global Sales, Manufacturing and Execution—ABB has successfully learned that as companies become global in scope, managers face increased responsibility for marketing and sales to foreign countries and managing adaptation to significant cultural differences. ABB helps key managers develop their cultural awareness and foreign language skills and provides them the opportunity to manage multi-national programs while fully utilizing the support of local subcontractors and local country hires to execute most of the actual work.

Global thinking is critical to the success of many companies. Globalization is not limited to large corporations like General Motors (GM), IBM, Sony, Phillips, Ikea, Honda, and McDonalds. Small firms tend to be more flexible, which allows them to quickly and effectively adapt to local markets often far better than large firms. In fact, over 80 percent of the more than 100,000 companies in the United States that export are small businesses.

Both large and small business throughout the United States and the world are forming partnerships or alliances to leverage strengths in order to help each of the partners sell more products and services. For example, in November 2002, Sun Microsystems and Lucent Technologies announced their global partnership to target sales of their products and related services for wireline, wireless, and enterprise customers worldwide.

MULTINATIONAL TRADE ORGANIZATION AND AGREEMENTS

The first real attempt to form a world trade organization after World War II failed because the U.S. Congress refused to ratify the proposed agreement. Later, in 1947, 23 nations signed a document called the General Agreement on Tariffs and Trade (GATT). Almost 40 years later, the Secretariat of the GATT effectively evolved into the World Trade Organization (WTO).

THE GATT

The GATT essentially served as an international forum focused on increasing international trade. It accomplished its mission by bringing member nations together in meetings called rounds to negotiate reductions in their respective import duties. The GATT also served as an important forum for discussion and settlement of trade disputes. The GATT expanded to cover more than 100 nations.

The Uruguay Round

The Uruguay Round of the GATT lasted for several years and resulted in numerous agreements, which were signed by 113 countries on May 3, 1994. Agreements were reached in the following areas of international trade.

- Agriculture;
- Preshipment inspection;
- Import licensing procedures;
- Rules of origin;
- Trade in services;
- Trade-related aspects of intellectual property rights;
- Rules and procedures governing settlement of disputes;
- Trade in civil aircraft;
- Government procurement;
- Dairy products; and
- Other areas.

THE WTO

The World Trade Organization (WTO) was on established April 15, 1995. Its mission is to provide a common framework for the conduct of international trade among member nations. The WTO holds a meeting of its trade ministers every two years. WTO meetings were held in 1996, 1998, 2000, 2002, and 2004 at various cities worldwide. Despite some protests at each of the meetings, the WTO has grown in both members and influence since its inception. Today 141 nations are members of the WTO, including China, who joined on January 1, 2002.

The WTO has numerous councils that meet more often than the general meeting. The WTO Councils include the General Council, which acts as a forum to settle trade disputes, a Council for Trade in Goods, and a Council for Trade-Related Aspects of Intellectual Property Rights. In addition, the WTO has established numerous committees including: Trade and Development Committee, Budget Committee, and Finance and Administration Committee. The former Secretariat of the GATT became the Secretariat of the WTO. Simply said, the WTO is a legal entity that serves as the champion of fair trade worldwide.

NAFTA

The North American Free Trade Agreement (NAFTA) was signed in December 1992 and was ratified by the United States, Canada, and Mexico on January 1, 1994. NAFTA to a large extent was an expansion of the U.S.–Canada Free Trade Agreement, which was ratified fives years earlier. The mission of NAFTA is to increase trilateral trade and investment through the elimination of both tariff and nontariff barriers over time.

NAFTA requires a special Certificate of Origin form, which must be used for all shipments for which NAFTA duty rates are requested. NAFTA also covers trade in services, investment, protection of intellectual property rights, and settlement of disputes. NAFTA has been successful in increasing both trade and investment between all three countries. For more information, see the official NAFTA website www.nafta-sec-alen.org.

EU AND EFTA

As of May 1, 2004, the European Union (EU) had grown to 25 nations and is likely to continue to grow. The EU cooperates closely with the European Free Trade Association (EFTA), which consists of four additional countries not currently in the EU. Clearly, the EU and EFTA have placed U.S. and Canadian exports to Europe at a disadvantage, because they face entry barriers that are not faced by any of the member nations of the EU and EFTA. Mexico faces far fewer barriers to its exports to Europe because it receives special consideration under the EU's Generalized System of Preferences. For more information about the EU, see the website, www.s700.uminho.pt/ec.html.

GLOBAL MARKETING AND SALES

In the late 1990s, the international business theme of ABB and other successful multinational enterprises was to "Think Globally, but, Act Locally." Today, the new global business theme is to "Think Globally and Locally, but Act Appropriately." It is far harder to sell many products and services worldwide than in just a single country. Globalization presents both great sales opportunities and significant business challenges and expenses.

Figure 10-1 illustrates the key determinants of market competitiveness in the globalizing industries and the external forces that act on each of the key determinants.

Figure 10-1.

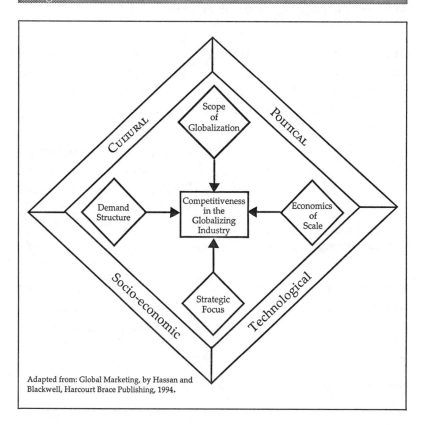

Adapted from: Global Marketing, by Hassan and
Blackwell, Harcourt Brace Publishing, 1994.

Scope of Globalization—A company's decision as to how much
or how far they want to expand their marketing and the sales
potential of their respective products or services in a particular
industry dictates the degree of standardization of the marketing
program and process. The greater the multi-national presence,
the more customized marketing and increased local investment
is required.

Economies of Scale—A company's decision to go global can expand the sourcing opportunities for labor and subcontracting. It
can also provide for increased economies of scale in research and
development, product design, manufacturing, assembly, testing,
and packaging procedures, thus reducing unit costs. However,
some savings associated with economies of scale will be offset

by increased costs associated with investments in localizing the product or services to a specific market.

Strategic Focus—When going global, a company must decide which countries to target, which market segments to focus on within the selected countries, and how much they are willing to spend to penetrate those markets to win more business.

Demand Structure—Real competitiveness in globalizing industries can be achieved only by understanding the needs of the customer, adapting to local requirements, and establishing close partnerships with the customer and suppliers. Local investments for manufacturing, subcontracting, local offices, local country hires, etc. are becoming more critical to global success.

External Forces—There are numerous factors that potentially impact a company's ability to successfully market and sell more products and services on a multinational scale, including the following:

Economic Forces

- Inflation rate;
- Unemployment rate;
- New and evolving markets;
- Labor rates;
- Tariffs/taxes;
- Standard of living;
- Customs process;
- Exchange rate;
- Stock market stability;
- Currency stability; and
- Degree of competition in the market.

Technological Forces

- Technology adaptation rate;
- Telecommunications infrastructure;
- Internet availability and usage;

- Rate of technological change;
- Degree of technical standards; and
- Technology transfer requirements.

Political Forces

- Protectionist laws and regulations;
- Support of multinational enterprises;
- Political stability:
  - Legislative changes;
  - Judicial changes; and
  - Executive changes;
- Local hiring regulations;
- Commercial sales code;
- Counter-trade requirements;
- Offset rules;
- Co-production requirements; and
- Licensing/taxes.

Cultural Forces

- Local Customs;
- Language;
- Need for local presence (office/facilities); and
- Local country hires

If a company is serious about going global, the aforementioned key determinants of market competitiveness and the related external forces must all be appropriately factored into the opportunity and risk assessment.

WHAT IT TAKES TO WIN BUSINESS GLOBALLY

Some people believe that globalization is an attitude, not knowledge or information. Stephen Rhinesmith has stated that a global mindset is a requirement of a global business manager who will guide institutions and organizations into the future. He defines a mindset as:

A predisposition to see the world in a particular way that sets boundaries and provides explanations for why things are the way they are, while at the same time establishing guidance for ways in which we should behave. In other words, a mindset is a filter through which we look at the world.

Rhinesmith explains that people with global mindsets approach the world in a number of specific ways, including:

- Looking for the big picture, they look for multiple possibilities;
- Understanding the world is very complex and business is interdependent;
- Being process-oriented, understanding that all business follows a process of inputs, tools and techniques, and outputs;
- Considering diversity in people as a real asset and valued resource, they know how to work effectively in multicultural teams;
- Being comfortable with change and ambiguity; and
- Being open to new experiences and enjoying a challenge.

While a global mindset or attitude is vital to winning business worldwide, there are several additional factors or competencies that are essential for success.

Clearly, globalization requires global thinking by both individuals and whole organizations working in harmony. Globalization for many organizations is a paradigm shift in both thinking and doing. Understanding key global trade agreements and how they impact your business either positively or negatively is critical to success. Understanding how to translate the knowledge of doing business internationally into a practical list of actions for both individuals and organizations is what will ultimately determine your success or failure in winning business on a multinational or global scale. As in all business, talk, while important is cheap—it is your execution and demonstrated performance that will help your company build trust and maintain customer loyalty both domestically and globally.

NEGOTIATING AROUND THE WORLD: BEST PRACTICES SCORECARD

After years of research, and many years of traveling around the world to six continents and more than 40 countries doing business, teaching, consulting, negotiating, and managing large complex contracts and projects, I have documented the following list of ten best practices for negotiating deals in various regions of the world. Further, I have created a scorecard of these ten best practices, so you can see how and when to apply the best practices when negotiating around the world. My research and experience have blended to form my perception of what are arguably some well documented business practices, all intended to help you to benefit from the combined experience of many others. To understand the color-coding on the respective regional best practices scorecard, I offer the following guidance:[1]

Red = R (Low - probability of success when using this best practice)

Yellow = Y (Moderate - probability of success when using this best practice)

Green = G (High - probability of success when using this best practice)

Form 10-1. Western Europe Contract Negotiation Best Practices

Scorecard	Red (low)	Yellow (moderate)	Green (high)
1. Focus on the business relationship		Y	
2. Get the deal done quickly		Y	
3. Use an agent/representative		Y	
4. Ensure detailed Ts and Cs			G
5. Document, document, document		Y to	G
6. Control the negotiation tone			G
7. Use a negotiation agenda			G
8. Ensure everyone saves face		Y	
9. Leverage personal relationships	R to	Y	
10. Obtain reviews & approvals		Y to	G

Form 10-2. Eastern Europe Contract Negotiation Best Practices

Scorecard	Red (low)	Yellow (moderate)	Green (high)
1. Focus on the business relationship	R		
2. Get the deal done quickly	R		
3. Use an agent/representative		Y	
4. Ensure detailed Ts and Cs		Y	
5. Document, document, document			G
6. Control the negotiation tone			G
7. Use a negotiation agenda			G
8. Ensure everyone saves face		Y to	G
9. Leverage personal relationships	R		
10. Obtain reviews & approvals			G

Form 10-3. Caribbean & Latin America Contract Negotiation Best Practices

Scorecard	Red (low)	Yellow (moderate)	Green (high)
1. Focus on the business relationship			G
2. Get the deal done quickly	R		
3. Use an agent/representative		Y	
4. Ensure detailed Ts and Cs		Y	
5. Document, document, document	R to	Y	
6. Control the negotiation tone		Y	
7. Use a negotiation agenda		Y	
8. Ensure everyone saves face			G
9. Leverage personal relationships			G
10. Obtain reviews & approvals			G

Form 10-4. Middle East & Africa Contract Negotiation Best Practices

Scorecard	Red (low)	Yellow (moderate)	Green (high)
1. Focus on the business relationship		Y	
2. Get the deal done quickly	R to	Y	
3. Use an agent/representative			G
4. Ensure detailed Ts and Cs		Y	
5. Document, document, document	R to	Y	
6. Control the negotiation tone		Y	
7. Use a negotiation agenda	R to	Y	
8. Ensure everyone saves face			G
9. Leverage personal relationships			G
10. Obtain reviews & approvals			G

Form 10-5. Asia/Pacific Contract Negotiation Best Practices

Scorecard	Red (low)	Yellow (moderate)	Green (high)
1. Focus on the business relationship		Y	
2. Get the deal done quickly	R		
3. Use an agent/representative		Y	
4. Ensure detailed Ts and Cs		Y to	G
5. Document, document, document		Y to	G
6. Control the negotiation tone		Y	
7. Use a negotiation agenda		Y	
8. Ensure everyone saves face			G
9. Leverage personal relationships			G
10. Obtain reviews & approvals		Y to	G

Form 10-6. North American Contract Negotiation Best Practices

Scorecard	Red (low)	Yellow (moderate)	Green (high)
1. Focus on the business relationship		Y to	G
2. Get the deal done quickly			G
3. Use an agent/representative	R		
4. Ensure detailed Ts and Cs		Y to	G
5. Document, document, document		Y to	G
6. Control the negotiation tone			G
7. Use a negotiation agenda			G
8. Ensure everyone saves face	R to	Y	
9. Leverage personal relationships		Y	
10. Obtain reviews & approvals		Y	

Twenty Best Practices When Using an Interpreter

Although English is indeed a global language, use the following best practices whenever it is necessary to use an interpreter:

■ Brief the interpreter in advance about the subject. Consult a dictionary ahead of time when working with technical material.

■ Speak clearly and slowly.

■ Avoid strange and little-known words.

■ Reiterate: Explain major points in two or three different ways so that they are clear.

■ Limit yourself to no more than 20 to 30 words, and then allow the interpreter time to interpret.

■ Do not begin speaking again until the interpreter has finished the previous sentences.

■ Do not lose confidence in an interpreter who uses a dictionary.

■ Permit the interpreter time to clarify complex points with obscure meanings.

■ Allow the interpreter time to take notes on what is said.

■ Do not interupt a translator who is interpreting, because it causes misunderstandings.

■ Avoid long sentences, double negatives in a sentence, and negative syntax when a positive form is available.

■ Avoid superfluous words; your main point may be obscured.

■ Try to be expressive and use gestures (within cultural bounds) to support your verbal messages.

■ During meetings, keep a list of the main points discussed. Both parties can confirm their understanding later.

■ After meetings, confirm in writing what was agreed to.

■ Provide the interpreter a rest period. Do not continue for more than two consecutive hours.

■ Consider using two interpreters for day-long meetings.

■ Do not be concerned if a speaker talks for five minutes and the interpreter's translation lasts 30 seconds.

■ Be understanding when interpreters make mistakes. They are under much pressure and must pay attention to a great deal of dialogue.

■ Ask the interpreter for advice if problems arise.

15 Best Practices for Cross-Cultural Negotiation

- Remain open-minded, step outside your own cultural biases.
- Have respect—this does not necessarily mean agreement.
- Tolerate ambiguity—certain cultures value vagueness and indirect communication.
- Strive for interpersonal communication.
- Be nonjudgmental.
- Practice empathy.
- Be persistent.
- Use appropriate humor.
- Be perceptive.
- Practice active listening.
- Don't try to do it alone.
- Understand that formality—rather than informality—is the rule.
- Understand each party's level of authority.
- Understand silence during negotiations is common to foreign negotiators.
- Be precise in your choice of language.

SUMMARY

This chapter has provided a broad but, information-packed overview of key topics related to multinational/global contract negotiations.

ENDNOTES

[1] The following Best Practices template has been adapted from the book *How to Negotiate Anything with Anyone Anywhere Around the World,* by Frank L. Acuff, AMA, 1997.

Appendix A

Seven Steps to Performance-Based Services Acquisition

INTRODUCTION

A Performance-Based Preference

Over the last decade, innovators in Congress and the executive branch have reformed the laws and policies that govern Federal acquisition. Among the most important of these reforms are the Government Performance and Results Act of 1993, the Federal Acquisition Streamlining Act of 1994 (FASA), and the Clinger-Cohen Act of 1996. All of these laws send an important message about performance in federal programs and acquisitions.

As is evident from the dates above, performance-based service acquisition is not new. Office of Federal Procurement Policy Pamphlet #4, "A Guide for Writing and Administering Performance Statements of Work for Service Contracts," (now rescinded) described "how to write performance into statements of work" and addressed job analysis, surveillance plans, and quality control in 1980. Eleven years later, OFPP Policy Letter 91-2, Service Contracting, established that:

> It is the policy of the Federal Government that (1) agencies use performance-based contracting methods to the maximum extent practicable when acquiring services, and (2) agencies carefully select acquisition and contract administration strategies, methods, and techniques that best accommodate the requirements.

The intent is for agencies to describe their needs in terms of what is to be achieved, not how it is to be done. These policies have been incorporated in the Federal Acquisition Regulation Subpart 37.6 (Performance-Based Contracting), and additional guidance is in the OFPP document, "A Guide to Best Practices for Performance-Based Service Contracting." (OFPP Policy Letter 91-2 was rescinded effective March 30, 2000.)

Law and regulation establish a preference for performance-based service acquisition. The new Administration continues a long line of support for this acquisition approach, as demonstrated in OMB Memorandum M-01-15 on performance goals and management initiatives. As cited in the Procurement Executives Council's Strategic Plan:

> *...over the next five years, a majority of the service contracts offered throughout the federal government will be performance-based. In other words, rather than micromanaging the details of how contractors operate, the government must set the standards, set the results and give the contractor the freedom to achieve it in the best way.*

—Presidential Candidate George W. Bush on June 9, 2000

Benefits of Performance-Based Acquisition

Performance-based service acquisition has many benefits. They include:

- Increased likelihood of meeting mission needs
- Focus on intended results, not process
- Better value and enhanced performance
- Less performance risk
- No detailed specification or process description needed
- Contractor flexibility in proposing solution
- Better competition: not just contractors, but solutions
- Contractor buy-in and shared interests
- Shared incentives permit innovation and cost effectiveness
- Less likelihood of a successful protest
- Surveillance: less frequent, more meaningful

- Results documented for Government Performance and Results Act reporting, as by-product of acquisition
- Variety of solutions from which to choose

Moving toward Performance-Based Competency

The federal acquisition workforce has not, to date, fully embraced performance-based acquisition. There are many reasons, such as workload demands, but more fundamentally, traditional "acquisition think" is entrenched in a workforce of dwindling numbers. The situation is complicated by lack of "push" from the program offices who have the mission needs and who fund the acquisitions... because there is where the true key to performance-based acquisition lies. It is not the procurement analyst, the contracting officer, or even the contracting office itself. Performance-based acquisition is a collective responsibility that involves representatives from budget, technical, contracting, logistics, legal, and program offices.

While there are leaders among us who understand the concept and its potential, it is difficult for an agency to assemble a team of people who together have the knowledge to drive such an acquisition through to successful contract performance. This is especially true today because many more types of people play a role in acquisition teams. These people add fresh perspective, insight, energy, and innovation to the process — but they may lack some of the rich contractual background and experience that acquisition often requires.

Performance-based service acquisition can be daunting, with its discussion of work breakdown structures, quality assurance plans, and contractor surveillance. Guides on the subject can easily run to and over 50, 75, or even 100 pages. This makes learning something new appear more complicated than it really is. The foundation for a successful acquisition involves a clear answer to three questions: *what do I need, when do I need it, and how do I know it's good when I get it?*

The virtual guide on which this downloadable guide is based breaks down performance-based service acquisition into seven easy steps, complete with "stories" (case studies). It is intended to make the subject of PBSC accessible for all and shift the paradigm from traditional "acquisition think" into one of collaborative performance-oriented teamwork with a focus on program performance and improvement, not simply contract compliance. Once the shift is made, the library and links sections interwoven in the virtual guide will lead you into the rich web of federal performance-based guidance.

Have a good journey!

EXECUTIVE SUMMARY

One of the most important challenges facing agencies today is the need for widespread adoption of performance-based acquisition to meet mission and program needs. This Administration has set a goal for FY 2002 in OMB Memorandum M-01-15 to "award contracts over $25,000 using PBSC techniques for not less than 20 percent of the total eligible service contracting dollars," increasing to 50 percent by FY 2005.

Although policies supporting performance-based contracting have been in place for more than 20 years, progress has been slow. The single most important reason for this is that the acquisition community is not the sole owner of the problem, nor can the acquisition community implement performance-based contracting on its own.

Laws, policies, and regulations have dramatically changed the acquisition process into one that must operate with a mission-based and program-based focus. Because of this, many more types of people must play a role in acquisition teams today. In addition to technical and contracting staff, for example, there is "value added" by including those from program and financial offices. These people add fresh perspective, insight, energy, and innovation to the process — but they may lack some of the rich contractual background and experience that acquisition often requires.

This guide, geared to the greater acquisition community (especially program offices), breaks down performance-based service acquisition into seven simple steps.

1. Establish an integrated solutions team
2. Describe the problem that needs solving
3. Examine private-sector and public-sector solutions
4. Develop a performance work statement (PWS) or statement of objectives (SOO)
5. Decide how to measure and manage performance

6. Select the right contractor

7. Manage performance

The intent is to make the subject of performance-based acquisition accessible and logical for all and shift the paradigm from traditional "acquisition think" into one of collaborative, performance-oriented teamwork with a focus on program performance, improvement, and innovation, not simply contract compliance. Performancebased acquisition offers the potential to dramatically transform the nature of service delivery, and permit the federal government to tap the enormous creative energy and innovative nature of private industry.

Let the acquisitions begin!

I. ESTABLISH AN INTEGRATED SOLUTIONS TEAM.

The trend today, given the statutory, policy, and regulatory mandates discussed in the introduction, is that acquisitions are conducted by teams of people, working cooperatively toward a common goal. This is the model used by leading or breakthrough organizations, which have come to recognize the limitations of clearly defined roles, responsibilities, and organizational boundaries... and have adopted the use of acquisition teams that integrate all stakeholders' efforts toward one goal: mission accomplishment. It is also the model that the Office of Management and Budget is seeking when it asks this question of agencies in their budget submissions: "Is there an Integrated Project Team? "

These principles are also reflected in the Federal Acquisition Regulation (FAR), which (1) recognizes that teams begin with the customer and end with the contractor and (2) outlines procurement policies and procedures that are used by members of the acquisition team. Note also that the FAR specifically provides that contracting officers "should take the lead in encouraging business process innovations and ensuring that business decisions are sound."

In this guide, we call such acquisition teams "integrated solutions teams" in acknowledgment of the fundamental purpose of performance-based acquisition: to find solutions to agency mission and program needs.

Tasks, Features, & Best Practices: Learn More

- Ensure senior management involvement and support.
- Tap multi-disciplinary expertise.
- Define roles and responsibilities.
- Develop rules of conduct.
- Empower team members.
- Identify stakeholders and nurture consensus.
- Develop and maintain the knowledge base over the project life.
- "Incent" the team: Establish link between program mission and team members' performance.

Ensure senior management involvement and support.

Most best-practice studies agree: senior management involvement and support is a predictor of success. For example, the CIO Council document, "Implementing Best Practices: Strategies at Work," cited "strong leadership at the top" as a "success factor" in the selection, evaluation and control processes associated with acquisition investment review. By its very nature, an integrated solutions team has members whose affiliations cut across organizational boundaries. "Turf" can become an issue unless there is strong, effective senior management support and a shared vision. Program decision makers should be on the team. Creating "buy in" from leadership and establishing the realms of authority are essential to project success.

Tap multi-disciplinary expertise.

Because of the mission-based and program-based focus of acquisition that has resulted from acquisition reform, many more types of people play a role in acquisition teams today. In addition to contracting staff, for example, are those from the program, financial, user, and even legal offices. All of these skills and more can be required to create a true performance-based approach to an agency's needs.

It is important to recognize that integrated solution teams are not a "training ground." They're a field of operation for not just 4 or 6 or 8 people, but 4 or 6 or 8 people who are among the best in their fields and have a grounding in, or have been trained in acquisition.

Team composition is a critical success factor in performance-based acquisition — so much so, in fact, that the Office of Management and Budget asks about team approach during the budget review process for acquisition funding.

Define roles and responsibilities.

It is important that the members of the team understand what their roles and responsibilities are. Regardless of its representation, the team is responsible for ensuring that the acquisition:

- Satisfies legal and regulatory requirements.
- Has performance and investment objectives consistent with the agency's strategic goals.
- Successfully meets the agency's needs and intended results.
- Remains on schedule and within budget.

Successful teams typically have a number of features: shared leadership roles, individual as well as mutual accountability, collective work-products, performance measures related to the collective workproduct, and other ingredients.

In a team environment, the roles and responsibilities of the members blur and merge, often with striking results.

Develop rules of conduct.

Seasoned facilitators and team leaders know this: It is important to develop rules of conduct for groups of people. Setting the rules... and then insisting on their use... is a key to effective team operation. Given a clear purpose and defined approach for working together, teams are much more likely to achieve the desired result.

The Monash University's Learning Centre has a website on teamwork, which puts the importance of the rules in perspective. It suggests that groups "pass through a sequence of five stages of development:

- forming, or coming together
- storming, or conflict
- norming, or working out the rules
- performing, or getting the job done
- mourning, or breaking up

The length of time different groups take to pass through each of these developmental stages will vary, but it is generally not possible to achieve high team performance until the group has passed through the first three stages."

Empower team members.

The "Statement of Guiding Principles for the Federal Acquisition System," says it most simply: *"Participants in the acquisition process should work together as a team and should be empowered to make decisions within their area of responsibility."* (FAR 1.102(a)) Clearly defined levels of empowerment are critical to success.

The Department of Commerce, in its CONOPS (Concept of Operations) acquisition program, has examined the concept of what "empowerment" means in detail. The Department believes that empowerment is tied to responsibility, authority, and autonomy. In the agency's project planning tool are the life-cycle tasks of an acquisition and an identification of where responsibility for the performance of that task typically resides.

Identify stakeholders and nurture consensus.

Stakeholders may include customers, the public, oversight organizations, and members and staff of Congress. It is important for the team to know who the stakeholders are and the nature of their interests, objectives, and possible objections. At a minimum, stakeholders should be consulted and, at times, may participate on the team.

In developing the acquisition, the key tools the team should use are consensus and compromise, without losing sight of the three key questions:
1. What do I need?
2. When do I need it?
3. How do I know it's good when I get it?

Develop and maintain the knowledge base over the project life.

"How do you predict the future... you create it." (Peter Drucker)

An emerging concern in the acquisition community is "knowledge management." There are many definitions, but the simplest may well be "the right knowledge in the right place at the right time and in the right context." Knowledge management is a people issue, not a technology issue.

Consider the need to manage the project's knowledge base in this light: Acquisitions often take months, and the contracts that are awarded are often performed over years. People join the team and people leave, taking their knowledge with them.

Further, those people that began the project and those that oversee the project are often different. All too often, when a contract is awarded, the acquisition team "pats itself on the back" and walks away. The project is passed into the care of a contract administrator who doesn't know the history of the project, why decisions were made, and why the contract is structured or worded the way it is. Modification may begin right away. And we wonder why contract performance is sometimes a problem?

The approach needs to shift from a focus on contracting to a focus on both acquisition and project management. Where possible, the same key members of the team (program manager, project manager, and contracting officer) should be part of the integrated solutions team from the initial discussions of mission-based need, through contract performance, and indeed to contract closeout. With this continuity, and a focus on maintaining the project's knowledge base, the likelihood of success is exponentially greater.

"Incent" the team: Link program mission and team members' performance.

If continuity is important, what can be done to keep a team together? Added to empowerment and a shared vision, incentives are key. The most fundamental incentives are those that link program mission and team members' performance, and then tie performance to pay. If the acquisition has performance objectives, and the contractor has performance objectives, then the Government team should also have performance objectives. Like contractor incentives, the team's objectives should carry a value in terms of pay, recognition, and awards.

Keep in mind that these performance objectives should be program-based, not acquisition-based. Who cares if the contract is awarded in two months if it takes two years to get deliverables in the hands of the users? Make sure the incentives are tied to the "right" results.

2. DESCRIBE THE PROBLEM THAT NEEDS SOLVING

Because a clearer, performance-based picture of the acquisition should be the team's first step, it is not yet time to retrieve the requirement's former solicitation, search for templates, think about contract type or incentives, decide on the contractor or the solution.

Planning for an acquisition should begin with business planning that focuses on the desired improvement. The first consideration is, what is the problem the agency needs to solve? What results are needed? Will it meet the organizational and mission objectives?

The Government Performance and Results Act of 1993 requires that agencies establish and "manage to" mission-related performance goals and objectives. It stands to reason that any significant, mission-critical acquisition should relate in some way to the Results Act objectives. Although many acquisitions do not make this link, performance-based acquisitions must make this connection to the agency's strategic plan and to employees' performance plans.

Tasks, Features, & Best Practices: Learn More

■ Link acquisition to mission and performance objectives.
■ Define (at a high level) desired results.
■ Decide what constitutes success.
■ Determine the current level of performance.

Link acquisition to mission and performance objectives.

The most effective foundation for an acquisition is the intended effect of the contract in supporting and improving an agency's mission and performance goals and objectives (reported to OMB and Congress under the Results Act's strategic and annual performance planning processes). Describing an acquisition in terms of how it supports these mission-based performance goals allows an agency to establish clearly the relationship of the acquisition to its business, and it sets the stage for crafting an acquisition in which the performance goals of the contractor and the government are in sync.

In addition to the Government Performance and Results Act, the President's Management Agenda has added the requirement for performance-based budgeting. This links funding to performance, and ensures that programs making progress towards achieving their goals will continue to receive funding. Conversely, programs unable to show adequate progress may lose option-year funding.

This mission-based foundation normally must be established by or in cooperation with people who work in the program area that the resources will support when they are acquired. (This is why assembling the team is the first step in a performance-based acquisition.) Again, note that the focus is not what resources are required; the focus is what outcome is required.

With this foundation, when the planning process is complete, an agency should be able to demonstrate clearly how an individual acquisition's performance objectives will assist in achieving the agency's mission and goals.

Define (at a high level) desired results.

Once the acquisition is linked to the agency's mission needs, the thoughts of the team should turn to what, specifically, are the desired results (outcomes) of contract performance? Is it a lower level of defaults on federal loans? Is it a reduction in benefit processing time? Is it broader dissemination of federal information? Is it a reduction in the average time it takes to get relief checks to victims? What is the ultimate intended result of the contract and how does it relate to the agency's strategic plan?

Note that these are questions that a former solicitation... or someone else's solicitation... cannot answer. This is one of the tough tasks that the integrated solutions team must face.

These answers can normally be found, not with an exhaustive analysis, but through facilitated work sessions with program staff, customers, and stakeholders. By taking the process away from a review of paper or an examination of the status quo, greater innovation and insight is possible. Once aired, those thoughts need to be captured in the performance work statement (PWS) or statement of objectives (SOO).

Note also that, to do this well, the team will need to plan to seek information from the private sector during market research (step three). Industry benchmarks and best practices from the "best in the business" may help sharpen the team's focus on what the performance objectives should be.

Decide what constitutes success.

Just as important as a clear vision of desired results is a clear vision of what will constitute success for the project. These are two distinct questions: Where do I want to go, and how will I know when I get there?

In the Joint Direct Attack Munitions (JDAM) research and development acquisition, for example, affordability (in terms of average unit production price) was a key element, along with "how well the product met the live-or-die criteria." Affordability was communicated in no uncertain terms from toplevel management to the acquisition team, and from the acquisition team to the competing contractors. As the project manager recalled— *I had a strong sense of empowerment... from the Air Force Chief of Staff who said basically, 'Do what you have to do to get the products under $40,000'.*

With that clear a mandate and the benefits of head-to-head contractor competition, the final, winning proposal included an average unit production price between $14,000 and $15,000... far lower than the original cost target of $40,000 and the original cost estimate of $68,000 per unit.

So it is important to establish a clear target for success, which will then serve to focus the efforts of the integrated solutions team in crafting the acquisition, the contractors in competing for award, and the government-industry team throughout contract performance.

Determine the current level of performance.

The main reason to determine the current level of performance is to establish the baseline against which future performance can be measured. If you don't know where you started, you can't tell how far you've come.

In order to think about taking measurements of current performance, think about what happens when you rent a car. The company will give you a piece of paper with an outline of a car on it. You're asked to go outside, and mark on the diagram every nick and scratch you see, so that when you return the car, the baseline is clear. This is precisely what we need to do with our current contracts or operations.

Keep in mind that the government doesn't necessarily have to do the baseline measurement. Another approach is to require a set of metrics as a deliverable under a current contract. Even if there were no existing provision, this could easily be done via contract modification. New solicitations can be written with provision for delivery of baseline and/or current performance levels, either annually, at the end of the contract, or both. The integrated solutions team must determine the adequacy of the baseline data for the new contract, to ensure they achieve the best results.

3. EXAMINE PRIVATE-SECTOR & PUBLIC-SECTOR SOLUTIONS.

Once the acquisition's intended results have been identified, the integrated solutions team should begin to examine both privatesector and public-sector solutions. This is called "market research," and it is a vital means of arming the team with the expertise needed to conduct an effective performancebased acquisition.

Market research is the continuous process of collecting information to maximize reliance on the commercial marketplace and to benefit from its capabilities, technologies, and competitive forces in meeting an agency need. Market research is essential to the government's ability to buy best-value products and services that solve missioncritical problems. Acquisition reform has opened the door to effective new approaches to market research that should be undertaken by the integrated solutions team long before attempting to write a performance work statement.

Tasks, Features, & Best Practices: Learn More

- Take a team approach to market research.
- Spend time learning from public-sector counterparts.
- Talk to private-sector companies before structuring the acquisition.
- Consider one-on-one meetings with industry.

- Look for existing contracts.
- Document market research.

Take a team approach to market research.

In the past, it was not unusual for technical staff to conduct market research about marketplace offerings, while contracting staff conducted market research more focused on industry practices and pricing. A better approach is for the entire integrated solutions team to be a part of the market research effort. This enables the members of the team to share an understanding and knowledge of the marketplace — an important factor in the development of the acquisition strategy — and a common understanding of what features, schedules, terms and conditions are key.

Spend time learning from public-sector counterparts.

While many are familiar with examining private-sector sources and solutions as part of market research, looking to the public-sector is not as common a practice. Yet it makes a great deal of sense on several levels.

First, there is an increased interest in cross-agency cooperation and collaboration. If the need is for payroll support, for example, many federal agencies have "solved" that problem and could potentially provide services through an interagency agreement. Alternatively, it could be that to provide seamless services to the public, two or more agencies need to team together to acquire a solution. (This is the model that may well evolve with e-Government solutions, given the President's proposal of a special fund for such initiatives.)

Second, agencies with similar needs may be able to provide lessons learned and best practices. For example, the Department of Commerce COMMITS office has frequently briefed other agencies on the process of establishing a Government-wide Agency Contract (GWAC). Another agency that we are aware of is now conducting public-sector market research about seat management implementation in the federal government. So it is important for the integrated solutions team to talk to their counterparts in other agencies. Taking the time to do so may help avert problems that could otherwise arise in the acquisition.

Talk to private-sector companies before structuring the acquisition.

With regard to the more traditional private-sector market research, it is important to be knowledgeable about commercial offerings, capabilities, and practices before structuring the acquisition in any detail. This is one of the more significant changes brought about by acquisition reform.

Some of the traditional ways to do this include issuing "sources sought" type notices at FedBizOps.gov, conducting "Industry Days," issuing Requests for Information, and holding pre-solicitation conferences. But it is also okay to simply pick up the phone and call private-sector company representatives.

Contact with vendors and suppliers for purposes of market research is now encouraged. In fact, FAR 15.201(a) specifically promotes the exchange of information "among all interested parties, from the earliest identification of a requirement through receipt of proposals." The limitations that apply (once a procurement is underway) are that prospective contractors be treated fairly and impartially and that standards of procurement integrity (FAR 3.104) be maintained. But the real key is to begin market research before a procurement is underway.

Consider one-on-one meetings with industry.

While many may not realize it, one-on-one meetings with industry leaders are not only permissible – see Federal Acquisition Regulation 15.201(c)(4)–they are more effective than pre-solicitation or preproposal conferences. Note that when market research is conducted before a solicitation or performance work statement is drafted, the rules are different. FAR 15.201(f) provides, for example: "General information about agency mission needs and future requirements may be disclosed at any time." Since the requirements have not (or should not have) been defined, disclosure of procurement-sensitive information is not an issue.

It is effective to focus on commercial and industry best practices, performance metrics and measurements, innovative delivery methods for the required services, and incentive programs that providers have found particularly effective.

This type of market research can expand the range of potential solutions, change the very nature of the acquisition, establish the performance-based approach, and represent the agency's first step on the way to an "incentivized" partnership with a contractor.

Look for existing contracts

FAR Part 10 requires that as part of market research, the Integrated Solutions Team must go to http://www.contractdirectory.gov to see if there is an existing contract available to meet agency requirements.

Document market research

FAR Part 10 requires that a written market research report be placed in the contract file. The amount of research, given the time and expense should be commensurate with the size of the acquisition.

4. DEVELOP PWS OR SOO.

There are two ways to develop a specification for a performance-based acquisition: by using a performance work statement (PWS) or an emerging methodology built around a statement of objectives (SOO).

The PWS process is discussed in most existing guides on performance-based service contracting and in the Federal Acquisition Regulation. Among its key processes are the conduct of a job analysis and development of a performance work statement and quality assurance and surveillance plan... When people talk about performance-based contracting, this is typically the model they have in mind.

The alternative process — use of a SOO — is an emerging methodology that turns the acquisition process around and requires competing contractors to develop the statement of work, performance metrics and measurement plan, and quality assurance plan... all of which should be evaluated before contract award. It is described briefly in the Department of Defense "Handbook for Preparation of Statement of Work (SOW)" for example:

The SOO is a Government prepared document incorporated into the RFP that states the overall solicitation objectives. It can be used in those solicitations where the intent is to provide the maximum flexibility to each offeror to propose an innovative development approach.

The SOO is a very short document (e.g., under ten pages) that provides the basic, high-level objectives of the acquisition. It is provided in the solicitation in lieu of a government-written statement of work or performance work statement.

In this approach, the contractors' proposals contain statements of work and performance metrics and measures (which are based on their proposed solutions and existing commercial practices). Clearly, use of a SOO opens the acquisition up to a wider range of potential solutions. The Veterans Benefits Administration loan servicing acquisition discussed under step two and in this step was conducted (very successfully) using a SOO.

The integrated solutions team should consider these two approaches and determine which is more suitable:

- Use of a PWS
- Use of a SOO

Tasks, Features, & Best Practices: Learn More

PWS

- Conduct an analysis.
- Apply the "so what?" test.
- Capture the results of the analysis in a matrix.
- Write the performance work statement.
- Let the contractor solve the problem, including the labor mix.

SOO

- Begin with the acquisition's "elevator message."
- Describe the scope.
- Write the performance objectives into the SOO.
- Make sure the government and the contractor share objectives.
- Identify the constraints.
- Develop the background.
- Make the final checks and maintain perspective.

USING A PWS

Conduct an analysis.

Preparing a PWS begins with an analytical process, often referred to as a "job analysis." It involves a close examination of the agency's requirements and tends to be a "bottom up" assessment with "re-engineering" potential. This analysis is the basis for establishing performance requirements, developing performance standards, writing the performance work statement, and producing the quality assurance plan. Those responsible for the mission or program are essential to the performance of the job analysis.

A different approach to the analytical process is described in the "Guidebook for Performance-Based Services Acquisition (PBSA) in the Department of Defense." It describes three "analysis-oriented steps" that are "top down" in nature:

- Define the desired outcomes: *What must be accomplished to satisfy the requirement?*
- Conduct an outcome analysis: *What tasks must be accomplished to arrive at the desired outcomes?*
- Conduct a performance analysis: *When or how will I know that the outcome has been satisfactorily achieved, and how much deviation from the performance standard will I allow the contractor, if any?*

The integrated solutions team should consider the various approaches. Neither the OFPP nor DoD guide is mandatory; both describe an approach to analysis. (There are other guides and other approaches in the "seven steps" library as well.) Regardless of the analytical process adopted, the team's task under step four is to develop certain information:

- A description of the requirement in terms of results or outcomes
- Measurable performance standards
- Acceptable quality levels (AQLs)

The AQL establishes the allowable error rate or variation from the standard. OFPP's best-practices guide cites this example: In a requirement for taxi services, the performance standard might be "pickup within five minutes of an agreed upon time." The AQL then might be five percent; i.e., the taxi could be more than five minutes late no more than five percent of the time. Failure to perform within the AQL could result in a contract price reduction or other action.

With regard to performance standards and AQLs, the integrated solutions team should remember that an option is to permit contractors to propose standards of service, along with appropriate price adjustment or other action. This approach fosters a reliance on standard commercial practices. (Remember that all these points — performance standards, quality levels, and price — are negotiable.)

Apply the "so what?" test.

There is nothing so useless as doing efficiently that which should not be done at all. (Peter Drucker)

An analysis of requirements is often, by its nature, a close examination of the status quo; that is, it is often an analysis of process and "how" things are done... exactly the type of detail that is not supposed to be in a PWS. The integrated solutions team needs to identify the essential inputs, processes, and outputs during job analysis. Otherwise, the danger is that contractors will bid back the work breakdown structure, and the agency will have failed to solicit innovative and streamlined approaches from the competitors.

One approach is to use the "so what?" test during job analysis. For example, once job analysis identifies outputs, the integrated solutions team should verify the continued need for the output. The team should ask questions like: Who needs the output? Why is the output needed? What is done with it? What occurs as a result? Is it worth the effort and cost? Would a different output be preferable? And so on...

Capture the results of the analysis in a matrix.

As the information is developed, the integrated solutions team should begin capturing the information in a performance matrix. The Department of Treasury guide, "Performance-Based Service Contracting" illustrates a six-column approach with the following:

- Desired Outcomes: What do we want to accomplish as the end result of this contract?
- Required Service: What task must be accomplished to give us the desired result? (Note: Be careful this doesn't become a "how" statement.)
- Performance Standard: What should the standards for completeness, reliability, accuracy, timeliness, customer satisfaction, quality and/or cost be?
- Acceptable Quality Level (AQL): How much error will we accept?

■ Monitoring Method: How will we determine that success has been achieved?
■ Incentives/Disincentives for Meeting or Not Meeting the Performance Standards:
  ■ What carrot or stick will best reward good performance or address poor performance? [This reflects priced and unpriced adjustments based on an established methodology. Reductions can be made for reduced value of performance.]

The Treasury guide provides templates for help desk, seat management, systems integration, software development, and system design/business process re-engineering services.

The Department of Defense approach is very similar: take the desired outcomes, performance objectives, performance standards, and acceptable quality levels that have been developed during the analytical process and document them in a Performance Requirements Summary (PRS). The PRS matrix has five columns: performance objective, performance standard, acceptable quality level, monitoring method, and incentive. The PRS serves as the basis for the performance work statement.

Write the performance work statement.

There is not a standard template or outline for a PWS. The Federal Acquisition Regulation only requires that agencies—
■ Describe requirements in terms of results rather than process.
■ Use measurable performance standards and quality assurance surveillance plans.
■ Provide for reductions of fees or price.
■ Include performance incentives where appropriate.

In terms of organization of information, a SOW-like approach is suitable for a performance work statement: introduction, background information, scope, applicable documents, performance requirements, special requirements (such as security), and deliverables. However, the team can adapt this outline as appropriate. Before finishing, there should be final checks:
■ Examine every requirement carefully and delete any that are not essential.
■ Search for process descriptions or "how" statements and eliminate them.

Many agencies have posted examples of performance-based so-licitations that can provide some guidance or helpful ideas. (See LINKS section) However, since the nature of performance-based acquisition is (or should be) tied to mission-unique or program-unique needs, keep in mind that another agency's solution may not be a good model.

Let the contractor solve the problem, including the labor mix.

FIRST, keep this important "lesson learned" in mind:

Don't spec the requirement so tightly that you get the same solution from each offeror.

SECOND, performance-based service acquisition requires that the integrated solutions team usually must jettison some traditional approaches to buying services... like specifying labor categories, educational requirements, or number of hours of support required. Those are "how" approaches. Instead, let contractors propose the best people with the best skill sets to meet the need and fit the solution. The government can then evaluate the proposal based both on the quality of the solution and the experience of the proposed personnel. In making the shift to performance-based acquisition, remember this:

The significant problems we face cannot be solved at the same level of thinking we were at when we created them. (Albert Einstein)

The Department of Defense addresses this in the "Guidebook for Performance-Based Services Acquisition (PBSA) in the Department of Defense." The guide provides as follows:

Prescribing manpower requirements limits the ability of offerors to propose their best solutions, and it could preclude the use of qualified contractor personnel who may be well suited for performing the requirement but may be lacking — for example — a complete college degree or the exact years of specified experience.

For some services, in fact, such practices are prohibited. Congress passed a provision (section 813) in the 2001 Defense Authorization Act, now implemented in the FAR (with government-wide applicability, of course). It prescribes that, when acquiring information technology services, solicitations may not describe any minimum experience or educational requirements for proposed contractor personnel unless the contracting officer determines that needs of the agency either (1) cannot be met without that requirement or (2) require the use of other than a performance-based contract.

Remember that how the performance work statement is written will either empower the private sector to craft innovative solutions... or limit or cripple that ability.

Using a SOO

As discussed previously, an alternative approach to development of the PWS is to develop a statement of objectives. There is no set format for a SOO, but one approach follows:

- Purpose
- Scope
- Period of Performance
- Place of Performance (if known, if required)
- Background
- Program Objectives
- Constraints (may include security, privacy, safety, and accessibility)

The Government-prepared SOO is usually incorporated into the RFP either as an attachment or as part of Section L. At contract award, the contractor-proposed statement of work (solution) can be incorporated by reference or integrated into Section C.

Begin with the acquisition's "elevator message."

How many solicitations have you seen that begin with a statement like, "This is a solicitation for a time-and-materials contract." Or what about this one: "The purpose of this solicitation is to acquire information technology hardware, software, and services." Or this one (true story): "This is a performance-based specification to acquire services on a time-and-materials basis." In the context of performance-based acquisition, all are bad starts.

The first statement made in a statement of objectives should be an explanation of how the acquisition relates to the agency's program or mission need and what problem needs solving (as identified under step two).

For example, in a recent task order solicitation by the Veterans Benefits Administration, this statement was made:

The purpose of this task order is to obtain loan servicing in support of VA's portfolio that will significantly improve loan guaranty operations and service to its customers.

This simple statement was a signal that the acquisition had made a huge break from the predecessor contract, which had started with something like, "This is a requirement for information technology resources." The turnaround was the realization that the need was for loan servicing support services; technology was the enabler.

Describe the scope.

A short description of scope in the SOO helps the competitors get a grasp on the size and range of the services needed. The Veteran's Benefits Administration's scope statement follows:

The purpose of this [task order] is to provide the full range of loan servicing support. This includes such activities as customer management, paying taxes and insurance, default management, accounting, foreclosure, bankruptcy, etc., as well as future actions associated with loan servicing. This Statement of Objectives reflects current VA policies and practices, allowing offerors to propose and price a solution to known requirements. It is anticipated that specific loan servicing requirements and resulting objectives will change over the life of this order. This will result in VA modifying this order to incorporate in-scope changes.

Another consideration for the integrated solutions team to consider is the budget authority (in dollars) available to fund the acquisition. In an acquisition approach as "wide open" as a statement of objectives, the competing contractors will need insight into funding authority so that they can size their solution to be both realistic and competitive. This may be listed as a constraint.

Write the performance objectives into the SOO.

In step two, the task of the integrated solutions team was to "decide what problem needs solving." The basis for that analysis was information in the agency's strategic and annual performance plans, program authorization documents, budget documents, and discussions with project owners and stakeholders. That information constitutes the core of the statement of objectives.

In the case of the Veterans Administration, for example, the acquisition's performance objectives were set forth in this opening statement:

VA expects to improve its current loan servicing operations through this task order in several ways. Primary among these is to increase the number and value of saleable loans. In addition, VA wants to be assured that all payments for such items as taxes and insurance are always paid on time. As part of these activities, the VA also has an objective to improve Information Technology information exchange and VA's access to automated information on an as required basis to have the information to meet customer needs and auditors' requirements.

What is immediately obvious is that these are mission-related, measurable objectives.

Make sure the government and the contractor share objectives.

When the acquisition's objectives are "grounded in" the plans and objectives found in agency strategic performance plans, program authorization documents, and budget and investment documents, then the government and the contractor are clearly working in a partnership toward shared goals. This is a far cry from the old-school acquisition approach, characterized by driving cost down and then berating the supplier to demand delivery. When the agency and the contractor share the same goals, the likelihood of successful performance rises dramatically.

Identify the constraints.

The purpose of a SOO is to provide contractors with maximum flexibility to conceive and propose innovative approaches and solutions. However, in some cases, there may be constraints that the government must place on those solutions. For example, core financial systems used by federal agencies must comply with requirements of OMB Circular A-127 and the guidance of the Joint Financial Management Improvement Program. Acquisitions related to technology will need to conform to the agency's information technology architecture and accessibility standards. In addition, there may be considerations of security, privacy, and safety that should be addressed. There may also be existing policies, directives, and standards that are constraining factors. The integrated solutions team should work with program managers, staff, customers, and stakeholders to identify these and to confirm their essentiality.

Develop the background.

The background and current environment set forth in a statement of objectives comprise important information for contractors. The Veterans Benefits Administration's statement of work included sections on—

- VA loan servicing history,
- Current VA Portfolio Origination/Acquisition Process, and
- Overview of the Current Servicing Process.

A best practice when using a SOO is to provide a brief overview of the program, listing links to webdelivered information on the current contract, government-controlled, government-furnished equipment, and a hardware configuration or enterprise architecture, as appropriate. The development of this information is essential so that contractors can perform meaningful due diligence.

Make the final checks and maintain perspective.

Before finalizing the document, the integrated solutions team should examine the entire SOO carefully and delete anything that is not essential.

Even more so than performance work statements, it is extremely unlikely that another agency's SOO would prove very useful, but several examples are provided in the library. Since this is an emerging technique, the integrated solutions team should examine them critically. New processes take time to perfect... and require ongoing experimentation and innovation.

5. DECIDE HOW TO MEASURE & MANAGE PERFORMANCE.

Developing an approach to measuring and managing performance is a complex process that requires consideration of many factors:

performance standards and measurement techniques, performance management approach, incentives, and more. This component of performance-based contracting is as important as developing the Statement of Work (SOW) or the Statement of Objectives (SOO), because this step establishes the strategy of managing the contract to achieve planned performance objectives.

Tasks, Features, & Best Practices: Learn More

- Review the success determinants.
- Rely on commercial quality standards.
- Have the contractor propose the metrics and the quality assurance plan.
- Select only a few meaningful measures on which to judge success.
- Include contractual language for negotiated changes to the metrics and measures.
- Apply the contract-type order of precedence carefully.
- Use incentive-type contracts.
- Consider "award term."
- Consider other incentive tools.
- Recognize the power of profit as motivator.
- Most importantly, consider the relationship.

Review the success determinants.

In Step Two, the integrated solutions team established a vision of what will constitute success for the project by answering two distinct questions: Where do I want to go, and how will I know when I get there?

The task now is to build the overall performance measurement and management approach on those success determinants.

Rely on commercial quality standards.

Rather than inventing metrics or quality or performance standards, the integrated solutions team should use existing commercial quality standards (identified during market research), such as International Standards Organization (ISO) 9000 or the Software Engineering Institute's Capability Maturity Models®.

ISO has established quality standards (the ISO 9000 series) that are increasingly being used by US firms to identify suppliers who meet the quality standards. The term "ISO 9001 2000" refers to a set of new quality management standards which apply to all kinds of organizations in all kinds of areas. Some of these areas include manufacturing, processing, servicing, printing, electronics, computing, legal services, financial services, accounting, banking, aerospace, construction, textiles, publishing, energy, telecommunications, research, health care, utilities, aviation, food processing, government, education, software development, transportation, design, instrumentation, communications, biotechnology, chemicals, engineering, farming, entertainment, horticulture, consulting, insurance, and so on.

The Carnegie Mellon Software Engineering Institute, a Federally funded research and development center, has developed Capability Maturity Models® (CMM) to "assist organizations in maturing their people, process, and technology assets to improve long-term business performance." SEI has developed CMMs for software, people, and software acquisition, and assisted in the development of CMMs for Systems Engineering and Integrated Product Development:

- SW-CMM® Capability Maturity Model for Software
- P-CMM People Capability Maturity Model
- SA-CMM Software Acquisition Capability Maturity Model
- SE-CMM Systems Engineering Capability Maturity Model
- IPD-CMM Integrated Product Development Capability Maturity Model

The Capability Maturity Models express levels of maturation: the higher the number, the greater the level of maturity. There are five levels. Solicitations that require CMMs typically specify only level two or three.

The integrated solutions team can incorporate such commercial quality standards in the evaluation and selection criteria.

Have the contractor propose the metrics and the quality assurance plan.

One approach is to require the contractor to propose performance metrics and the quality assurance plan (QAP) , rather than have the government develop it. This is especially suitable when using a SOO because the solution is not known until proposed. With a SOO, offerors are free to develop their own solutions, so it makes sense for them to develop and propose a QAP that is tailored to their solution and commercial practices. If the agency were to develop the QAP, it could very well limit what contractors can propose.

As the integrated solutions team considers what is required in a QAP, it may be useful to consider how the necessity for quality control and assurance has changed over time, especially as driven by acquisition reform. In short, QAPs were quite necessary when federal acquisition was dominated by low-cost selections. Think about the incentives at work: To win award but still protect some degree of profit margin, the contractor had to shave his costs, an action that could result in use of substandard materials or processes. With best-value selection and an emphasis on past-performance evaluation and reporting, entirely different incentives are at work.

The regulations have changed to some degree to reflect this reality. FAR 46.102 provides that contracts for commercial items "shall rely on a contractor's existing quality assurance system as a substitute for compliance with Government inspection and testing before tender for acceptance unless customary market practices for the commercial item being acquired permit in-process inspection."

Air Force Instruction 63-124 (1 April 1999) goes farther. Among others, the AFI suggests these considerations in implementing a quality management system:

- Tailor the system to management risks and costs associated with the requirement.
- Use source selection criteria that promise the most potential to reduce government oversight and ensure the government is only receiving and paying for the services required.
- Rely on customer feedback where contract nonconformance can be validated.
- Allow variation in the extent of oversight to match changes in the quality of the contractor's performance.
- Allow the contractor to perform and report on surveillance of services as part of their quality assurance system. Some form of oversight (government QA, third party audit) is needed to confirm surveillance results.

Remember the following key aspects. Performance metrics are negotiable and, wherever possible, address quality concerns by exception not inspection. Also, when contractors propose the metrics and the QAP, these become true discriminators among the proposals in best-value evaluation and source selection.

Select only a few meaningful measures on which to judge success.

Whether the measures are developed by the proposing contractor or by the integrated solutions team, it is important to limit the measures to those that are truly important and directly tied to the program objectives. The measures should be selected with some consideration of cost. For example, the team will want to determine that the cost of measurement does not exceed the value of the information... and that more expensive means of measurement are used for only the most risky and missioncritical requirements.

The American Productivity and Quality Center website states that performance measures come in many types, including economic and financial measures such as return on investment, and other quantitative and qualitative measures. "Organizations are investing energy in developing measures that cover everything from capital adequacy and inventory turns to public image, innovation, customer value, learning, competency, error rate, cost of quality, customer contact, perfect orders, training hours, and re-engineering results." Each measure should relate directly to the objectives of the acquisition.

Include contractual language for negotiated changes to the metrics and measures.

One important step the integrated solutions team can take is to reserve the right to change the metrics and measures. One effective way to do this is for the agency and the contractor to meet regularly to review performance. The first question at each meeting should be, "Are we measuring the right thing?"

This requires that the contractual documents include such provisions as value engineering change provisions, share-in-savings options, or other provisions preserving the government's right to review and revise.

Apply the contract-type order of precedence carefully.

Under law and regulation, there is an order of preference in contract types used for performancebased contracting, as follows:

(i) A firm-fixed price performance-based contract or task order.

(ii) A performance-based contract or task order that is not firm-fixed price.

(iii) A contract or task order that is not performance-based.

Agencies must take care implementing this order of precedence. Be aware that a firm-fixed price contract is not the best solution for every requirement. "Force fitting" the contract type can actually result in much higher prices as contractors seek to cover their risks.

This view is upheld by FAR 16.103(b) which indicates, "A firm-fixed-price contract, which best utilizes the basic profit motive of business enterprise, shall be used when the risk involved is minimal or can be predicted with an acceptable degree of certainty. However, when a reasonable basis for firm pricing does not exist, other contract types should be considered, and negotiations should be directed toward selecting a contract type (or combination of types) that will appropriately tie profit to contractor performance."

Clearly, the decision about the appropriate type of contract to use is closely tied to the agency's need and can go a long way to motivating superior performance — or contributing to poor performance and results. Market research, informed business decision, and negotiation will determine the best contract type.

One final point: The decision on contract type is not necessarily either-or. Hybrid contracts — those with both fixed-price and cost-type tasks — are common.

Use incentive-type contracts.

Although determining the type of contract to use is often the first type of incentive considered, it is important to understand that contract type is only part of the overall incentive approach and structure of a performance-based acquisition. Other aspects have become increasingly important as agencies and contractors have moved closer to partnering relationships.

Contract types differ in their allocation and balance of cost, schedule, and technical risks between government and contractor. As established by FAR Part 16 (Types of Contracts), contract types vary in terms of:

- The degree and timing of the risk and responsibility assumed by the contractor for the costs of performance, and
- The amount and nature of the profit incentive offered to the contractor for achieving or exceeding specified standards or goals.

The government's obligation is to assess its requirements and the uncertainties involved in contract performance and select from the contractual spectrum a contract type and structure that places an appropriate degree of risk, responsibility, and incentives on the contractor for performance.

At one end of the contractual spectrum is the firm-fixed-price contract, under which the contractor is fully responsible for performance costs and enjoys (or suffers) resulting profits (or losses). At the other end of the spectrum is the cost-plus-fixed-fee contract, in which allowable and allocable costs are reimbursed and the negotiated fee (profit) is fixed — consequently, the contractor has minimal responsibility for, or incentive to control, performance costs. In between these extremes are various incentive contracts, including:

- *Fixed-price incentive contracts* (in which final contract price and profit are calculated based on a formula that relates final negotiated cost to target cost): these may be either firm target or successive targets.
- *Fixed-price contracts with award fees* (used to "motivate a contractor" when contractor performance cannot be measured objectively, making other incentives inappropriate).
- Cost-reimbursement incentive contracts (used when fixed-price contracts are inappropriate, due to uncertainty about probable costs): these may be either cost-plus-incentive-fee or cost-plusaward-fee.

Use of certain types of incentives may be limited by availability of funds. Fortunately, there are other types of incentives that can tailored to the acquisition and performance goals, requirements, and risks. For example, agencies can also incorporate delivery incentives and performance incentives — the latter related to contractor performance and/or specific products' technical performance characteristics, such as speed or responsiveness. Incentives are based on meeting target performance standards, not minimum contractual requirements. These, too, are negotiable.

Consider "award term."

"Award term" is a contract performance incentive feature that ties the length of a contract's term to the performance of the contractor. The contract can be extended for "good" performance or reduced for "poor" performance.

Award term is a contracting tool used to promote efficient and quality contractor performance. In itself, it is not an acquisition strategy, nor is it a performance solution. As with any tool, its use requires careful planning, implementation, and management/measurement to ensure its success in incentivizing contractors and improving performance.

The award term feature is similar to award fee (FAR 16.405-2) contracting where contract performance goals, plans, assessments, and awards are made regularly during the life of a contract. Award term solicitations and contracts should include a base period (e.g., 3 years) and a maximum term (e.g., 10 years), similar to quantity estimates used in indefinite quantity/indefinite delivery contracts for supplies (FAR 16.504).

When applying the award term feature, agencies need to identify and understand the project or task:

- Conditions, constraints, assumptions, and complexities
- Schedule, performance, and cost critical success factors
- Schedule, performance, and cost risks

They also need to understand marketplace conditions and pricing realities. Only then can agencies establish meaningful and appropriate schedule, performance, and cost measures/parameters for a specific contract. These measures must be meaningful, accurate, and quantifiable to provide the right incentives and contract performance results. Specifics need to be incorporated and integrated in an award term plan.

Award term is best applied when utilizing performance or solution-based requirements where a SOW or SOO describes the agency's required outcomes or results (the "what" and "when" of the agency's requirement) and where the contractor has the freedom to apply its own management and best performance practices (the "how" of the requirement) towards performing the contract. The award term plan must specify success measurement criteria, regarding how performance will be measured (i.e., defines what is "good" or "poor" performance) and the award term decision made.

There should also be a clear indication of the consequences of various levels of performance in terms of the contract's minimum, estimated, and maximum terms — and the agency needs to be prepared to follow up with those consequences. If contractor performance is below the standard set, the contract ends at the completion of the base period. The agency must be prepared to re-procure in a timely fashion.

The effort applied in managing an award term contract after award is critical. Too often, agencies and contractors don't invest the right people (numbers and skills) and management attention during the contract performance phase. Managing contracts with features like award term is not a "last minute," incidental, or a fill-out-a-survey job. As in the case of its "sister" award fee approach, communication needs to be constant and clear with contractors, and not include so many evaluation elements that it dilutes the critical success factors.

Consider other incentive tools.

Incentives can be monetary or nonmonetary. They should be positive, but include remedies, as appropriate, when performance targets or objectives are missed.

Creating an incentive strategy is much the same as crafting an acquisition strategy. There is no single, perfect, "one size fits all" approach; instead, the incentive structure should be geared to the acquisition, the characteristics of the marketplace, and the objectives the government seeks to achieve. While cost incentives are tied to a degree to contract-type decisions, there are other cost and noncost incentives for the integrated solutions team to consider, such as—

- Contract length considerations (options and award term)
- Strategic supplier alliances
- Performance-based payments
- Performance incentive bonus
- Schedule incentives
- Past performance evaluation
- Agency "supplier of the year" award programs
- Competitive considerations
- Nonperformance remedies
- Value engineering change provisions
- Share-in-savings strategies
- Letters of commendation

Remember that performance incentives are negotiable. Developing an incentive strategy is a "study unto itself," and there are some excellent guides on the subject. See Step 5 Additional Information.

Recognize the power of profit as motivator.

One of the keys to effective incentives involves recognizing... then acting on... the private sector's chief motivator: profit. It is a simple fact that companies are motivated by generating return for their investors. One contractor was heard to say, "You give us the incentive, we will earn every available dollar."

The real opportunity is to make that work to the government's advantage. For example, link the incentive program to the mutually agreed-to contract performance measures and metrics. Then, incorporate value engineering change provisions (VECP) or share-in-savings strategies that reward the contractor for suggesting innovations that improve performance and reduce total overall cost. Put more simply: Set up the acquisition so that a contractor and the government can benefit from economies, efficiencies, and innovations delivered in contract performance.

If the incentives are right, and if the contractor and the agency share the same goals, risk is largely controlled and effective performance is almost the inevitable outcome. This approach will help ensure that the contractor is just as concerned — generated by self-interest in winning all available award fees and award terms — about every element of contract performance, whether maximizing operational efficiency overall, reducing subcontract costs, or ensuring the adequacy of post-award subcontractor competition and reasonableness of prices, as is the agency.

Most importantly, consider the relationship.

With regard to overall approach to contract performance management, the integrated solutions team should plan to rely less on management by contract and more on management by relationship. At its most fundamental level, a contract is much like a marriage. It takes work by both parties throughout the life of the relationship to make it successful. Consider, for example, the public-private partnership that was the Apollo Program. Other, more recent examples exist, but they all share the same common characteristics:

- Trust and open communication
- Strong leadership on both sides
- Ongoing, honest self-assessment
- Ongoing interaction
- Creating and maintaining mutual benefit or value throughout the relationship

There are several means to shift the focus from management by contract to management by relationship. For example, plan on meeting with the contractor to identify ways to improve efficiency and reduce the effect of the "cost drivers." Sometimes agencies require management reporting based on policy *without considering what the cost of the requirement is.* For example, in one contract, an agency required that certain reports be delivered regularly on Friday. When asked to recommend changes, the contractor suggested that report due date be shifted to Monday because weekend processing time costs less. An example is requiring earned-value reporting on every contractual process. For tasks of lesser risk, complexity, and expense, a less costly approach to measuring cost, schedule, and performance can be used. This type of collaborative action will set the stage for the contractor and government to work together to identify more effective and efficient ways to measure and manage the program.

Another effective means is to establish a Customer Process Improvement Working Group that includes contractor, program, and contracting representatives. This works especially well when the integrated solutions team's tasks migrate into contract performance and they take part in the working group. These meetings should always start with the question, are we measuring the right thing?

For major acquisitions, the team can consider the formation of a higher-level "Board of Directors," comprised of top officials from the government and its winning partner, with a formal charter that requires continual open communication, self-assessment, and ongoing interaction.

The intent to "manage by relationship" should be documented in a contract administration plan that lays out the philosophies and approach to managing this effort, placing special emphasis on techniques that enhance the ability to adapt and incorporate changes.

6. SELECT THE RIGHT CONTRACTOR.

Developing an acquisition strategy that will lead to selection of the "right contractor" is especially important in performance-based acquisition. The contractor must understand the performance-based approach, know or develop an understanding of the agency's requirement, have a history of performing exceptionally in the field, and have the processes and resources in place to support the mission. This goes a long way to successful mission accomplishment. In fact, selecting the right contractor and developing a partnership automatically solves many potential performance issues.

Keep in mind that large businesses have not "cornered the market" on good ideas. Small firms can be nimble, quick thinking, and very dedicated to customer service. While there is a cost in proposing solutions, a small business with a good solution can win performance-based awards.

Also, do not think you are limited to companies that specialize in the federal market. Information obtained from market research sessions has shown that often commercial companies — or commercial divisions of companies that do federal and commercial business — have significantly more experience with performance-based service delivery methods and techniques.

While there are many aspects to crafting an acquisition strategy, among the most important for performance-based acquisition are to "compete the solution," use downselection and "due diligence," evaluate heavily on past performance information, and make a best-value source selection decision.

Tasks, Features, & Best Practices: Learn More

- Compete the solution Use downselection and "due diligence."
- Use oral presentations and other opportunities to communicate.
- Emphasize past performance in evaluation.
- Use best-value evaluation and source selection.
- Assess solutions for issues of conflict of interest.

Compete the solution.

Too many government-issued statements of work try to "solve the problem." In such cases, the agency issues a detailed SOW, often with the assumption that "the tighter the spec the better," without realizing that this approach increases the government's risk. The agency SOW establishes what to do, how to do it, what labor categories to provide, what minimum qualifications to meet, and how many hours to work. The agency then asks vendors to respond with a "mirror image" of the specifications in the proposal. The result is that the "competing" vendors bid to the same government-directed plan, and the agency awards the contract to the company with the best proposal writers... not the best ideas.

So the first key to selecting the right contractor is to structure the acquisition so that the government describes the problem that needs to be solved and vendors compete by proposing solutions. The quality of the solution and the contractor-proposed performance measures and methodology then become true discriminators in best-value evaluation.

Use downselection and "due diligence."

Responding to a performance-based solicitation, especially a SOO that seeks contractor-developed solutions, is substantial work for contractors. Likewise, evaluation of what may be significantly different approaches or solutions is much more substantial work for the integrated solutions team. The team will have to understand the contractor-proposed solutions, assess the associated risks and likelihood of success, identify the discriminators, and do the best-value tradeoff analysis.

Because of this, the acquisition strategy should consider some means of "downselection," so that only those contractors with a significant likelihood of winning award will go through the expense of developing proposals. As to the integrated solutions team, evaluating dozens of solution-type proposals would be overly burdensome.

"Downselection" is a means of limiting the competitive pool to those contractors most likely to offer a successful solution. There are four primary means of downselection in current acquisition methodology: using the Federal Supply Service (FSS) Multiple Award Schedule (MAS) competitive process, using the "fair opportunity" competitive process under an existing Government-wide Agency Contract (GWAC) or multiple-award contract (MAC), using the multistep advisory process in a negotiated procurement, or using a competitive range determination in a negotiated procurement. All these methods provide a means to establish a small pool of the most qualified contractors, competing to provide the solution.

Once the competing pool of contractors is established, those contractors enter a period called due diligence. "Due diligence" is used in acquisitions to describe the period and process during which competitors take the time and make the effort to become knowledgeable about an agency's needs in order to propose a competitive solution. It usually includes site visits, meetings with key agency people, and research and analysis necessary to develop a competitive solution tailored to agency requirements.

During this time, the competing contractors must have access to the integrated solutions team and program staff so that the contractors can learn as much as possible about the requirement. It is a far more open period of communication than is typical in more traditional acquisitions.

Use oral presentations and other opportunities to communicate.

One streamlining tool that eases the job of evaluation is the use of oral presentations (characterized by "real-time interactive dialogue"). These presentations provide information about the contractor's management and/or technical approach that the integrated solutions team will use in evaluation, selection, and award.

Oral presentations provide "face time," permitting the integrated solutions team to assess prospective contractors. Agencies have said that oral presentations remove the "screen" that professional proposal writers can erect in front of the contractor's key personnel. The integrated solutions team should take full advantage of "face time" by requiring that the project manager and key personnel (those who will do the work) make the presentations. This gives agency evaluators an opportunity to see part of the vendor-proposed solution team, to ask specific questions, and to gauge how well the team works together and would be likely to work with the agency.

Oral presentations can lay out the proposed solution and the contractor's capability and understanding of the requirement. Oral presentations *may substitute for, or augment, written information.* However, it's important to remember that statements made in oral presentations are not binding unless written into the contract. Note that oral presentations should be recorded in some way.

Communication with offerors is an important element of selecting the right contractor. Despite this fact, it is "trendy" in negotiated procurements to announce the intent to award without discussions. Given the complexities associated with performance-based proposals (i.e., different approaches and different performance metrics), it is nearly impossible to award without conducting discussions. While it may reduce time, it is important to use discussions to fully understand the quality of the solution, the pricing approach, incentive structure, and even the selection itself.

Emphasize past performance in evaluation.

A contractor's past performance record is arguably the key indicator for predicting future performance. As such, it is to the agency's advantage to use past performance in evaluating and selecting contractors for award. Evaluation of past performance is particularly important for service contracts. Properly conducted, the collection and use of such information provides significant benefits. It enhances the government's ability to predict both the performance quality and customer satisfaction. It also provides a powerful incentive for current contractors to maximize performance and customer satisfaction.

Past performance information can come from multiple sources. The two most familiar methods are asking the offerors to provide references and seeking information from past performance information databases. The Past Performance Information Retrieval System, or PPIRS, is the Government-wide repository for past performance information. It ties together a number of data bases formerly independent of one another. (Reference: http://www.ppirs.gov.)

There are other means of obtaining past performance information for evaluation. One very important means is through market research. Call counterparts in other agencies with similar work and ask them for the names of the best contractors they've worked with. Are there industry awards in the field of work? Who has won them? In fact, ask offerors to identify their awards and events of special recognition. Look for industry quality standards and certifications, such as ISO 9000 and SEI CMM® (discussed in Step Five). Ask offerors what they do to track customer satisfaction and to resolve performance issues. Is there an established and institutionalized approach? In short, the integrated solutions team must take past performance more seriously than just calling a few references. Make the answers to these questions part of the request for proposals. Rather than have a separate past performance team, integrate this evaluation into the technical and management proposal evaluation effort.

When used in the source selection evaluation process, past performance evaluation criteria must provide information that allows the source selection official to compare the "quality" of offerors against the agency requirement and assess the risk and likelihood of success of the proposed solution and success of contractor performance. This requires the information to be relevant, current and accurate. For example, the information requested of the contractor and evaluated by the integrated solutions team should be designed to determine how well, in contracts of similar size, scope and complexity, the contractor—

- Conformed to the contract requirements and standards of good workmanship.
- Adhered to contract schedules.

- Forecasted and controlled costs.
- Managed risk.
- Provided reasonable and cooperative behavior and commitment to customer satisfaction.
- Demonstrated business-like concern for the interest of the customer.

The answers to the above list provide the source selection authority with information to make a comparative assessment for the award decision.

Use best-value evaluation and source selection.

"Best value" is a process used to select the most advantageous offer by evaluating and comparing factors in addition to cost or price. It allows flexibility in selection through tradeoffs which the agency makes between the cost and non-cost evaluation factors with the intent of awarding to the contractor that will give the government the greatest or best value for its money.

Note that "the rules" for the best-value and tradeoff process (and the degree of documentation required) depend on two factors: the rules for the specific acquisition process being used and the rules the agency sets in the solicitation. For example, when conducting a negotiated procurement, the complex processes of FAR Subpart 15.1, "Source Selection Processes and Techniques," and FAR Subpart 15.3, "Source Selection," apply. When using Federal Supply Schedule contracts, the simpler provisions at FAR 8.404 apply. However, if the agency writes FAR 15-type rules into a Request for Quote under Federal Supply Schedule contracts, the rules in the RFQ control.

The integrated solutions team should consider including factors such as the following in the evaluation model:

- Quality and benefits of the solution
- Quality of the performance metrics and measurement approach
- Risks associated with the solution
- Management approach and controls
- Management team (limited number of key personnel)
- Past performance (how well the contractor has performed)
- Past experience (what the contractor has done)

The General Accounting Office acknowledges broad agency discretion in selection; therefore, the integrated solution team evaluators and the source selection authority should expect to exercise good judgment. Quite simply, best-value source selection involves subjective analysis. It cannot, and should not, be reduced to a mechanical, mathematical exercise. The following, derived from GAO protest decision B-284270, reflects just how broad agency discretion is.

- Source selection officials have broad discretion to determine the manner and extent to which they will make use of the technical and price evaluation results in negotiated procurements.
- In deciding between competing proposals, price/technical tradeoffs may be made; the propriety of such tradeoffs turns not on the difference in technical scores or ratings per se, but on whether the source selection official's judgment concerning the significance of that difference was reasonable and adequately justified in light of the RFP evaluation scheme.
- The discretion to determine whether the technical advantages associated with a higher-priced proposal are worth the price premium exists notwithstanding the fact that price is equal to or more important than other factors in the evaluation scheme.
- In a best-value procurement, an agency's selection of a higher-priced, higher-rated offer should be supported by a determination that the technical superiority of the higher-priced offer warrants the additional cost involved.

Assess solutions for issues of conflict of interest.

An "organizational conflict of interest" exists when a contractor is or may be unable or unwilling to provide the government with impartial or objective assistance or advice. An organizational conflict of interest may result when factors create an actual or potential conflict of interest on a current contract or a potential future procurement.

While concerns about organizational conflict of interest are important, they should be tempered by good business sense. For example, sometimes software development is done in stages. Organizational conflict of interest would suggest that the contractor that does the initial systems design work be precluded from the follow-on code development due to unfair competitive advantage. However, this would also mean that the agency is excluding from consideration the contractor with the best understanding of the requirement. In this case, perhaps the acquisition approach should be reconsidered to allow the definer of the requirements to continue with the development.

7. MANAGE PERFORMANCE.

The final step of the seven steps of performance-based acquisition is the most important. Unlike legacy processes where the contract is awarded and the team disperses, there is a growing realization that "the real work" of acquisition is in contract management. This requires that agencies allocate sufficient resources, in both the contracting or program offices, to do the job well.

This is largely a problem of resource allocation and education. Again, legacy processes are much to blame. Many contracting staff learned their job when the culture was to maintain an arm's length distance (or more) from contractors... and, by all means, limit the amount of contact the contractor has with program people. That approach won't work in today's environment and especially not in performance-based acquisition. The contractor must be part of the acquisition team itself... a reality recognized by the guiding principles of the federal acquisition system. FAR 1.102(c) provides:

The Acquisition Team consists of all participants in Government acquisition including not only representatives of the technical, supply, and procurement communities but also the customers they serve, and the contractors who provide the products and services.

Effective contract management is a missioncritical agency function. This goes to the heart of the need to maintain sufficient core capability in the federal government to manage its programs. If the contractor is flying blind in performance, then the agency will soon fly blind and without landing gear when the contract is over.

This step, contract performance, is guided far less by law, regulation, and policy than those described in the preceding steps. To a large degree, the management of contract performance is guided by the contract's terms and conditions and is achieved with the support of the business relationships and communications established between the contractor and the integrated solutions team. It is in the best interest of all parties concerned that the contract be successful.

Tasks, Features, & Best Practices: Learn More

- Keep the team together.
- Adjust roles and responsibilities.
- Assign accountability for managing contract performance.
- Add the contractor to the team at a formal "kick-off" meeting.
- Regularly review performance in a Contract Performance Improvement Working Group.
- Ask the right questions.
- Report on the contractor's "past performance."

Keep the team together.

To be successful in performance-based acquisition, the agency must retain at least a core of the integrated solutions team on the project for contract management. Those on the team have the most knowledge, experience, and insight into what needs to happen next and what is expected during contract performance. Contract award is not the measure of success or even an especially meaningful metric. Effective and efficient contract performance that delivers a solution is the goal. The team should stay together to see that end reached.

Adjust roles and responsibilities.

Often the members of the acquisition team take on new roles during the contract performance phase. Typically, these responsibilities are shared between the program office and contracting office.

Given that the purpose of any acquisition (in part) is "to deliver on a timely basis the best value product or service to the customer" (as provided in FAR 1.102), meeting this objective requires the continued involvement of the program office in duties classified as contract administration as well as those more accurately described as program (or project) management.

Program management is concerned with maintaining the project's strategic focus and monitoring and measuring the contractor's performance. The integrated solutions team is ultimately responsible for ensuring that the contractor performs on time and within budget. On smaller acquisitions, the contracting officer's technical representative (COTR) may fill this role.

Contract administration involves the execution of the administrative processes and tasks necessary to see that the contractual requirements are met, by both contractor and agency. FAR Subpart 42.3 identifies the numerous but specific contract administration functions that may be delegated by the contracting office to a contract administration office, and in turn to a specific individual.

Assign accountability
for managing contract performance.

Just as important as keeping the team together is assigning roles and responsibilities to the parties. Contracting officers have certain responsibilities that can't be delegated or assumed by the other members of the team. These include, for example, making any commitment relating to an award of a task, modification, or contract; negotiating technical or pricing issues with the contractor; or modifying the stated terms and conditions of the contract. Some roles and responsibilities are decreed... for example, agencies are required to establish capability and training requirements for contracting officers technical representatives (COTRs).

Make sure the people assigned the most direct roles for monitoring contract performance have read and understand the contract and have the knowledge, experience, skills, and ability to perform their roles. In performance-based organizations, they are held accountable for the success or failure of the program they lead. They should know the program needs in depth, understand the contractor's marketplace, have familiarity with the tools the contractor is using to perform, have good interpersonal skills... and the capability to disagree constructively.

Enhanced professionalism in contract performance management is on the horizon. In November 2003, the Services Acquisition Reform Act (SARA) was passed with a number of noteworthy provisions. A fund is to be established in FY2005 to ensure Government program managers are properly trained and certified to manage large projects. Certified project managers' names will appear on OMB Form 300 submissions. See http://www.pubklaw.com/legis/SARA2003ssa.pdf. Information certification programs can be found at http://www.pmi.org. These requirements are part of a larger effort to link budget to performance, and to improve project management in order to reduce or eliminate wasteful spending.

Add the contractor to the team at a formal "kick-off" meeting.

It is often advisable — and sometimes required by the contract — to conduct a "kick-off meeting" or, more formally, a "post-award conference," attended by those who will be involved in contract performance. Even though a post-award conference may not be required by the contract, it is an especially good idea for performance-based contracts. This meeting can help both agency and contractor personnel achieve a clear and mutual understanding of contract requirements and further establish the foundation for good communications and a win-win relationship.

It is very important that the contractor be part of the integrated solutions team, and that agency and contractor personnel work closely together to fulfill the mission and program needs.

Regularly review performance in a Contract Performance Improvement Working Group.

Performance reviews should take place regularly, and that means much more than the annual "past performance" reviews required by regulation. These are contract management performance reviews, not for formal reporting and rebutting, but for keeping the project on course, measuring performance levels, and making adjustments as necessary. For most contracts, monthly or bimonthly performance reviews would be appropriate. For contracts of extreme importance or contracts in performance trouble, more frequent meetings may be required.

Measuring and managing a project to the attainment of performance goals and objectives requires the continued involvement of the acquisition team, especially the program manager. It also requires considerable involvement by the acquisition team's new members — contractor personnel.

Ask the right questions.

It is important to keep the focus of the meetings on improving performance, not evaluating people. Each meeting should start with the questions, "Are we measuring the right thing?" and "How are we doing?" It is important to continually revisit the success measures the team identified during Step Two. Other important questions are—

- Is the acquisition achieving its cost, schedule, and performance goals?
- Is the contractor meeting or exceeding the contract's performance-based requirements?
- How effective is the contractor's performance in meeting or contributing to the agency's program performance goals?
- Are there problems or issues that we can address to mitigate risk?

There should be time in each meeting where the agency asks, "Is there anything we are requiring that is affecting the job you can do in terms of quality, cost, schedule, or delivering the solution?" Actions discussed should be recorded for the convenience of all parties, with responsibilities and due dates assigned.

Report on the contractor's "past performance"

There are many types of performance reporting that may be required of the integrated solutions team. For example, agency procedures may establish special requirements for acquisition teams to report to the agency's investment review board regarding the status of meeting a major acquisition's cost, schedule, and performance goals (as required by the Federal Acquisition Streamlining Act). The team may also be responsible for performance reporting under the Government Performance and Results Act, if the contractor's performance directly supports a GPRA performance goal. Refer to internal agency guidance on these processes.

However, one type of performance reporting requirement — evaluation of the contractor's performance — is dictated by the contract terms and conditions and by FAR 42.15. This requirement is generally referred to as past-performance evaluation.

The FAR now requires that agencies evaluate contractor performance for each contract in excess of $100,000. The performance evaluation and report is shared with the contractor, who has an opportunity to respond before the contracting officer finalizes the performance report. In well managed contracts, there has been continual feedback and adjustment, so there should be no surprises on either side.

CONCLUSION

The intent of this guide is to make the subject of performance-based acquisition accessible and logical for all and shift the paradigm from traditional "acquisition think" into one of collaborative, performance-oriented teamwork with a focus on program performance, improvement, and innovation, not simply contract compliance. Performance-based acquisition offers the potential to dramatically transform the nature of service delivery, and permit the federal government to tap the enormous creative energy and innovative nature of private industry.

Let the acquisitions begin!

Appendix B

UNITED NATIONS CONVENTION ON CONTRACTS FOR THE INTERNATIONAL SALE OF GOODS (1980) [CISG]

For U.S. citation purposes, the UN-certified English text is published in 52 Federal Register 6262, 6264-6280 (March 2, 1987); United States Code Annotated, Title 15, Appendix (Supp. 1987).

The States Parties to this Convention,

Bearing in mind the broad objectives in the resolutions adopted by the sixth special session of the General Assembly of the United Nations on the establishment of a New International Economic Order, considering that the development of international trade on the basis of equality and mutual benefit is an important element in promoting friendly relations among States, being of the opinion that the adoption of uniform rules which govern contracts for the international sale of goods and take into account the different social, economic and legal systems would contribute to the removal of legal barriers in international trade and promote the development of international trade, have decreed as follows:

Part I

SPHERE OF APPLICATION AND GENERAL PROVISIONS

Chapter I
Sphere Of Application

Article I

(1) This Convention applies to contracts of sale of goods between parties whose places of business are in different States:

(a) when the States are Contracting States; or

(b) when the rules of private international law lead to the application of the law of a Contracting State.

(2) The fact that the parties have their places of business in different States is to be disregarded whenever this fact does not appear either from the contract or from any dealings between, or from information disclosed by, the parties at any time before or at the conclusion of the contract.

(3) Neither the nationality of the parties nor the civil or commercial character of the parties or of the contract is to be taken into consideration in determining the application of this Convention.

Article 2

This Convention does not apply to sales:

(a) of goods bought for personal, family or household use, unless the seller, at any time before or at the conclusion of the contract, neither knew nor ought to have known that the goods were bought for any such use;

(b) by auction;

(c) on execution or otherwise by authority of law;

(d) of stocks, shares, investment securities, negotiable instruments or money;

(e) of ships, vessels, hovercraft or aircraft;

(f) of electricity.

Article 3

(1) Contracts for the supply of goods to be manufactured or produced are to be considered sales unless the party who orders the goods undertakes to supply a substantial part of the materials necessary for such manufacture or production.

(2) This Convention does not apply to contracts in which the preponderant part of the obligations of the party who furnishes the goods consists in the supply of labour or other services.

Article 4

This Convention governs only the formation of the contract of sale and the rights and obligations of the seller and the buyer arising from such a contract. In particular, except as otherwise expressly provided in this Convention, it is not concerned with:

(a) the validity of the contract or of any of its provisions or of any usage;

(b) the effect which the contract may have on the property in the goods sold.

Article 5

This Convention does not apply to the liability of the seller for death or personal injury caused by the goods to any person.

Article 6

The parties may exclude the application of this Convention or, subject to article 12, derogate from or vary the effect of any of its provisions.

Chapter II
General Provisions

Article 7

(1) In the interpretation of this Convention, regard is to be had to its international character and to the need to promote uniformity in its application and the observance of good faith in international trade.

(2) Questions concerning matters governed by this Convention which are not expressly settled in it are to be settled in conformity with the general principles on which it is based or, in the absence of such principles, in conformity with the law applicable by virtue of the rules of private international law.

Article 8

(1) For the purposes of this Convention statements made by and other conduct of a party are to be interpreted according to his intent where the other party knew or could not have been unaware what that intent was.

(2) If the preceding paragraph is not applicable, statements made by and other conduct of a party are to be interpreted according to the understanding that a reasonable person of the same kind as the other party would have had in the same circumstances.

(3) In determining the intent of a party or the understanding a reasonable person would have had, due consideration is to be given to all relevant circumstances of the case including the negotiations, any practices which the parties have established between themselves, usages and any subsequent conduct of the parties.

Article 9

(1) The parties are bound by any usage to which they have agreed and by any practices which they have established between themselves.

(2) The parties are considered, unless otherwise agreed, to have impliedly made applicable to their contract or its formation a usage of which the parties knew or ought to have known and which in international trade is widely known to, and regularly observed by, parties to contracts of the type involved in the particular trade concerned.

Article 10

For the purposes of this Convention:

(a) if a party has more than one place of business, the place of business is that which has the closest relationship to the contract and its performance, having regard to the circumstances known to or contemplated by the parties at any time before or at the conclusion of the contract;

(b) if a party does not have a place of business, reference is to be made to his habitual residence.

Article 11

A contract of sale need not be concluded in or evidenced by writing and is not subject to any other requirement as to form. It may be proved by any means, including witnesses.

Article 12

Any provision of article 11, article 29 or Part II of this Convention that allows a contract of sale or its modification or termination by agreement or any offer, acceptance or other indication of intention to be made in any form other than in writing does not apply where any party has his place of business in a Contracting State which has made a declaration under article 96 of this Convention. The parties may not derogate from or vary the effect or this article.

Article 13

For the purposes of this Convention "writing" includes telegram and telex.

Part II

FORMATION OF THE CONTRACT

Article 14

(1) A proposal for concluding a contract addressed to one or more specific persons constitutes an offer if it is sufficiently definite and indicates the intention of the offeror to be bound in case of acceptance. A proposal is sufficiently definite if it indicates the goods and expressly or implicitly fixes or makes provision for determining the quantity and the price.

(2) A proposal other than one addressed to one or more specific persons is to be considered merely as an invitation to make offers, unless the contrary is clearly indicated by the person making the proposal.

Article 15

(1) An offer becomes effective when it reaches the offeree.

(2) An offer, even if it is irrevocable, may be withdrawn if the withdrawal reaches the offeree before or at the same time as the offer.

Article 16

(1) Until a contract is concluded an offer may be revoked if the revocation reaches the offeree before he has dispatched an acceptance.

(2) However, an offer cannot be revoked:

(a) if it indicates, whether by stating a fixed time for acceptance or otherwise, that it is irrevocable; or

(b) if it was reasonable for the offeree to rely on the offer as being irrevocable and the offeree has acted in reliance on the offer.

Article 17

An offer, even if it is irrevocable, is terminated when a rejection reaches the offeror.

Article 18

(1) A statement made by or other conduct of the offeree indicating assent to an offer is an acceptance. Silence or inactivity does not in itself amount to acceptance.

(2) An acceptance of an offer becomes effective at the moment the indication of assent reaches the offeror. An acceptance is not effective if the indication of assent does not reach the offeror within the time he has fixed or, if no time is fixed, within a reasonable time, due account being taken of the circumstances of the transaction, including the rapidity of the means of communication employed by the offeror. An oral offer must be accepted immediately unless the circumstances indicate otherwise.

(3) However, if, by virtue of the offer or as a result of practices which the parties have established between themselves or of usage, the offeree may indicate assent by performing an act, such as one relating to the dispatch of the goods or payment of the price, without notice to the offeror, the acceptance is effective at the moment the act is performed, provided that the act is performed within the period of time laid down in the preceding paragraph.

Article 19

(1) A reply to an offer which purports to be an acceptance but contains additions, limitations or other modifications is a rejection of the offer and constitutes a counter-offer.

(2) However, a reply to an offer which purports to be an acceptance but contains additional or different terms which do not materially alter the terms of the offer constitutes an acceptance, unless the offeror, without undue delay, objects orally to the discrepancy or dispatches a notice to that effect. If he does not so object, the terms of the contract are the terms of the offer with the modifications contained in the acceptance.

(3) Additional or different terms relating, among other things, to the price, payment, quality and quantity of the goods, place and time of delivery, extent of one party's liability to the other or the settlement of disputes are considered to alter the terms of the offer materially.

Article 20

(1) A period of time for acceptance fixed by the offeror in a telegram or a letter begins to run from the moment the telegram is handed in for dispatch or from the date shown on the letter or, if no such date is shown, from the date shown on the envelope. A period of time for acceptance fixed by the offeror by telephone, telex or other means of instantaneous communication, begins to run from the moment that the offer reaches the offeree.

(2) Official holidays or non-business days occurring during the period for acceptance are included in calculating the period. However, if a notice of acceptance cannot be delivered at the address of the offeror on the last day of the period because that day falls on an official holiday or a non-business day at the place of business of the offeror, the period is extended until the first business day which follows.

Article 21

(1) A late acceptance is nevertheless effective as an acceptance if without delay the offeror orally so informs the offeree or dispatches a notice to that effect.

(2) If a letter or other writing containing a late acceptance shows that it has been sent in such circumstances that if its transmission had been normal it would have reached the offeror in due time, the late acceptance is effective as an acceptance unless, without delay, the offeror orally informs the offeree that he considers his offer as having lapsed or dispatches a notice to that effect.

Article 22

An acceptance may be withdrawn if the withdrawal reaches the offeror before or at the same time as the acceptance would have become effective.

Article 23

A contract is concluded at the moment when an acceptance of an offer becomes effective in accordance with the provisions of this Convention.

Article 24

For the purposes of this Part of the Convention, an offer, declaration of acceptance or any other indication of intention "reaches" the addressee when it is made orally to him or delivered by any other means to him personally, to his place of business or mailing address or, if he does not have a place of business or mailing address, to his habitual residence.

Part III

SALE OF GOODS

Chapter I
General Provisions

Article 25

A breach of contract committed by one of the parties is fundamental if it results in such detriment to the other party as substantially to deprive him of what he is entitled to expect under the contract, unless the party in breach did not foresee and a reasonable person of the same kind in the same circumstances would not have foreseen such a result.

Article 26

A declaration of avoidance of the contract is effective only if made by notice to the other party.

Article 27

Unless otherwise expressly provided in this Part of the Convention, if any notice, request or other communication is given or made by a party in accordance with this Part and by means appropriate in the circumstances, a delay or error in the transmission of the communication or its failure to arrive does not deprive that party of the right to rely on the communication.

Article 28

If, in accordance with the provisions of this Convention, one party is entitled to require performance of any obligation by the other party, a court is not bound to enter a judgement for specific performance unless the court would do so under its own law in respect of similar contracts of sale not governed by this Convention.

Article 29

(1) A contract may be modified or terminated by the mere agreement of the parties.

(2) A contract in writing which contains a provision requiring any modification or termination by agreement to be in writing may not be otherwise modified or terminated by agreement. However, a party may be precluded by his conduct from asserting such a provision to the extent that the other party has relied on that conduct.

Chapter II
Obligations Of The Seller
Article 30

The seller must deliver the goods, hand over any documents relating to them and transfer the property in the goods, as required by the contract and this Convention.

Section I.
Delivery of the goods and handing over of documents
Article 31

If the seller is not bound to deliver the goods at any other particular place, his obligation to deliver consists:

(a) if the contract of sale involves carriage of the goods - in handing the goods over to the first carrier for transmission to the buyer;

(b) if, in cases not within the preceding subparagraph, the contract relates to specific goods, or unidentified goods to be drawn from a specific stock or to be manufactured or produced, and at the time of the conclusion of the contract the parties knew that the goods were at, or were to be manufactured or produced at, a particular place - in placing the goods at the buyer's disposal at that place;

(c) in other cases - in placing the goods at the buyer's disposal at the place where the seller had his place of business at the time of the conclusion of the contract.

Article 32

(1) If the seller, in accordance with the contract or this Convention, hands the goods over to a carrier and if the goods are not clearly identified to the contract by markings on the goods, by shipping documents or otherwise, the seller must give the buyer notice of the consignment specifying the goods.

(2) If the seller is bound to arrange for carriage of the goods, he must make such contracts as are necessary for carriage to the place fixed by means of transportation appropriate in the circumstances and according to the usual terms for such transportation.

(3) If the seller is not bound to effect insurance in respect of the carriage of the goods, he must, at the buyer's request, provide him with all available information necessary to enable him to effect such insurance.

Article 33

The seller must deliver the goods:

(a) if a date is fixed by or determinable from the contract, on that date;

(b) if a period of time is fixed by or determinable from the contract, at any time within that period unless circumstances indicate that the buyer is to choose a date; or

(c) in any other case, within a reasonable time after the conclusion of the contract.

Article 34

If the seller is bound to hand over documents relating to the goods, he must hand them over at the time and place and in the form required by the contract. If the seller has handed over documents before that time, he may, up to that time, cure any lack of conformity in the documents, if the exercise of this right does not cause the buyer unreasonable inconvenience or unreasonable expense. However, the buyer retains any right to claim damages as provided for in this Convention.

Section II.
Conformity of the goods and third party claims

Article 35

(1) The seller must deliver goods which are of the quantity, quality and description required by the contract and which are contained or packaged in the manner required by the contract.

(2) Except where the parties have agreed otherwise, the goods do not conform with the contract unless they:

(a) are fit for the purposes for which goods of the same description would ordinarily be used;

(b) are fit for any particular purpose expressly or impliedly made known to the seller at the time of the conclusion of the contract, except where the circumstances show that the buyer did not rely, or that it was unreasonable for him to rely, on the seller's skill and judgement;

(c) possess the qualities of goods which the seller has held out to the buyer as a sample or model;

(d) are contained or packaged in the manner usual for such goods or, where there is no such manner, in a manner adequate to preserve and protect the goods.

(3) The seller is not liable under subparagraphs (a) to (d) of the preceding paragraph for any lack of conformity of the goods if at the time of the conclusion of the contract the buyer knew or could not have been unaware of such lack of conformity.

Article 36

(1) The seller is liable in accordance with the contract and this Convention for any lack of conformity which exists at the time when the risk passes to the buyer, even though the lack of conformity becomes apparent only after that time.

(2) The seller is also liable for any lack of conformity which occurs after the time indicated in the preceding paragraph and which is due to a breach of any of his obligations, including a breach of any guarantee that for a period of time the goods will remain fit for their ordinary purpose or for some particular purpose or will retain specified qualities or characteristics.

Article 37

If the seller has delivered goods before the date for delivery, he may, up to that date, deliver any missing part or make up any deficiency in the quantity of the goods delivered, or deliver goods in replacement of any non-conforming goods delivered or remedy any lack of conformity in the goods delivered, provided that the exercise of this right does not cause the buyer unreasonable inconvenience or unreasonable expense. However, the buyer retains any right to claim damages as provided for in this Convention.

Article 38

(1) The buyer must examine the goods, or cause them to be examined, within as short a period as is practicable in the circumstances.

(2) If the contract involves carriage of the goods, examination may be deferred until after the goods have arrived at their destination.

(3) If the goods are redirected in transit or redispatched by the buyer without a reasonable opportunity for examination by him and at the time of the conclusion of the contract the seller knew or ought to have known of the possibility of such redirection or redispatch, examination may be deferred until after the goods have arrived at the new destination.

Article 39

(1) The buyer loses the right to rely on a lack of conformity of the goods if he does not give notice to the seller specifying the nature of the lack of conformity within a reasonable time after he has discovered it or ought to have discovered it.

(2) In any event, the buyer loses the right to rely on a lack of conformity of the goods if he does not give the seller notice thereof at the latest within a period of two years from the date on which the goods were actually handed over to the buyer, unless this time-limit is inconsistent with a contractual period of guarantee.

Article 40

The seller is not entitled to rely on the provisions of articles 38 and 39 if the lack of conformity relates to facts of which he knew or could not have been unaware and which he did not disclose to the buyer.

Article 41

The seller must deliver goods which are free from any right or claim of a third party, unless the buyer agreed to take the goods subject to that right or claim. However, if such right or claim is based on industrial property or other intellectual property, the seller's obligation is governed by article 42.

Article 42

(1) The seller must deliver goods which are free from any right or claim of a third party based on industrial property or other intellectual property, of which at the time of the conclusion of the contract the seller knew or could not have been unaware, provided that the right or claim is based on industrial property or other intellectual property:

(a) under the law of the State where the goods will be resold or otherwise used, if it was contemplated by the parties at the time of the conclusion of the contract that the goods would be resold or otherwise used in that State; or

(b) in any other case, under the law of the State where the buyer has his place of business.

(2) The obligation of the seller under the preceding paragraph does not extend to cases where:

(a) at the time of the conclusion of the contract the buyer knew or could not have been unaware of the right or claim; or

(b) the right or claim results from the seller's compliance with technical drawings, designs, formulae or other such specifications furnished by the buyer.

Article 43

(1) The buyer loses the right to rely on the provisions of article 41 or article 42 if he does not give notice to the seller specifying the nature of the right or claim of the third party within a reasonable time after he has become aware or ought to have become aware of the right or claim.

(2) The seller is not entitled to rely on the provisions of the preceding paragraph if he knew of the right or claim of the third party and the nature of it.

Article 44

Notwithstanding the provisions of paragraph (1) of article 39 and paragraph (1) of article 43, the buyer may reduce the price in accordance with article 50 or claim damages, except for loss of profit, if he has a reasonable excuse for his failure to give the required notice.

Section III.
Remedies for breach of contract by the seller
Article 45

(1) If the seller fails to perform any of his obligations under the contract or this Convention, the buyer may:

(a) exercise the rights provided in articles 46 to 52;

(b) claim damages as provided in articles 74 to 77.

(2) The buyer is not deprived of any right he may have to claim damages by exercising his right to other remedies.

(3) No period of grace may be granted to the seller by a court or arbitral tribunal when the buyer resorts to a remedy for breach of contract.

Article 46

(1) The buyer may require performance by the seller of his obligations unless the buyer has resorted to a remedy which is inconsistent with this requirement.

(2) If the goods do not conform with the contract, the buyer may require delivery of substitute goods only if the lack of conformity constitutes a fundamental breach of contract and a request for substitute goods is made either in conjunction with notice given under article 39 or within a reasonable time thereafter.

(3) If the goods do not conform with the contract, the buyer may require the seller to remedy the lack of conformity by repair, unless this is unreasonable having regard to all the circumstances. A request for repair must be made either in conjunction with notice given under article 39 or within a reasonable time thereafter.

Article 47

(1) The buyer may fix an additional period of time of reasonable length for performance by the seller of his obligations.

(2) Unless the buyer has received notice from the seller that he will not perform within the period so fixed, the buyer may not, during that period, resort to any remedy for breach of contract. However, the buyer is not deprived thereby of any right he may have to claim damages for delay in performance.

Article 48

(1) Subject to article 49, the seller may, even after the date for delivery, remedy at his own expense any failure to perform his obligations, if he can do so without unreasonable delay and without causing the buyer unreasonable inconvenience or uncertainty of reimbursement by the seller of expenses advanced by the buyer. However, the buyer retains any right to claim damages as provided for in this Convention.

(2) If the seller requests the buyer to make known whether he will accept performance and the buyer does not comply with the request within a reasonable time, the seller may perform within the time indicated in his request. The buyer may not, during that period of time, resort to any remedy which is inconsistent with performance by the seller.

(3) A notice by the seller that he will perform within a specified period of time is assumed to include a request, under the preceding paragraph, that the buyer make known his decision.

(4) A request or notice by the seller under paragraph (2) or (3) of this article is not effective unless received by the buyer.

Article 49

(1) The buyer may declare the contract avoided:

(a) if the failure by the seller to perform any of his obligations under the contract or this Convention amounts to a fundamental breach of contract; or

(b) in case of non-delivery, if the seller does not deliver the goods within the additional period of time fixed by the buyer in accordance with paragraph (1) of article 47 or declares that he will not deliver within the period so fixed.

(2) However, in cases where the seller has delivered the goods, the buyer loses the right to declare the contract avoided unless he does so:

(a) in respect of late delivery, within a reasonable time after he has become aware that delivery has been made;

(b) in respect of any breach other than late delivery, within a reasonable time:

(i) after he knew or ought to have known of the breach;

(ii) after the expiration of any additional period of time fixed by the buyer in accordance with paragraph (1) of article 47, or after the seller has declared that he will not perform his obligations within such an additional period; or

(iii) after the expiration of any additional period of time indicated by the seller in accordance with paragraph (2) of article 48, or after the buyer has declared that he will not accept performance.

Article 50

If the goods do not conform with the contract and whether or not the price has already been paid, the buyer may reduce the price in the same proportion as the value that the goods actually delivered had at the time of the delivery bears to the value that conforming goods would have had at that time. However, if the seller remedies any failure to perform his obligations in accordance with article 37 or article 48 or if the buyer refuses to accept performance by the seller in accordance with those articles, the buyer may not reduce the price.

Article 51

(1) If the seller delivers only a part of the goods or if only a part of the goods delivered is in conformity with the contract, articles 46 to 50 apply in respect of the part which is missing or which does not conform.

(2) The buyer may declare the contract avoided in its entirety only if the failure to make delivery completely or in conformity with the contract amounts to a fundamental breach of the contract.

Article 52

(1) If the seller delivers the goods before the date fixed, the buyer may take delivery or refuse to take delivery.

(2) If the seller delivers a quantity of goods greater than that provided for in the contract, the buyer may take delivery or refuse to take delivery of the excess quantity. If the buyer takes delivery of all or part of the excess quantity, he must pay for it at the contract rate.

Chapter III
Obligations Of The Buyer

Article 53

The buyer must pay the price for the goods and take delivery of them as required by the contract and this Convention.

Section I.
Payment of the price

Article 54

The buyer's obligation to pay the price includes taking such steps and complying with such formalities as may be required under the contract or any laws and regulations to enable payment to be made.

Article 55

Where a contract has been validly concluded but does not expressly or implicitly fix or make provision for determining the price, the parties are considered, in the absence of any indication to the contrary, to have impliedly made reference to the price generally charged at the time of the conclusion of the contract for such goods sold under comparable circumstances in the trade concerned.

Article 56

If the price is fixed according to the weight of the goods, in case of doubt it is to be determined by the net weight.

Article 57

(1) If the buyer is not bound to pay the price at any other particular place, he must pay it to the seller:

(a) at the seller's place of business; or

(b) if the payment is to be made against the handing over of the goods or of documents, at the place where the handing over takes place.

(2) The seller must bear any increases in the expenses incidental to payment which is caused by a change in his place of business subsequent to the conclusion of the contract.

Article 58

(1) If the buyer is not bound to pay the price at any other specific time, he must pay it when the seller places either the goods or documents controlling their disposition at the buyer's disposal in accordance with the contract and this Convention. The seller may make such payment a condition for handing over the goods or documents.

(2) If the contract involves carriage of the goods, the seller may dispatch the goods on terms whereby the goods, or documents controlling their disposition, will not be handed over to the buyer except against payment of the price.

(3) The buyer is not bound to pay the price until he has had an opportunity to examine the goods, unless the procedures for delivery or payment agreed upon by the parties are inconsistent with his having such an opportunity.

Article 59

The buyer must pay the price on the date fixed by or determinable from the contract and this Convention without the need for any request or compliance with any formality on the part of the seller.

Section II.
Taking delivery

Article 60

The buyer's obligation to take delivery consists:

(a) in doing all the acts which could reasonably be expected of him in order to enable the seller to make delivery; and

(b) in taking over the goods.

Section III.
Remedies for breach of contract by the buyer

Article 61

(1) If the buyer fails to perform any of his obligations under the contract or this Convention, the seller may:

(a) exercise the rights provided in articles 62 to 65;

(b) claim damages as provided in articles 74 to 77.

(2) The seller is not deprived of any right he may have to claim damages by exercising his right to other remedies.

(3) No period of grace may be granted to the buyer by a court or arbitral tribunal when the seller resorts to a remedy for breach of contract.

Article 62

The seller may require the buyer to pay the price, take delivery or perform his other obligations, unless the seller has resorted to a remedy which is inconsistent with this requirement.

Article 63

(1) The seller may fix an additional period of time of reasonable length for performance by the buyer of his obligations.

(2) Unless the seller has received notice from the buyer that he will not perform within the period so fixed, the seller may not, during that period, resort to any remedy for breach of contract. However, the seller is not deprived thereby of any right he may have to claim damages for delay in performance.

Article 64

(1) The seller may declare the contract avoided:

(a) if the failure by the buyer to perform any of his obligations under the contract or this Convention amounts to a fundamental breach of contract; or

(b) if the buyer does not, within the additional period of time fixed by the seller in accordance with paragraph (1) of article 63, perform his obligation to pay the price or take delivery of the goods, or if he declares that he will not do so within the period so fixed.

(2) However, in cases where the buyer has paid the price, the seller loses the right to declare the contract avoided unless he does so:

(a) in respect of late performance by the buyer, before the seller has become aware that performance has been rendered; or

(b) in respect of any breach other than late performance by the buyer, within a reasonable time:

(i) after the seller knew or ought to have known of the breach; or

(ii) after the expiration of any additional period of time fixed by the seller in accordance with paragraph (1) of article 63, or after the buyer has declared that he will not perform his obligations within such an additional period.

Article 65

(1) If under the contract the buyer is to specify the form, measurement or other features of the goods and he fails to make such specification either on the date agreed upon or within a reasonable time after receipt of a request from the seller, the seller may, without prejudice to any other rights he may have, make the specification himself in accordance with the requirements of the buyer that may be known to him.

(2) If the seller makes the specification himself, he must inform the buyer of the details thereof and must fix a reasonable time within which the buyer may make a different specification. If, after receipt of such a communication, the buyer fails to do so within the time so fixed, the specification made by the seller is binding.

Chapter IV
Passing Of Risk

Article 66

Loss of or damage to the goods after the risk has passed to the buyer does not discharge him from his obligation to pay the price, unless the loss or damage is due to an act or omission of the seller.

Article 67

(1) If the contract of sale involves carriage of the goods and the seller is not bound to hand them over at a particular place, the risk passes to the buyer when the goods are handed over to the first carrier for transmission to the buyer in accordance with the contract of sale. If the seller is bound to hand the goods over to a carrier at a particular place, the risk does not pass to the buyer until the goods are handed over to the carrier at that place. The fact that the seller is authorized to retain documents controlling the disposition of the goods does not affect the passage of the risk.

(2) Nevertheless, the risk does not pass to the buyer until the goods are clearly identified to the contract, whether by markings on the goods, by shipping documents, by notice given to the buyer or otherwise.

Article 68

The risk in respect of goods sold in transit passes to the buyer from the time of the conclusion of the contract. However, if the circumstances so indicate, the risk is assumed by the buyer from the time the goods were handed over to the carrier who issued the documents embodying the contract of carriage. Nevertheless, if at the time of the conclusion of the contract of sale the seller knew or ought to have known that the goods had been lost or damaged and did not disclose this to the buyer, the loss or damage is at the risk of the seller.

Article 69

(1) In cases not within articles 67 and 68, the risk passes to the buyer when he takes over the goods or, if he does not do so in due time, from the time when the goods are placed at his disposal and he commits a breach of contract by failing to take delivery.

(2) However, if the buyer is bound to take over the goods at a place other than a place of business of the seller, the risk passes when delivery is due and the buyer is aware of the fact that the goods are placed at his disposal at that place.

(3) If the contract relates to goods not then identified, the goods are considered not to be placed at the disposal of the buyer until they are clearly identified to the contract.

Article 70

If the seller has committed a fundamental breach of contract, articles 67, 68 and 69 do not impair the remedies available to the buyer on account of the breach.

Chapter V
Provisions Common To The Obligations Of The Seller And Of The Buyer

Section I.
Anticipatory breach and instalment contracts

Article 71

(1) A party may suspend the performance of his obligations if, after the conclusion of the contract, it becomes apparent that the other party will not perform a substantial part of his obligations as a result of:

(a) a serious deficiency in his ability to perform or in his credit-worthiness; or

(b) his conduct in preparing to perform or in performing the contract.

(2) If the seller has already dispatched the goods before the grounds described in the preceding paragraph become evident, he may prevent the handing over of the goods to the buyer even though

the buyer holds a document which entitles him to obtain them. The present paragraph relates only to the rights in the goods as between the buyer and the seller.

(3) A party suspending performance, whether before or after dispatch of the goods, must immediately give notice of the suspension to the other party and must continue with performance if the other party provides adequate assurance of his performance.

Article 72

(1) If prior to the date for performance of the contract it is clear that one of the parties will commit a fundamental breach of contract, the other party may declare the contract avoided.

(2) If time allows, the party intending to declare the contract avoided must give reasonable notice to the other party in order to permit him to provide adequate assurance of his performance.

(3) The requirements of the preceding paragraph do not apply if the other party has declared that he will not perform his obligations.

Article 73

(1) In the case of a contract for delivery of goods by instalments, if the failure of one party to perform any of his obligations in respect of any instalment constitutes a fundamental breach of contract with respect to that instalment, the other party may declare the contract avoided with respect to that instalment.

(2) If one party's failure to perform any of his obligations in respect of any instalment gives the other party good grounds to conclude that a fundamental breach of contract will occur with respect to future instalments, he may declare the contract avoided for the future, provided that he does so within a reasonable time.

(3) A buyer who declares the contract avoided in respect of any delivery may, at the same time, declare it avoided in respect of deliveries already made or of future deliveries if, by reason of their interdependence, those deliveries could not be used for the purpose contemplated by the parties at the time of the conclusion of the contract.

Section II.
Damages
Article 74

Damages for breach of contract by one party consist of a sum equal to the loss, including loss of profit, suffered by the other party as a consequence of the breach. Such damages may not exceed the loss which the party in breach foresaw or ought to have foreseen at the time of the conclusion of the contract, in the light of the facts and matters of which he then knew or ought to have known, as a possible consequence of the breach of contract.

Article 75

If the contract is avoided and if, in a reasonable manner and within a reasonable time after avoidance, the buyer has bought goods in replacement or the seller has resold the goods, the party claiming damages may recover the difference between the contract price and the price in the substitute transaction as well as any further damages recoverable under article 74.

Article 76

(1) If the contract is avoided and there is a current price for the goods, the party claiming damages may, if he has not made a purchase or resale under article 75, recover the difference between the price fixed by the contract and the current price at the time of avoidance as well as any further damages recoverable under article 74. If, however, the party claiming damages has avoided the contract after taking over the goods, the current price at the time of such taking over shall be applied instead of the current price at the time of avoidance.

(2) For the purposes of the preceding paragraph, the current price is the price prevailing at the place where delivery of the goods should have been made or, if there is no current price at that place, the price at such other place as serves as a reasonable substitute, making due allowance for differences in the cost of transporting the goods.

Article 77

A party who relies on a breach of contract must take such measures as are reasonable in the circumstances to mitigate the loss, including loss of profit, resulting from the breach. If he fails to take such measures, the party in breach may claim a reduction in the damages in the amount by which the loss should have been mitigated.

Section III.
Interest
Article 78

If a party fails to pay the price or any other sum that is in arrears, the other party is entitled to interest on it, without prejudice to any claim for damages recoverable under article 74.

Section IV.
Exemptions
Article 79

(1) A party is not liable for a failure to perform any of his obligations if he proves that the failure was due to an impediment beyond his control and that he could not reasonably be expected to have taken the impediment into account at the time of the conclusion of the contract or to have avoided or overcome it or its consequences.

(2) If the party's failure is due to the failure by a third person whom he has engaged to perform the whole or a part of the contract, that party is exempt from liability only if:

(a) he is exempt under the preceding paragraph; and

(b) the person whom he has so engaged would be so exempt if the provisions of that paragraph were applied to him.

(3) The exemption provided by this article has effect for the period during which the impediment exists.

(4) The party who fails to perform must give notice to the other party of the impediment and its effect on his ability to perform. If the notice is not received by the other party within a reasonable time after the party who fails to perform knew or ought to have

known of the impediment, he is liable for damages resulting from such non-receipt.

(5) Nothing in this article prevents either party from exercising any right other than to claim damages under this Convention.

Article 80

A party may not rely on a failure of the other party to perform, to the extent that such failure was caused by the first party's act or omission.

Section V.
Effects of avoidance

Article 81

(1) Avoidance of the contract releases both parties from their obligations under it, subject to any damages which may be due. Avoidance does not affect any provision of the contract for the settlement of disputes or any other provision of the contract governing the rights and obligations of the parties consequent upon the avoidance of the contract.

(2) A party who has performed the contract either wholly or in part may claim restitution from the other party of whatever the first party has supplied or paid under the contract. If both parties are bound to make restitution, they must do so concurrently.

Article 82

(1) The buyer loses the right to declare the contract avoided or to require the seller to deliver substitute goods if it is impossible for him to make restitution of the goods substantially in the condition in which he received them.

(2) The preceding paragraph does not apply:

(a) if the impossibility of making restitution of the goods or of making restitution of the goods substantially in the condition in which the buyer received them is not due to his act or omission;

(b) if the goods or part of the goods have perished or deteriorated as a result of the examination provided for in article 38; or

(c) if the goods or part of the goods have been sold in the normal course of business or have been consumed or transformed by the buyer in the course of normal use before he discovered or ought to have discovered the lack of conformity.

Article 83

A buyer who has lost the right to declare the contract avoided or to require the seller to deliver substitute goods in accordance with article 82 retains all other remedies under the contract and this Convention.

Article 84

(1) If the seller is bound to refund the price, he must also pay interest on it, from the date on which the price was paid.

(2) The buyer must account to the seller for all benefits which he has derived from the goods or part of them:

(a) if he must make restitution of the goods or part of them; or

(b) if it is impossible for him to make restitution of all or part of the goods or to make restitution of all or part of the goods substantially in the condition in which he received them, but he has nevertheless declared the contract avoided or required the seller to deliver substitute goods.

Section VI.
Preservation of the goods

Article 85

If the buyer is in delay in taking delivery of the goods or, where payment of the price and delivery of the goods are to be made concurrently, if he fails to pay the price, and the seller is either in possession of the goods or otherwise able to control their disposition, the seller must take such steps as are reasonable in the circumstances to preserve them. He is entitled to retain them until he has been reimbursed his reasonable expenses by the buyer.

Article 86

(1) If the buyer has received the goods and intends to exercise any right under the contract or this Convention to reject them, he must take such steps to preserve them as are reasonable in the circumstances. He is entitled to retain them until he has been reimbursed his reasonable expenses by the seller.

(2) If goods dispatched to the buyer have been placed at his disposal at their destination and he exercises the right to reject them, he must take possession of them on behalf of the seller, provided that this can be done without payment of the price and without unreasonable inconvenience or unreasonable expense. This provision does not apply if the seller or a person authorized to take charge of the goods on his behalf is present at the destination. If the buyer takes possession of the goods under this paragraph, his rights and obligations are governed by the preceding paragraph.

Article 87

A party who is bound to take steps to preserve the goods may deposit them in a warehouse of a third person at the expense of the other party provided that the expense incurred is not unreasonable.

Article 88

(1) A party who is bound to preserve the goods in accordance with article 85 or 86 may sell them by any appropriate means if there has been an unreasonable delay by the other party in taking possession of the goods or in taking them back or in paying the price or the cost of preservation, provided that reasonable notice of the intention to sell has been given to the other party.

(2) If the goods are subject to rapid deterioration or their preservation would involve unreasonable expense, a party who is bound to preserve the goods in accordance with article 85 or 86 must take reasonable measures to sell them. To the extent possible he must give notice to the other party of his intention to sell.

(3) A party selling the goods has the right to retain out of the proceeds of sale an amount equal to the reasonable expenses of

preserving the goods and of selling them. He must account to the other party for the balance.

Part IV

FINAL PROVISIONS

Article 89

The Secretary-General of the United Nations is hereby designated as the depositary for this Convention.

Article 90

This Convention does not prevail over any international agreement which has already been or may be entered into and which contains provisions concerning the matters governed by this Convention, provided that the parties have their places of business in States parties to such agreement.

Article 91

(1) This Convention is open for signature at the concluding meeting of the United Nations Conference on Contracts for the International Sale of Goods and will remain open for signature by all States at the Headquarters of the United Nations, New York until 30 September 1981.

(2) This Convention is subject to ratification, acceptance or approval by the signatory States.

(3) This Convention is open for accession by all States which are not signatory States as from the date it is open for signature.

(4) Instruments of ratification, acceptance, approval and accession are to be deposited with the Secretary-General of the United Nations.

Article 92

(1) A Contracting State may declare at the time of signature, ratification, acceptance, approval or accession that it will not be bound

by Part II of this Convention or that it will not be bound by Part III of this Convention.

(2) A Contracting State which makes a declaration in accordance with the preceding paragraph in respect of Part II or Part III of this Convention is not to be considered a Contracting State within paragraph (1) of article 1 of this Convention in respect of matters governed by the Part to which the declaration applies.

Article 93

(1) If a Contracting State has two or more territorial units in which, according to its constitution, different systems of law are applicable in relation to the matters dealt with in this Convention, it may, at the time of signature, ratification, acceptance, approval or accession, declare that this Convention is to extend to all its territorial units or only to one or more of them, and may amend its declaration by submitting another declaration at any time.

(2) These declarations are to be notified to the depositary and are to state expressly the territorial units to which the Convention extends.

(3) If, by virtue of a declaration under this article, this Convention extends to one or more but not all of the territorial units of a Contracting State, and if the place of business of a party is located in that State, this place of business, for the purposes of this Convention, is considered not to be in a Contracting State, unless it is in a territorial unit to which the Convention extends.

(4) If a Contracting State makes no declaration under paragraph (1) of this article, the Convention is to extend to all territorial units of that State.

Article 94

(1) Two or more Contracting States which have the same or closely related legal rules on matters governed by this Convention may at any time declare that the Convention is not to apply to contracts of sale or to their formation where the parties have their places of business in those States. Such declarations may be made jointly or by reciprocal unilateral declarations.

(2) A Contracting State which has the same or closely related legal rules on matters governed by this Convention as one or more non-Contracting States may at any time declare that the Convention is not to apply to contracts of sale or to their formation where the parties have their places of business in those States.

(3) If a State which is the object of a declaration under the preceding paragraph subsequently becomes a Contracting State, the declaration made will, as from the date on which the Convention enters into force in respect of the new Contracting State, have the effect of a declaration made under paragraph (1), provided that the new Contracting State joins in such declaration or makes a reciprocal unilateral declaration.

Article 95

Any State may declare at the time of the deposit of its instrument of ratification, acceptance, approval or accession that it will not be bound by subparagraph (1)(b) of article 1 of this Convention.

Article 96

A Contracting State whose legislation requires contracts of sale to be concluded in or evidenced by writing may at any time make a declaration in accordance with article 12 that any provision of article 11, article 29, or Part II of this Convention, that allows a contract of sale or its modification or termination by agreement or any offer, acceptance, or other indication of intention to be made in any form other than in writing, does not apply where any party has his place of business in that State.

Article 97

(1) Declarations made under this Convention at the time of signature are subject to confirmation upon ratification, acceptance or approval.

(2) Declarations and confirmations of declarations are to be in writing and be formally notified to the depositary.

(3) A declaration takes effect simultaneously with the entry into force of this Convention in respect of the State concerned. However, a dec-

laration of which the depositary receives formal notification after such entry into force takes effect on the first day of the month following the expiration of six months after the date of its receipt by the depositary. Reciprocal unilateral declarations under article 94 take effect on the first day of the month following the expiration of six months after the receipt of the latest declaration by the depositary.

(4) Any State which makes a declaration under this Convention may withdraw it at any time by a formal notification in writing addressed to the depositary. Such withdrawal is to take effect on the first day of the month following the expiration of six months after the date of the receipt of the notification by the depositary.

(5) A withdrawal of a declaration made under article 94 renders inoperative, as from the date on which the withdrawal takes effect, any reciprocal declaration made by another State under that article.

Article 98

No reservations are permitted except those expressly authorized in this Convention.

Article 99

(1) This Convention enters into force, subject to the provisions of paragraph (6) of this article, on the first day of the month following the expiration of twelve months after the date of deposit of the tenth instrument of ratification, acceptance, approval or accession, including an instrument which contains a declaration made under article 92.

(2) When a State ratifies, accepts, approves or accedes to this Convention after the deposit of the tenth instrument of ratification, acceptance, approval or accession, this Convention, with the exception of the Part excluded, enters into force in respect of that State, subject to the provisions of paragraph (6) of this article, on the first day of the month following the expiration of twelve months after the date of the deposit of its instrument of ratification, acceptance, approval or accession.

(3) A State which ratifies, accepts, approves or accedes to this Convention and is a party to either or both the Convention relating to

a Uniform Law on the Formation of Contracts for the International Sale of Goods done at The Hague on 1 July 1964 (1964 Hague Formation Convention) and the Convention relating to a Uniform Law on the International Sale of Goods done at The Hague on 1 July 1964 (1964 Hague Sales Convention) shall at the same time denounce, as the case may be, either or both the 1964 Hague Sales Convention and the 1964 Hague Formation Convention by notifying the Government of the Netherlands to that effect.

(4) A State party to the 1964 Hague Sales Convention which ratifies, accepts, approves or accedes to the present Convention and declares or has declared under article 52 that it will not be bound by Part II of this Convention shall at the time of ratification, acceptance, approval or accession denounce the 1964 Hague Sales Convention by notifying the Government of the Netherlands to that effect.

(5) A State party to the 1964 Hague Formation Convention which ratifies, accepts, approves or accedes to the present Convention and declares or has declared under article 92 that it will not be bound by Part III of this Convention shall at the time of ratification, acceptance, approval or accession denounce the 1964 Hague Formation Convention by notifying the Government of the Netherlands to that effect.

(6) For the purpose of this article, ratifications, acceptances, approvals and accessions in respect of this Convention by States parties to the 1964 Hague Formation Convention or to the 1964 Hague Sales Convention shall not be effective until such denunciations as may be required on the part of those States in respect of the latter two Conventions have themselves become effective. The depositary of this Convention shall consult with the Government of the Netherlands, as the depositary of the 1964 Conventions, so as to ensure necessary co-ordination in this respect.

Article 100

(1) This Convention applies to the formation of a contract only when the proposal for concluding the contract is made on or after the date when the Convention enters into force in respect of the Contracting States referred to in subparagraph (1)(a) or the Contracting State referred to in subparagraph (1)(b) of article 1.

(2) This Convention applies only to contracts concluded on or after the date when the Convention enters into force in respect of the Contracting States referred to in subparagraph (1)(a) or the Contracting State referred to in subparagraph (1)(b) of article 1.

Article 101

(1) A Contracting State may denounce this Convention, or Part II or Part III of the Convention, by a formal notification in writing addressed to the depositary.

(2) The denunciation takes effect on the first day of the month following the expiration of twelve months after the notification is received by the depositary. Where a longer period for the denunciation to take effect is specified in the notification, the denunciation takes effect upon the expiration of such longer period after the notification is received by the depositary.

DONE at Vienna, this day of eleventh day of April, one thousand nine hundred and eighty, in a single original, of which the Arabic, Chinese, English, French, Russian and Spanish texts are equally authentic.

IN WITNESS WHEREOF the undersigned plenipotentiaries, being duly authorized by their respective Governments, have signed this Convention.

Glossary

absolute standards

A type of standard used in competitive negotiations to evaluate a proposal. Includes both the maximum acceptable value and the minimum acceptable value for all selected evaluation criteria.

acceptance

(1) The taking and receiving of anything in good part, and as if it were a tacit agreement to a preceding act, which might have been defeated or avoided if such acceptance had not been made. (2) Agreement to the terms offered in a contract. An acceptance must be communicated, and (in common law) it must be the mirror image of the offer.

acquisition cost

The money invested up front to bring in new customers

acquisition plan

A plan for an acquisition that serves as the basis for initiating the individual contracting actions necessary to acquire a system or support a program.

acquisition strategy

The conceptual framework for conducting systems acquisition. It encompasses the broad concepts and objectives that direct and control the overall development, production, and deployment of a system.

act of God

An inevitable, accidental, or extraordinary event that cannot be foreseen and guarded against, such as lightning, tornadoes, or earthquakes.

actual authority

The power that the principal intentionally confers on the agent or allows the agent to believe he or she possesses.

actual damages

See *compensatory damages.*

affidavit

A written and signed statement sworn to under oath.

agency

A relationship that exists when there is a delegation of authority to perform all acts connected within a particular trade, business, or company. It gives authority to the agent to act in all matters relating to the business of the principal.

agent

An employee (usually a contract manager) empowered to bind his or her organization legally in contract negotiations.

allowable cost

A cost that is reasonable, allocable, and within accepted standards, or otherwise conforms to generally accepted accounting principles, specific limitations or exclusions, or agreed-on terms between contractual parties.

alternative dispute resolution

Any procedure that is used, in lieu of litigation, to resolve issues in controversy, including but not limited to, settlement negotiations, conciliation, facilitation, mediation, fact finding, mini-trials and arbitration.

amortization

Process of spreading the cost of an intangible asset over the expected useful life of the asset.

apparent authority

The power that the principal permits the perceived agent to exercise, although not actually granted.

as is

A contract phrase referring to the condition of property to be sold or leased; generally pertains to a disclaimer of liability; property sold in as-is condition is generally not guaranteed.

assign

To convey or transfer to another, as to assign property, rights, or interests to another.

assignment

The transfer of property by an assignor to an assignee.

audits

The systematic examination of records and documents and/ or the securing of other evidence by confirmation, physical inspection, or otherwise, for one or more of the following purposes: determining the propriety or legality of proposed or completed transactions; ascertaining whether all transactions have been recorded and are reflected accurately in accounts; determining the existence of recorded assets and inclusiveness of recorded liabilities; determining the accuracy of financial or statistical statements or reports and the fairness of the facts they represent; determining the degree of compliance with established policies and procedures in terms of financial transactions and business management; and appraising an account system and making recommendations concerning it.

base profit

The money a company is paid by a customer, which exceeds the company's cost.

best value

The best trade-off between competing factors for a particular purchase requirement. The key to successful best-value contracting is consideration of life-cycle costs, including the use of quantitative as well as qualitative techniques to measure price and technical performance trade-offs between various proposals. The best-value concept applies to acquisitions in which price or price-related factors are *not* the primary determinant of who receives the contract award.

bid

An offer in response to an invitation for bids (IFB).

bid development

All of the work activities required to design and price the product and service solution and accurately articulate this in a proposal for a customer.

bid phase

The period of time a seller of goods and/or services uses to develop a bid/proposal, conduct internal bid reviews, and obtain stakeholder approval to submit a bid/proposal.

bilateral contract

A contract formed if an offer states that acceptance requires only for the accepting party to promise to perform. In contrast, a *unilateral contract* is formed if an offer requires actual performance for acceptance.

bond

A written instrument executed by a seller and a second party (the surety or sureties) to ensure fulfillment of the principal's obligations to a third party (the obligee or buyer), identified in the bond. If the principal's obligations are not met, the bond ensures payment, to the extent stipulated, of any loss sustained by the obligee.

breach of contract

(1) The failure, without legal excuse, to perform any promise that forms the whole or part of a contract. (2) The ending of a contract that occurs when one or both of the parties fail to keep their promises; this could lead to arbitration or litigation.

buyer

The party contracting for goods and/or services with one or more sellers.

cancellation

The withdrawal of the requirement to purchase goods and/or services by the buyer.

capture management

The art and science of winning more business

capture management life cycle

The art and science of winning more business throughout the entire business cycle

capture project plan

A document or game plan of who needs to do what, when, where, how often and how much to win business.

change in scope

An amendment to approved program requirements or specifications after negotiation of a basic contract. It may result in an increase or decrease.

change order/purchase order amendment

A written order directing the seller to make changes according to the provisions of the contract documents.

claim

A demand by one party to contract for something from another party, usually but not necessarily for more money or more time. Claims are usually based on an argument that the party making the demand is entitled to an adjustment by virtue of the contract terms or some violation of those terms by the other party. The word does not imply any disagreement between the parties, although claims often lead to disagreements. This book uses the term *dispute* to refer to disagreements that have become intractable.

clause

A statement of one of the rights and/or obligations of the parties to a contract. A contract consists of a series of clauses.

collaboration software

Automated tools that allow for the real-time exchange of visual information using personal computers.

collateral benefit

The degree to which pursuit of an opportunity will improve the existing skill level or develop new skills which will positively affect other or future business opportunities.

compensable delay

A delay for which the buyer is contractually responsible that excuses the seller's failure to perform and is compensable.

compensatory damages

Damages that will compensate the injured party for the loss sustained and nothing more. They are awarded by the court as the measure of actual loss, and not as punishment for outrageous conduct or to deter future transgressions. Compensatory damages are often referred to as "actual damages." See also *incidental* and *punitive damages*.

competitive intelligence

Information on competitors or competitive teams which is specific to an opportunity.

competitive negotiation

A method of contracting involving a request for proposals that states the buyer's requirements and criteria for evaluation; submission of timely proposals by a maximum number of offerors; discussions with those offerors found to be within the competitive range; and award of a contract to the one offeror whose offer, price, and other consideration factors are most advantageous to the buyer.

condition precedent

A condition that activates a term in a contract.

condition subsequent

A condition that suspends a term in a contract.

conflict of interest

Term used in connection with public officials and fiduciaries and their relationships to matters of private interest or gain to them. Ethical problems connected therewith are covered by statutes in most jurisdictions and by federal statutes on the federal level. A conflict of interest arises when an employee's personal or financial interest conflicts or appears to conflict with his or her official responsibility.

consideration

(1) The thing of value (amount of money or acts to be done or not done) that must change hands between the parties to a contract. (2) The inducement to a contract — the cause, motive, price, or impelling influence that induces a contracting party to enter into a contract.

contract negotiation

Is the process of unifying different positions into a unanimous joint decision, regarding the buying and selling of products and/or services.

contract negotiation process

A three phased approach composed of planning, negotiating, and documenting a contractual agreement between two or more parties to buy or sell products and/or services.

constructive change

An oral or written act or omission by an authorized or unauthorized agent that is of such a nature that it is construed to have the same effect as a written change order.

contingency

The quality of being contingent or casual; an event that may but does not have to occur; a possibility.

contingent contract

A contract that provides for the possibility of its termination when a specified occurrence takes place or does not take place.

contra proferentem

A legal phrase used in connection with the construction of written documents to the effect that an ambiguous provision is construed most strongly against the person who selected the language.

contract

(1) A relationship between two parties, such as a buyer and seller, that is defined by an agreement about their respective rights and responsibilities. (2) A document that describes such an agreement.

contract administration

The process of ensuring compliance with contractual terms and conditions during contract performance up to contract closeout or termination.

contract closeout

The process of verifying that all administrative matters are concluded on a contract that is otherwise physically complete — in other words, the seller has delivered the required supplies or performed the required services, and the buyer has inspected and accepted the supplies or services.

contract fulfillment

The joint Buyer/Seller actions taken to successfully perform and administer a contractual agreement and met or exceed all contract obligations, including effective changes management and timely contract closeout.

contract interpretation

The entire process of determining what the parties agreed to in their bargain. The basic objective of contract interpretation is to determine the intent of the parties. Rules calling for interpretation of the documents against the drafter, and imposing a duty to seek clarification on the drafter, allocate risks of contractual ambiguities by resolving disputes in favor of the party least responsible for the ambiguity.

contract management

The art and science of managing a contractual agreement(s) throughout the contracting process.

contract type

A specific pricing arrangement used for the performance of work under the contract.

contractor

The seller or provider of goods and/or services.

controversy

A litigated question. A civil action or suit may not be instigated unless it is based on a "justifiable" dispute. This term is important in that judicial power of the courts extends only to cases and "controversies."

copyright

A royalty-free, nonexclusive, and irrevocable license to reproduce, translate, publish, use, and dispose of written or recorded material, and to authorize others to do so.

cost

The amount of money expended in acquiring a product or obtaining a service, or the total of acquisition costs plus all expenses related to operating and maintaining an item once acquired.

cost of good sold (COGS)

Direct costs of producing finished goods for sale.

cost accounting standards

Federal standards designed to provide consistency and coherency in defense and other government contract accounting.

cost-plus-award fee (CPAF) contract

A type of cost-reimbursement contract with special incentive fee provisions used to motivate excellent contract performance in such areas as quality, timeliness, ingenuity, and cost-effectiveness.

cost-plus-fixed fee (CPFF) contract

A type of cost-reimbursement contract that provides for the payment of a fixed fee to the contractor. It does not vary with actual costs, but may be adjusted if there are any changes in the work or services to be performed under the contract.

cost-plus-incentive fee (CPIF) contract

A type of cost-reimbursement contract with provision for a fee that is adjusted by a formula in accordance with the relationship between total allowable costs and target costs.

cost-plus-a-percentage-of-cost (CPPC) contract

A type of cost-reimbursement contract that provides for a reimbursement of the allowable cost of services performed plus an agreed-on percentage of the estimated cost as profit.

cost-reimbursement (CR) contract

A type of contract that usually includes an estimate of project cost, a provision for reimbursing the seller's expenses, and a provision for paying a fee as profit. CR contracts are often used when there is high uncertainty about costs. They normally also include a limitation on the buyer's cost liability.

cost-sharing contract

A cost-reimbursement contract in which the seller receives no fee and is reimbursed only for an agreed-on portion of its allowable costs.

cost contract

The simplest type of cost-reimbursement contract. Governments commonly use this type when contracting with universities and nonprofit organizations for research projects. The contract provides for reimbursing contractually allowable costs, with no allowance given for profit.

cost proposal

The instrument required of an offeror for the submission or identification of cost or pricing data by which an offeror submits to the buyer a summary of estimated (or incurred) costs, suitable for detailed review and analysis.

counteroffer

An offer made in response to an original offer that changes the terms of the original.

customer revenue growth

The increased revenues achieved by keeping a customer for an extended period of time.

customer support costs

Costs expended by a company to provide information and advice concerning purchases.

default termination

The termination of a contract, under the standard default clause, because of a buyer's or seller's failure to perform any of the terms of the contract.

defect

The absence of something necessary for completeness or perfection. A deficiency in something essential to the proper use of a thing. Some structural weakness in a part or component that is responsible for damage.

defect, latent

A defect that existed at the time of acceptance but would not have been discovered by a reasonable inspection.

defect, patent

A defect that can be discovered without undue effort. If the defect was actually known to the buyer at the time of acceptance, it is patent, even though it otherwise might not have been discoverable by a reasonable inspection.

definite-quantity contract

A contractual instrument that provides for a definite quantity of supplies or services to be delivered at some later, unspecified date.

delay, excusable

A contractual provision designed to protect the seller from sanctions for late performance. To the extent that it has been excusably delayed, the seller is protected from default termination or liquidated damages. Examples of excusable delay are acts of God, acts of the government, fire, flood, quarantines, strikes, epidemics, unusually severe weather, and embargoes. See also *forbearance* and *force majeure clause.*

depreciation

Amount of expense charged against earnings by a company to write off the cost of a plant or machine over its useful live, giving consideration to wear and tear, obsolescence, and salvage value.

design specification

(1) A document (including drawings) setting forth the required characteristics of a particular component, part, subsystem, system, or construction item. (2) A purchase description that establishes precise measurements, tolerances, materials, in-process and finished product tests, quality control, inspection requirements, and other specific details of the deliverable.

direct cost

The costs specifically identifiable with a contract requirement, including but not restricted to costs of material and/or labor directly incorporated into an end item.

direct labor

All work that is obviously related and specifically and conveniently traceable to specific products.

direct material

Items, including raw material, purchased parts, and subcontracted items, directly incorporated into an end item, which are identifiable to a contract requirement.

discount rate

Interest rate used in calculating present value.

discounted cash flow (DCF)

Combined present value of cash flow and tangible assets minus present value of liabilities.

discounts, allowances and returns

Price discounts, returned merchandise.

dispute

A disagreement not settled by mutual consent that could be decided by litigation or arbitration. Also see *claim*.

e-business

Technology-enabled business that focuses on seamless integration between each business, the company, and its supply partners.

EBITDA

Earnings Before Interest, Taxes, Depreciation and Amortization, but after all product/service, sales and overhead (SG&A) costs are accounted for. Sometimes referred to as Operating Profit.

EBITDARM

Acronym for Earnings Before Interest, Taxes, Depreciation, Amortization. Rent and Management fees.

e-commerce

A subset of e-business, Internet-based electronic transactions.

electronic data interchange (EDI)

Private networks used for simple data transactions, which are typically batch- processed.

elements of a contract

The items that must be present in a contract if the contract is to be binding, including an offer, acceptance (agreement), consideration, execution by competent parties, and legality of purpose.

enterprise resource planning (ERP)

An electronic framework for integrating all organizational functions, evolved from Manufacturing Resource Planning (MRP).

entire contract

A contract that is considered entire on both sides and cannot be made severable.

e-procurement

Technology-enabled buying and selling of goods and services.

estimate at completion (EAC)

The actual direct costs, plus indirect costs allocable to the contract, plus the estimate of costs (direct or indirect) for authorized work remaining.

estoppel

A rule of law that bars, prevents, and precludes a party from alleging or denying certain facts because of a previous allegation or denial or because of its previous conduct or admission.

ethics

Of or relating to moral action, conduct, motive, or character (such as ethical emotion). Also, treating of moral feelings, duties, or conduct; containing precepts of morality; moral. Professionally right or befitting; conforming to professional standards of conduct.

e-tool

An electronic device, program, system, or software application used to facilitate business.

exculpatory clause

The contract language designed to shift responsibility to the other party. A "no damages for delay" clause would be an example of one used by buyers.

excusable delay

See *delay, excusable.*

executed contract

A contract that is formed and performed at the same time. If performed in part, it is partially executed and partially executory.

executed contract (document)

A written document, signed by both parties and mailed or otherwise furnished to each party, that expresses the requirements, terms, and conditions to be met by both parties in the performance of the contract.

executory contract

A contract that has not yet been fully performed.

express

Something put in writing, for example, "express authority."

fair and reasonable

A subjective evaluation of what each party deems as equitable consideration in areas such as terms and conditions, cost or price, assured quality, timeliness of contract performance, and/or any other areas subject to negotiation.

Federal Acquisition Regulation (FAR)

The government-wide procurement regulation mandated by Congress and issued by the Department of Defense, the General Services Administration, and the National Aeronautics and Space Administration. Effective April 1, 1984, the FAR supersedes both the Defense Acquisition Regulation (DAR) and the Federal Procurement Regulation (FPR). All federal agencies are authorized to issue regulations implementing the FAR.

fee

An agreed-to amount of reimbursement beyond the initial estimate of costs. The term "fee" is used when discussing cost-reimbursement contracts, whereas the term "profit" is used in relation to fixed-price contracts.

firm-fixed-price (FFP) contract

The simplest and most common business pricing arrangement. The seller agrees to supply a quantity of goods or to provide a service for a specified price.

fixed cost

Operating expenses that are incurred to provide facilities and organization that are kept in readiness to do business without regard to actual volumes of production and sales. Examples of fixed costs consist of rent, property tax, and interest expense.

fixed price

A form of pricing that includes a ceiling beyond which the buyer bears no responsibility for payment.

fixed-price incentive (FPI) contract

A type of contract that provides for adjusting profit and establishing the final contract price using a formula based on the relationship of total final negotiated cost to total target cost. The final price is subject to a price ceiling, negotiated at the outset.

fixed-price redeterminable (FPR) contract

A type of fixed-price contract that contains provisions for subsequently negotiated adjustment, in whole or in part, of the initially negotiated base price.

fixed-price with economic price adjustment

A fixed-price contract that permits an element of cost to fluctuate to reflect current market prices.

forbearance

An intentional failure of a party to enforce a contract requirement, usually done for an act of immediate or future consideration from the other party. Sometimes forbearance is referred to as a nonwaiver or as a onetime waiver, but not as a relinquishment of rights.

force majeure clause

Major or irresistible force. Such a contract clause protects the parties in the event that a part of the contract cannot be performed due to causes outside the control of the parties and could not be avoided by exercise of due care. Excusable conditions for nonperformance, such as strikes and acts of God (e.g., typhoons) are contained in this clause.

fraud

An intentional perversion of truth to induce another in reliance upon it to part with something of value belonging to him or her or to surrender a legal right. A false representation of a matter of fact, whether by words or conduct, by false or misleading allegations, or by concealment of that which should have been disclosed, that deceives and is intended to deceive another so that he or she shall act upon it to his or her legal injury. Anything calculated to deceive.

free on board (FOB)

A term used in conjunction with a physical point to determine (a) the responsibility and basis for payment of freight charges and (b) unless otherwise agreed, the point at which title for goods passes to the buyer or consignee. *FOB origin* — The seller places the goods on the conveyance by which they are to be transported. Cost of shipping and risk of loss are borne by the buyer. *FOB destination* — The seller delivers the goods on the seller's conveyance at destination. Cost of shipping and risk of loss are borne by the seller.

functional specification

A purchase description that describes the deliverable in terms of performance characteristics and intended use, including those characteristics that at minimum are necessary to satisfy the intended use.

general and administrative (G&A)

(1) The indirect expenses related to the overall business. Expenses for a company's general and executive offices, executive compensation, staff services, and other miscellaneous support purposes. (2) Any indirect management, financial, or other expense that (a) is not assignable to a program's direct overhead charges for engineering, manufacturing, material, and so on, but (b) is routinely incurred by or allotted to a business unit, and (c) is for the general management and administration of the business as a whole.

general accepted accounting principles (GAAP)

A term encompassing conventions, rules, and procedures of accounting that are "generally accepted" and have "substantial authoritative support." The GAAP have been developed by agreement on the basis of experience, reason, custom, usage, and to a certain extent, practical necessity, rather than being derived from a formal set of theories.

General Agreement on Tariffs and Trade (GATT)

A multi-national trade agreement, signed in 1947 by 23 nations.

gross profit margin

Net Sales minus Cost of Goods Sold. Also called Gross Margin, Gross Profit or Gross Loss

gross profit margin % or ratio

Gross Profit Margin $ divided by Net Sales.

gross sales

Total revenues at invoice value before any discounts or allowances.

horizontal exchange

A marketplace that deals with goods and services that are not specific to one industry.

imply

To indirectly convey meaning or intent; to leave the determination of meaning up to the receiver of the communication based on circumstances, general language used, or conduct of those involved.

incidental damages

Any commercially reasonable charges, expenses, or commissions incurred in stopping delivery; in the transportation, care and custody of goods after the buyer's breach; or in connection with the return or resale of the goods or otherwise resulting from the breach.

indefinite-delivery/indefinite-quantity (IDIQ) contract

A type of contract in which the exact date of delivery or the exact quantity, or a combination of both, is not specified at the time the contract is executed; provisions are placed in the contract to later stipulate these elements of the contract.

indemnification clause

A contract clause by which one party engages to secure another against an anticipated loss resulting from an act or forbearance on the part of one of the parties or of some third person.

indemnify

To make good; to compensate; to reimburse a person in case of an anticipated loss.

indirect cost

Any cost not directly identifiable with a specific cost objective but subject to two or more cost objectives.

indirect labor

All work that is not specifically associated with or cannot be practically traced to specific units of output.

intellectual property

The kind of property that results from the fruits of mental labor.

internet

The World Wide Web.

interactive chat

A feature provided by automated tools that allow for users to establish a voice connection between one or more parties and exchange text or graphics via a virtual bulletin board.

intranet

An organization specific internal secure network.

joint contract

A contract in which the parties bind themselves both individually and as a unit.

liquidated damages

A contract provision providing for the assessment of damages on the seller for its failure to comply with certain performance or delivery requirements of the contract; used when the time of delivery or performance is of such importance that the buyer may reasonably expect to suffer damages if the delivery or performance is delinquent.

mailbox rule

The idea that the acceptance of an offer is effective when deposited in the mail if the envelope is properly addressed.

marketing

Activities that direct the flow of goods and services from the producer to the consumers.

market intelligence

Information on your competitors or competitive teams operating in the marketplace or industry.

market research

The process used to collect and analyze information about an entire market to help determine the most suitable approach to acquiring, distributing, and supporting supplies and services.

memorandum of agreement (MOA)/ memorandum of understanding (MOU)

The documentation of a mutually agreed-to statement of facts, intentions, procedures, and parameters for future actions and matters of coordination. A "memorandum of understanding" may express mutual understanding of an issue without implying commitments by parties to the understanding.

method of procurement

The process used for soliciting offers, evaluating offers, and awarding a contract.

modifications

Any written alterations in the specification, delivery point, rate of delivery, contract period, price, quantity, or other provision of an existing contract, accomplished in accordance with a contract clause; may be unilateral or bilateral.

monopoly

A market structure in which the entire market for a good or service is supplied by a single seller or firm.

monopsony

A market structure in which a single buyer purchases a good or service.

NCMA CMBOK

Definitive descriptions of the elements making up the body of professional knowledge that applies to contract management.

negotiation

A process between buyers and sellers seeking to reach mutual agreement on a matter of common concern through fact-finding, bargaining, and persuasion.

net marketplace

Two-sided exchange where buyers and sellers negotiate prices, usually with a bid-and-ask system, and where prices move both up and down.

net present value (NPV)

The lifetime customer revenue stream discounted by the investment costs and operations costs.

net sales

Gross sales minus discounts, allowances and returns.

North America Free Trade Agreement (NAFTA)

A trilateral trade and investment agreement, between Canada, Mexico, and the United States ratified on January 1, 1994.

novation agreement

A legal instrument executed by (a) the contractor (transferor), (b) the successor in interest (transferee), and (c) the buyer by which, among other things, the transferor guarantees performance of the contract, the transferee assumes all obligations under the contract, and the buyer recognizes the transfer of the contract and related assets.

offer

(1) The manifestation of willingness to enter into a bargain, so made as to justify another person in understanding that his or her assent to that bargain is invited and will conclude it. (2) An unequivocal and intentionally communicated statement of proposed terms made to another party. An offer is presumed revocable unless it specifically states that it is irrevocable. An

offer once made will be open for a reasonable period of time and is binding on the offeror unless revoked by the offeror before the other party's acceptance.

oligopoly

A market dominated by a few sellers.

operating expenses

SG&A plus depreciation and amortization.

opportunity

A potential or actual favorable event

opportunity engagement

The degree to which your company or your competitors were involved in establishing the customer's requirements.

opportunity profile

A stage of the Capture Management Life Cycle, during which a seller evaluates and describes the opportunity in terms of what it means to your customer, what it means to your company, and what will be required to succeed.

option

A unilateral right in a contract by which, for a specified time, the buyer may elect to purchase additional quantities of the supplies or services called for in the contract, or may elect to extend the period of performance of the contract.

order of precedence

A solicitation provision that establishes priorities so that contradictions within the solicitation can be resolved.

Organizational Breakdown Structure (OBS)

A organized structure which represents how individual team members are grouped to complete assigned work tasks.

outsourcing

A contractual process of obtaining another party to provide goods and/or services that were previously done internal to an organization.

overhead

An accounting cost category that typically includes general indirect expenses that are necessary to operate a business but are not directly assignable to a specific good or service produced. Examples include building rent, utilities, salaries of corporate officers, janitorial services, office supplies, and furniture.

overtime

The time worked by a seller's employee in excess of the employee's normal workweek.

parol evidence

Oral or verbal evidence; in contract law, the evidence drawn from sources exterior to the written instrument.

parol evidence rule

A rule that seeks to preserve the integrity of written agreements by refusing to permit contracting parties to attempt to alter a written contract with evidence of any contradictory prior or contemporaneous oral agreement (*parol* to the contract).

payments

The amount payable under the contract supporting data required to be submitted with invoices, and other payment terms such as time for payment and retention.

payment bond

A bond that secures the appropriate payment of subcontracts for their completed and acceptable goods and/or services.

Performance-based contract (PBC)

A documented business arrangement, in which the buyer and seller agree to use: a Performance work statement, performance-based metrics, and a quality assurance plant o ensure contract requirements are met or exceeded.

performance bond

A bond that secures the performance and fulfillment of all the undertakings, covenants, terms, conditions, and agreements contained in the contract.

performance specification

A purchase description that describes the deliverable in terms of desired operational characteristics. Performance specifications tend to be more restrictive than functional specifications, in that they limit alternatives that the buyer will consider and define separate performance standards for each such alternative.

Performance Work Statement (PWS)

A statement of work expressed in terms of desired performance results, often including specific measurable objectives.

post-bid phase

The period of time after a seller submits a bid/proposal to a buyer through source selection, negotiations, contract formation, contract fulfillment, contract closeout, and follow-on opportunity management.

pre-bid phase

The period of time a seller of goods and/or services uses to identify business opportunities prior to the release of a customer solicitation.

pricing arrangement

An agreed-to basis between contractual parties for the payment of amounts for specified performance; usually expressed in terms of a specific cost-reimbursement or fixed-price arrangement.

prime/prime contractor

The principal seller performing under the contract.

private exchange

A marketplace hosted by a single company inside a company's firewall and used for procurement from among a group of preauthorized sellers.

privity of contract

The legal relationship that exists between the parties to a contract that allows either party to (a) enforce contractual rights against the other party and (b) seek remedy directly from the other party.

procurement

The complete action or process of acquiring or obtaining goods or services using any of several authorized means.

procurement planning

The process of identifying which business needs can be best met by procuring products or services outside the organization.

profit

The net proceeds from selling a product or service when costs are subtracted from revenues. May be positive (profit) or negative (loss).

program management

Planning and execution of multiple projects that are related to one another.

progress payments

An interim payment for delivered work in accordance with contract terms; generally tied to meeting specified performance milestones.

project management

Planning and ensuring the quality, on-time delivery, and cost of a specific set of related activities with a definite beginning and end.

promotion

Publicizing the attributes of the product/service through media and personal contacts and presentations, e.g., technical articles/presentations, new releases, advertising, and sales calls.

proposal

Normally, a written offer by a seller describing its offering terms. Proposals may be issued in response to a specific request or may be made unilaterally when a seller feels there may be an interest in its offer (which is also known as an unsolicited proposal).

proposal evaluation

An assessment of both the proposal and the offeror's ability (as conveyed by the proposal) to successfully accomplish the prospective contract. An agency shall evaluate competitive proposals solely on the factors specified in the solicitation.

protest

A written objection by an interested party to (a) a solicitation or other request by an agency for offers for a contract for the procurement of property or services, (b) the cancellation of the solicitation or other request, (c) an award or proposed award of the contract, or (d) a termination or cancellation of an award of the contract, if the written objection contains an allegation that the termination or cancellation is based in whole or in part on improprieties concerning the award of the contract.

punitive damages

Those damages awarded to the plaintiff over and above what will barely compensate for his or her loss. Unlike compensatory damages, punitive damages are based on actively different public policy consideration, that of punishing the defendant or of setting an example for similar wrongdoers.

purchasing

The outright acquisition of items, mostly off-the-shelf or catalog, manufactured outside the buyer's premises.

quality assurance

The planned and systematic actions necessary to provide adequate confidence that the performed service or supplied goods will serve satisfactorily for the intended and specified purpose.

quotation

A statement of price, either written or oral, which may include, among other things, a description of the product or service; the terms of sale, delivery, or period of performance; and payment. Such statements are usually issued by sellers at the request of potential buyers.

reasonable cost

A cost is reasonable if, in its nature and amount, it does not exceed that which would be incurred by a prudent person in the conduct of competitive business.

request for information (RFI)

A formal invitation to submit general and/or specific information concerning the potential future purchase of goods and/or services.

request for proposals (RFP)

A formal invitation that contains a scope of work and seeks a formal response (proposal), describing both methodology and compensation, to form the basis of a contract.

request for quotations (RFQ)

A formal invitation to submit a price for goods and/or services as specified.

request for technical proposals (RFTP)

Solicitation document used in two-step sealed bidding. Normally in letter form, it asks only for technical information; price and cost breakdowns are forbidden.

revenue value

The monetary value of an opportunity.

risk

Exposure or potential of an injury or loss

sealed-bid procedure

A method of procurement involving the unrestricted solicitation of bids, an opening, and award of a contract to the lowest responsible bidder.

selling, general & administrative (SG&A) expenses

Administrative costs of running business.

severable contract

A contract divisible into separate parts. A default of one section does not invalidate the whole contract.

several

A circumstance when more than two parties are involved with the contract.

single source

One source among others in a competitive marketplace that, for justifiable reason, is found to be most worthy to receive a contract award.

small business concerns

A small business is one that is independently owned and operated, and is not dominant in its field; a business concern that meets government size standards for its particular industry type.

socioeconomic programs

Programs designed to benefit particular groups. They represent a multitude of program interests and objectives unrelated to procurement objectives. Some examples of these are preferences for small business and for American products, required sources for specific items, and minimum labor pay levels mandated for contractors.

solicitation

A process through which a buyer requests, bids, quotes, tenders, or proposes orally, in writing, or electronically. Solicitations can take the following forms: request for proposals (RFP), request for quotations (RFQ), request for tenders, invitation to bid (ITB), invitation for bids, and invitation for negotiation.

solicitation planning

The preparation of the documents needed to support a solicitation.

source selection

The process by which the buyer evaluates offers, selects a seller, negotiates terms and conditions, and awards the contract.

Source Selection Advisory Council

A group of people who are appointed by the Source Selection Authority (SSA). The Council is responsible for reviewing and approving the source selection plan (SSP) and the solicitation of competitive awards for major and certain less-than-major procurements. The Council also determines what proposals are in the competitive range and provides recommendations to the SSA for final selection.

source selection plan (SSP)

The document that describes the selection criteria, the process, and the organization to be used in evaluating proposals for competitively awarded contracts.

specification

A description of the technical requirements for a material, product, or service that includes the criteria for determining that the requirements have been met. There are generally three types of specifications used in contracting: performance, functional, and design.

stakeholders

Individuals who control the resources in a company needed to pursue opportunities or deliver solutions to customers.

standard

A document that establishes engineering and technical limitations and applications of items, materials, processes, methods, designs, and engineering practices. It includes any related criteria deemed essential to achieve the highest practical degree of uniformity in materials or products, or interchangeability of parts used in those products.

standards of conduct

The ethical conduct of personnel involved in the acquisition of goods and services. Within the federal government, business shall be conducted in a manner above reproach and, except as authorized by law or regulation, with complete impartiality and without preferential treatment.

statement of work (SOW)

That portion of a contract describing the actual work to be done by means of specifications or other minimum requirements, quantities, performance date, and a statement of the requisite quality.

statute of limitations

The legislative enactment prescribing the periods within which legal actions may be brought upon certain claims or within which certain rights may be enforced.

stop work order

A request for interim stoppage of work due to nonconformance, funding, or technical considerations.

subcontract

A contract between a buyer and a seller in which a significant part of the supplies or services being obtained is for eventual use in a prime contract.

subcontractor

A seller who enters into a contract with a prime contractor or a subcontractor of the prime contractor.

supplementary agreement

A contract modification that is accomplished by the mutual action of parties.

technical factor

A factor other than price used in evaluating offers for award. Examples include technical excellence, management capability, personnel qualifications, prior experience, past performance, and schedule compliance.

technical leveling

The process of helping a seller bring its proposal up to the level of other proposals through successive rounds of discussion, such as by pointing out weaknesses resulting from the seller's lack of diligence, competence, or inventiveness in preparing the proposal.

technical/management proposal

That part of the offer that describes the seller's approach to meeting the buyer's requirement.

technical transfusion

The disclosure of technical information pertaining to a proposal that re-suits in improvement of a competing proposal. This practice is not allowed in federal government contracting.

term

A part of a contract that addresses a specific subject.

termination

An action taken pursuant to a contract clause in which the buyer unilaterally ends all or part of the work.

terms and conditions (Ts and Cs)

All clauses in a contract, including time of delivery, packing and shipping, applicable standard clauses, and special provisions.

unallowable cost

Any cost that, under the provisions of any pertinent law, regulation, or contract, cannot be included in prices, cost-reimbursements, or settlements under a government contract to which it is allocable.

uncompensated overtime

The work that exempt employees perform above and beyond 40 hours per week. Also known as competitive time, deflated hourly rates, direct allocation of salary costs, discounted hourly rates, extended work week, full-time accounting, and green time.

Uniform Commercial Code (UCC)

A U.S. model law developed to standardize commercial contracting law among the states. It has been adopted by 49 states (and in significant portions by Louisiana). The UCC comprises articles that deal with specific commercial subject matters, including sales and letters of credit.

unilateral

See *bilateral contract*.

unsolicited proposal

A research or development proposal that is made by a prospective contractor without prior formal or informal solicitation from a purchasing activity.

variable costs

Costs associated with production that change directly with the amount of production, e.g., the direct material or labor required to complete the build or manufacturing of a product.

variance

The difference between projected and actual performance, especially relating to costs.

vertical exchange

A marketplace that is specific to a single industry.

waiver

The voluntary and unilateral relinquishment a person of a right that he or she has. See also *forbearance*.

warranty

A promise or affirmation given by a seller to a buyer regarding the nature, usefulness, or condition of the goods or services furnished under a contract. Generally, a warranty's purpose is to delineate the rights and obligations for defective goods and services and to foster quality performance.

warranty, express

A written statement arising out of a sale to the consumer of a consumer good, pursuant to which the manufacturer, distributor, or retailer undertakes to preserve or maintain the utility or performance of the consumer good or provide compensation if there is a failure in utility or performance. It is not necessary to the creation of an express warranty that formal words such as "warrant" or "guarantee" be used, or that a specific intention to make a warranty be present.

warranty, implied

A promise arising by operation of law that something that is sold shall be fit for the purpose for which the seller has reason to know that it is required. Types of implied warranties include implied warranty of merchantability, of title, and of wholesomeness.

warranty of fitness

A warranty by the seller that goods sold are suitable for the special purpose of the buyer.

warranty of merchantability

A warranty that goods are fit for the ordinary purposes for which such goods are used and conform to the promises or affirmations of fact made on the container or label.

warranty of title

An express or implied (arising by operation of law) promise that the seller owns the item offered for sale and, therefore, is able to transfer a good title and that the goods, as delivered, are free from any security interest of which the buyer at the time of contracting has no knowledge.

web portals

A public exchange in which a company or group of companies list products or services for sale or provide other transmission of business information.

win strategy

A collection of messages or points designed to guide the customer's perception of you, your solution, and your competitors.

Work Breakdown Structure (WBS)

A logical, organized, decomposition of the work tasks within a given project, typically uses a hierarchical numeric coding scheme.

World Trade Organization (WTO)

A multi-national legal entity which serves as the champion of fair trade globally, established April 15, 1995.

Bibliography

Acuff, Frank L., *How to Negotiate Everything with Anyone Anywhere Around the World,* (New York: American Management Association, 1997).

Badgerow, Dana B., Gregory A. Garrett, Dominic F. DiClementi, and Barbara M. Weaver, *Managing Contracts for Peak Performance* (Vienna, Va.: National Contract Management Association, 1990).

Barlow, C. Wayne, and Glenn P. Eisen, *Purchasing Negotiations* (Boston: CBI Publishing Company, Inc., 1983).

Bazerman, Max, and Margaret A. Neale, *Negotiating Rationally* (New York: The Free Press, 1992).

Berry, Wayne, *Negotiating in the Age of Integrity* (London: Nicholas Brealey Publishing, 1996).

Binnendijk, Hans, ed., *National Negotiating Styles* (Washington, D.C.: Foreign Service Institute, U.S. Department of State, 1987).

Black, Henry Campbell, Joseph R. Nolan, Jacqueline M. Nolan-Haley, M.J. Connolly, Stephan C. Hicks, and Martina N. Alibrandi, *Black's Law Dictionary,* 6th ed. (St. Paul, Minn: West Publishing Co., 1990).

Bunnik, Ed C., and Garrett, Gregory A., "Creating a World-Class PM Organization: A Success Story," *PM Network Magazine,* September 2000 (Project Management Institute).

Clarkson, Kenneth W., Roger LeRoy Miller, Stephen A. Chaplin, and Bonnie Blaire, *West's Business Law: Alternate UCC Comprehensive Edition* (St. Paul, Minn.: West Publishing Company, 1981).

Cohen, Herb, *You Can Negotiate Anything,,* 1st ed. (Secaucus, N.J.: L. Stuart, 1980).

Corbin, Arthur L., *Corbin on Contract* (St. Paul, Minn.: West Publishing Company, 1993).

Covey, Stephen R., *The Seven Habits of Highly Effective People* (New York: Simon and Schuster, Inc., 1989).

Dobler, Donald W., David N. Burt, and Lamar Lee, Jr., "Types of Contracts and Ordering Agreements," in *Purchasing and Materials Management: Text and Cases,* 5th ed. (New York: McGraw-Hill Publishing Company, 1990).

Dawson, Roger, *Secrets of Power Negotiating for Salespeople,* (Franklin Lakes, NJ: Career Press, 1999)

Fifer, Bob, *Double Your Profits,* (New York: Harper Collins Publishers, 1995).

Fisher, Roger, *Getting Ready to Negotiate: The Getting to Yes Workbook* (New York: Penguin Books, 1995).

Fisher, Roger, and Scott Brown, *Getting Together* (New York: Penguin Books, 1989).

Fisher, Roger, and William Ury, *Getting to Yes: Negotiating Agreement Without Giving In,* 2d ed. (New York: Penguin Books, 1991).

Fisher, Roger, Elizabeth Kopelman, and Andrea K. Schneider, *Beyond Machiavelli: Tools for Coping with Conflict* (Cambridge: Harvard University Press, 1994).

Fuller, George, *The Negotiator's Handbook,* (Englewood Cliffs, NJ Prentice Hall, 1991).

Garrett, Gregory A. and Reginald J. Kipke, *The Capture Management Life-Cycle: Winning More Business,* (Chicago, IL: CCH Incorporated, 2003).

Garrett, Gregory A., *Managing Complex Outsourced Projects*, (Chicago, IL: CCH, Incorporated, 2004).

Garrett, Gregory A., *World Class Contracting*, (Chicago, IL: CCH, Incorporated, Third Edition, 2003).

Gates, Bill, *Business @ The Speed of Thought: Using a Digital Nervous System* (New York: Warner Books USA, 1999).

Goodpaster, Gary, *A Guide to Negotiation and Mediation*, (New York: Transnational Publishers, Inc., 1997).

Harris, Phillip R., and Robert T. Moran, *Managing Cultural Differences* (Houston: Gulf Publishing Company, 1996).

Hendon, Donald W., and Rebecca A. Hendon, *World-Class Negotiating: Dealmaking in the Global Marketplace* (New York: John Wiley & Sons, 1990).

Hernandez, Richard J., and Delane F. Moeller, *Negotiating a Quality Contract*, (Vienna, VA: National Contract Management Association, 1992).

Karrass, Chester L., *Give and Take: The Complete Guide to Negotiating Strategies and Tactics* (New York: Harper Collins Pubs., Inc., 1993).

Karrass, Gary, *Negotiate to Close: How to Make More Successful Deals* (New York: Simon and Schuster, 1985).

Kirk, Dorthy, "Managing Expectations,"*PM Network Magazine*, August 2000 (Project Management Institute).

Koren, Leonard, and Peter Goodman, *The Haggler's Handbook: One Hour to Negotiating Power* (New York: W.W. Norton & Co., Inc., 1992).

LeBoeuf, Michael, *Fast Forward*, (New York: Berkley Books, 1995).

Leenders, Michael R., Harold E. Fearon, and Wilbur B. England, *Purchasing and Materials Management*, 9th ed. (Homewood, Ill: Richard D. Irwin, Inc., 1989).

Levinson, Jay Conrad, Mark S. Smith, and Orvel R. Wilson, *Guerrilla Negotiating*, (New York: John Wiley & Sons, Inc. 1999).

Liebesny, Herbert J., *Foreign Legal Systems: A Comparative Analysis*, 4th rev. ed. (Washington, D.C.: The George Washington University, 1981).

Monroe, Kent B., *Pricing: Making Profitable Decisions*, 2d ed. (New York: McGraw-Hill Publishing Company, 1990).

McCormack, Mark H., *Mark H. McCormack on Negotiating*, (Los Angeles: Dove Books, 1995).

Nash, Ralph C., Jr., and John Cibinic, *Formation of Government Contracts*, 3d ed (Washington, D.C.: The George Washington University & CCH Incorporated, 1998).

Nash, Ralph C., Jr., and John Cibinic, *Administration of Government Contracts*, 3d ed (Washington, D.C.: The George Washington University & CCH Incorporated, 1995).

Nash, Ralph C., Jr., Karen R. O'Brien, and Steven L. Schooner, *The Government Contracts Reference Book: A Comprehensive Guide to the Language of Procurement*, 2d ed. (Washington, D.C.: The George Washington University & CCH Incorporated, 1998).

The National Contract Management Association, *The Desktop Guide to Basic Contracting Terms*, 4th ed. (1912 Woodford Road, Vienna, Virginia 22182, 1994).

Nierenberg, Gerard, *The Art of Negotiating* (New York: Penguin Books, 1989).

O'Connell, Brian, *B2B.com: Cashing-in on the Business-to-Business E-commerce Bonanza* (Holbrook, Massachusetts: Adams Media Corp., 2000).

Ohmae, Kenichi, *The Borderless World: Power and Strategy in the Inter-linked Economy* (New York: Harper Collins Pubs., Inc., 1991).

Project Management Institute Standards Committee, *A Guide to the Project Management Body of Knowledge* (Upper Darby, Pa.: Project Management Institute, 2003).

Shapiro, Ronald M., and Mark A. Jankowski, *The Power of Nice,* (New York: John Wiley & Sons, Inc., 2001).

Stein, Janice Gross, ed., *Getting to the Table: The Processes of International Prenegotiation* (Baltimore: Johns Hopkins University Press, 1989).

Stark, Peter B., and Jane Flaherty, *The Only Negotiating Guide You'll Ever Need,* (New York: Broadway Books, 2003).

Ury, William, *Getting Past No: Negotiating Your Way from Confrontation to Cooperation* (New York: Bantam Books, 1993).

Zartman, I. William, *The Fifty Percent Solution* (New Haven: Yale University Press, 1987).

Zartman, I. William, ed., *The Negotiation Process* (Beverly Hills, Calif.: Sage Publications, 1978).

Index